CHILD CARE IN THE EC

Child Care in the EC

A country-specific guide to foster and residential care

edited by
M.J. Colton
W. Hellinckx

arena

Published by
Arena
Ashgate Publishing Limited
Gower House
Croft Road
Aldershot
Hants GU11 3HR
England

Ashgate Publishing Company
Old Post Road
Brookfield
Vermont 05036
USA

British Library Cataloguing in Publication Data

Child Care in the EC: Country-specific Guide to
Foster and Residential Care
    I. Colton, M.J. II. Hellinckx, W.
    362.7094

ISBN 1 85742 178 7 (hardback)
     1 85742 179 5 (paperback)

Printed in Great Britain at the University Press, Cambridge

Contents

Preface

W. Hellinckx and M. Colton

The roots of this book lie in EUSARF - *European Scientific Association on Residential and Foster Care for Children and Adolescents* - and in the Erasmus student exchange scheme, *Residential Care For Children and Young People with Behavioural Problems.* EUSARF is a body of researchers voluntarily banded together and concerned with the advancement of knowledge in the field of residential care, foster care and their alternatives for children and young people with psycho-social problems, including young addicts. The objects of the Association include the promotion and development within Europe of empirical and theoretical research on residential and foster care, and the interchange between the European members and other researchers throughout the world of information relating to this subject area.

Before developing a European research network for residential and foster care, one should have a thorough knowledge of contemporary policy and practice in the different European countries. This is the origin of the idea for this overview of residential and foster care for children and adolescents in the European Community. The need for such a survey was further evidenced in the operation of the Erasmus exchange scheme referred to above. The development of this scheme has been impeded by the fact that the students concerned often lack sufficient knowledge about the nature of services provided in host countries.

This book attempts to offer a systematic description of residential and foster care in each of the constituent countries of the EC. In addition, a concise account of the research on residential and foster care undertaken in each country is presented. The book is, therefore, unique in that it represents the first coherent account of policy, practice and research in the field of residential and foster care in all the countries of the EC. As far as we know, the only other recent work that has attempted to compare child care provision across national frontiers is FICE's, *Residential Child Care : An International Reader* (edited by Gottesman, M., 1991, London, Whiting and Birch). However, the present work is distinguished from the latter in that this book embraces all EC countries, examines foster care as well as residential care, and devotes a good deal of attention to research.

We are proud that we have managed to present an account of residential and foster care in the 12 member states of the EC. That the scope of the book is limited to the EC reflects the fact that it is, among other things, the product of an agreement between different European universities participating in the Erasmus programme initiated and financed by the EC. This should not be construed as meaning that we are not concerned about residential and foster care in the other countries of Europe and the CIS. The situation in the East European countries and in the former Soviet Union affects us deeply. Moreover, it is our earnest intention that our colleagues in non-EC countries will contribute to future information exchanges and joint publications.

Apart from the necessary geographical limitation mentioned, we have also been obliged to restrict our attention to residential, foster care and their alternatives for children and young people who are placed away from home as a result of adverse family circumstances, or because of their emotional or behavioural problems, or a combination of both. Boarding-schools, provisions for children with disabilities (mental or physical) and services for children with psychiatric disturbances are beyond the scope of this book.

In order to have the information on each country conveniently arranged, and to facilitate comparisons between countries, the authors were requested to structure their contributions according to a standard framework. First, attention is given to the current nature of residential and foster care services, and their alternatives. By this we mean the types and number of provisions and children cared for in the various forms of residential and foster care, their historical antecedents, the legal and administrative framework of services, fundings arrangements, ideas and theories which have helped to shape policy and practice, recent innovations and trends, and critical issues and major problems. Second, research on residential and foster care is reviewed. This includes an examination of the following topics : major research funding agencies, present research trends, the impact of research findings on policy and practice, and issues for future research. Most authors have followed this structure, not always as faithfully as we had hoped, but to the extent permitted by the specific circumstances in their individual countries.

This leads us to the principal obstacles that must be overcome in producing a work of this kind. With the exception of those on Ireland and the United Kingdom, the chapters on individual EC countries comprising this book were written by authors whose first language is not English. Most, therefore, required very extensive revision. This complex and arduous task (undertaken by Matthew Colton) meant that the book took considerably longer to complete than was originally envisaged.

Davies Jones, who served as style editor for the FICE publication referred to above, presents a full discussion of the difficulties associated with producing a text of this sort in English from an originally multilingual work. He distinguishes three major problems. First, ... 'the linguistic task of finding appropriate words in the various languages to describe the features of a distinctive system' ... Second, ... 'the problem of understanding the different frameworks of reference and intellectual traditions that inform thinking and action within national cultures' ... Third ... 'the need to make sense of the separate professional maps which show the various ways in which professional duties are distributed in the different countries' ... (Davies Jones, 1991; see Gottesman, 1991).

With regard to the linguistic task, Davies Jones (1991) indicates that the well documented problems associated with the translation of professional and technical terms in residential child care have so far not been overcome by the use of glossaries. In part, this is because ... 'real problems arise when quite fundamental words in one language have no ¤precise equivalence' in others... The versatility of many key words adds to the problem. Words such as 'care' and 'community' are good examples' ...

Turning to frames of reference and intellectual traditions, Davies Jones (1991) points out that ... 'current practice ... makes it difficult in English to link education with the wider range of nurturing services (social, psychological, family), associated with the term' ... in other European countries; and that ... 'the same is broadly true of 'pedagogy''.

In discussing different professional maps, Davies Jones (1991) relates that the main profession of residential child care in Europe - the social pedagogue or educateur specialisé - does not exist in the United

Kingdom, where the work is carried out by a variety of groups, including social workers, youth and community workers, and teachers. Consequently, ... 'the learning, scholarship and vocabulary directly associated with the development of a distinctive residential child care profession is ... missing'.

Notwithstanding the problems of communication identified, we hope that we have succeeded in delineating residential and foster care in the EC. The knowledge and expertise of those who have contributed ensures the reliability of this volume, and its usefulness for policy makers, researchers, practitioners and students.

This book would not have been possible without the dedication of Mrs Anne Vanden Berge, who time and again with infinite patience had to see to it that the deadlines for correcting the proofs were kept by the manifold authors, and who made an enormous contribution to the task of editing the book. We also wish to thank Wilfried Erkens for his help with translation. He was ably assisted in this by Mrs Lieve Reusens. Finally, we are also grateful to Benedikte Van den Bruel for her help in preparing our concluding remarks.

1 Belgium and Luxembourg

*W. Hellinckx, B. van den Bruel
and C. vander Borght*

Recent political history : **Belgium** : Belgium is a parliamentary monarchy, and is divided into three regions and three communities : the Flemish region (with the Flemish Community), the Walloon region (with the French Community and a very small German Community), and the region of Brussels (with a Flemish and a French Community). Since 1980, the unitary state has gradually been reformed into a federal state, in which regions and communities have more autonomy and powers. **Luxembourg** : Luxembourg is an independent Grand Duchy which became fully autonomous in 1839. It has a democratic parliamentary government under a constitutional monarchy. Luxembourg is a strong supporter of European cooperation. The average income and the purchasing power of the people are among the highest in Europe.
Geographical size : **Belgium** : 30,518 Km². **Luxembourg** : 2,586 Km².
Principal industries : **Belgium** : Steel, metallurgy, textiles and chemicals were the traditional major components of Belgian industry. In recent years the textile and steel sectors have declined in importance, while the capacity of the chemical sector has expanded. **Luxembourg** : Although traditionally Luxembourg's principle industry, steel production declined in the 1970s. The industrial sector is now dominated by US multi-national companies, which primarily produce tires, chemicals and fabricated metals.
Date of EC membership : **Belgium and Luxembourg** : 1958.
Numbers of inhabitants : **Belgium** : Flemish-speaking community : 5,722,000 (57.6%); Brussels : 971,000 (9.7%); French-speaking community : 3,169,000 (31.9%); German-speaking community : 66,000 (0.7%); Total : 9,928,000. **Luxembourg** (01.01.1990) : 378,400.
Age of majority : **Belgium** : 18 years. **Luxembourg** : 18 years.
Numbers under the age of majority : **Belgium** : Flemish-speaking community : 1,250,120; Brussels : 199,873; French- and German-speaking communities : 738,913; Total : 2,188,906. **Luxembourg** (under the age of 20) : 87,712.
Numbers of children and young people :

in residential care :	**Belgium** :	Flanders (31.12.1991) :	3,381
		Wallonia(31.03.1992) :	4,258
	Luxembourg (31.12.1991) :		514
in foster care :	**Belgium** :	Flanders (31.12.1991) :	2,139
		Wallonia (31.03.1992) :	1,364
	Luxembourg (31.12.1991) :		248

Introduction

Belgium has a long tradition of care for troubled children. In the first part of this contribution, we outline developments in residential and foster care in Belgium up to 1980, when responsibility for child welfare was delegated to the three communities, namely, the Flemish, the French-speaking and the German-speaking communities. This led to differences in the development of welfare provision in the three communities. In the second part of this chapter an account is given of current tendencies in the Flemish community with regard to residential and foster care. In the third part, we discuss residential and foster care in the French-speaking community. The German-speaking community is very small, and is therefore outside the scope of this chapter[1].

In the fourth part, we present a brief overview of residential and foster care in Luxembourg. Because it is a very small country, child care never became a matter for nationwide discussion in Luxembourg (Soisson, 1991). Child care professionals in Luxembourg borrowed ideas from elsewhere, notably Belgium. Thus, there are clear similarities in the issues surrounding residential and foster care for children in the two countries.

Part I : Historical antecedents of services

As in other European countries, the historical antecedents of residential and foster care in Belgium are to be found in the care of orphans and abandoned children. From the early Middle Ages, abandoned children were taken care of in institutions set up by the clergy or charitable foundations. However, not all orphans and abandoned children were accommodated in institutions. Many were boarded out with private individuals who agreed to raise the children and provide them with vocational training. This may be considered an early precursor of foster care.

In the eighteenth and nineteenth centuries, the number of orphanages grew significantly. For example, by the early years of the twentieth century, the number of orphanages had grown to 278 in the area corresponding with the present-day Flemish language region.

Until the middle of the nineteenth century, the aim of institutions was to protect the defenceless child from unfavourable influences in the outside world. An all-embracing institutional climate was the norm : the children lived in large groups, education consisted almost exclusively of drill, the social climate was impersonal, and contact with the outside world was almost non-existent.

From 1850 onwards, a new type of institution developed for destitute and delinquent children : the reform school. The purpose of these establishments was to 'reform' children and young people, thus turning them into useful citizens and docile workers. The regime was severe, almost military.

Measures for the protection of vulnerable children and young people were first introduced by the law of 15 May 1912. At that point, Belgium was a leading nation in the field of child protection. For the first time in Europe, the child was protected from the severity of criminal law and a special court for children was set up - the juvenile court (Dupont and Vander Auwera, 1988). Residential and foster care also made their first appearance in legislation. Juvenile court magistrates were empowered to board out children with 'dependable private persons' or to place them in residential care, which often meant the reform schools.

One negative result of the law of 1912 was that the number of placements grew enormously. Another problem was that something had to go wrong before the juvenile court magistrate was permitted to intervene. As long as the child did not do anything that could be construed as a criminal offence, the juvenile court judge was unable to take preventive action.

It was not until 1965 that a new law was passed shifting the focus of intervention towards safeguarding the 'child's interest'. The dominant idea was that no stone should be left unturned to prevent the child's removal from his or her family environment. Preventative action was the aim with regard to both the parents and the child. A new organisation, the 'Committee for Youth Protection', was given responsibility for these activities. 'Judicial protection' was exercised via the juvenile court. Although the 1965 law was intended to reduce the number of placements, it had the opposite effect. The residential sector further expanded, and the number of foster care placements also increased significantly.

Up to the 1960s, residential homes admitted far too many children. The basic training given to residential staff was inadequate, and little attention was paid to in-service-training. By the late 1960s, a variety of factors had led to serious questioning of residential care. These factors included research suggesting that long-term residential care adversely effected children's development (Bowlby, 1951; Pringle and Bossio, 1960), Goffman's work on total institutions, the critical studies of King, Raynes and Tizard (1971), the emergence of systemic thinking in care, the broadening of social criticism from 1968, the protests of caregivers and young people in care against the often inhuman conditions prevailing in some institutions, and the high financial costs of residential care at a time of economic crisis (Hellinckx, 1991).

These factors contributed to a qualitative improvement in residential care homes. For example, they became smaller, more and better trained personnel were recruited and greater attention was paid to in-service-training. Moreover, from the 1970s, the number and size of private institutions decreased sharply. In the Flemish Community, for example, a 33 per cent reduction in residential capacity occurred between 1978 and 1987. Alternative forms of care, such as foster care, day-care, independant living under supervision and home-based treatment were expanded with government support (D'hoker et al., 1986; Lammertyn and Antoons, 1990).

Part II : Residential and foster care in the Flemish Community[2]

The nature of residential and foster care provisions

The administrative and legal system

The majority of children placed away from home (97 per cent) under the Flemish community's recent by-laws concerning 'special youth assistance' (4 April 1990), are accommodated in foster homes or in private institutions approved by the government and subsidised by the Ministry of Family and Welfare. Only a small proportion of children in substitute care (3 per cent) are accommodated in facilities directly administered by the Flemish Community (Bestuur Bijzondere Jeugdbijstand, 1991). The latter are regarded as a 'safety net' for the most difficult or disturbed children.

In recent years, the provision of alternatives to residential and foster care, such a day-centres, independent living under supervision and home based treatment, has increased.

In order to be subsidised, a child must have been placed in the above mentioned facilities by the Juvenile court of the 'Committee for special youth care'. This is a body that has developed out of the former 'Committee for youth protection', and was established by the recent by-laws on special youth assistance to prevent the need for judicial intervention in problematic parenting situations. To this end, different measures can be taken. The Committee may, with the consent of the parents and the child, decide to place the child away from home.

The 'Committee for youth protection' was replaced by the 'Committee for special youth care' because the former blurred the distinction between voluntary admission to care and compulsory committal by the Juvenile court. This was because the 'Committee for youth protection' had the authority to refer certain cases to the Juvenile court. By no longer permitting the present Committee to act under orders from the Juvenile court, a clearer distinction has been made between voluntary and compulsory care. A new body was created, the Mediation Committee, which mediates when voluntary care is in danger of failing, and which ensures that compulsion is used only when there really is no other choice.

In 1984, the Flemish community (the Ministry of Family and Welfare) became responsible for private care provisions. The Flemish community's new policy not only stresses the prevention of problems, but also seeks to empower parents and children and to improve the quality of services. Flemish legislation comprises the so-called by-laws on Special youth assistance (4 April 1990).

Central to these by-laws is the concept of 'the problematic parenting situation'. This phrase conveys that the problems of troubled children lie neither solely with the child nor exclusively with the parents, but rather in the parenting process. All those involved in such cases (parents, children, welfare workers, Committee of special youth assistance, juvenile court magistrates or Mediation committee) perceive the parenting situation as problematic. Therefore, practical help, support and guidance must be given not only to the child, but also to the parents and others involved in the parenting process (Lammertyn and Antoons, 1990).

Types of facilities

Some 6,000 young people in Flanders are placed in residential care or with foster families. This represents about four per thousand of young people aged under 19. About 2,000 are placed with foster families, and some 4,000 are accommodated in institutions. In 1991, the Juvenile court was responsible for making around two-thirds of placements into care, the remaining third were made by the Committee (Bestuur Bijzondere Jeugdbijstand, 1991).

As previously mentioned, a distinction can be drawn between different types of facilities : those administered by the Flemish community, private residential homes authorised and subsidised by government, and foster families.

5

In Flanders, 4 institutions are run directly by the Flemish Community, and 145 establishments are privately administered (Bestuur Bijzondere Jeugdbijstand, 1991).

Facilities of the Flemish Community[3] The aim of the facilities administered by the Flemish community is to reintegrate young people as quickly as possible into their natural environment, or transfer them to less restrictive forms of residential care. Some facilities provide vocational training, which may enhance the chances of a fresh start for the young people concerned (Lammertyn and Antoons, 1990). All those placed in facilities of the Flemish community have been committed to care by the court (Vereecke, 1990).

The organisation of the Flemish community's facilities is based on two principles : regionalisation and multi-dimensionality. Regionalisation means that an attempt is made to place young people in facilities situated in their home regions. Multi-dimensionality indicates that every facility consists of different sections, each of which performs a specific function in the reintegration process. In the observation section, for instance, young people spend a period of time undergoing multi-disciplinary tests designed to assess their needs. Following this, young people may be transferred to an 'educational section', which comprise open and closed regimes. Closed regimes are characterised by fairly rigid daily routines and a structured approach (Lammertyn and Antoons, 1990; Geukens, 1989; Hellinckx et al., 1989).

Generally speaking, the structure and overall climate of the Flemish community's facilities involve a greater degree of restrictiveness than the private facilities. The pattern of daily life experienced by young people at the beginning of their stay is particularly structured (Gryspeerdt, 1987).

The age of children and young people entrusted to the Flemish community's facilities varies between 12 and 18, with a heavy concentration of youngsters aged between 15 and 17 years[4].

Young people are placed in Flemish community facilities for a variety of reasons. The majority of such youngsters have committed offences. In practice, there is a tendency to consider placement in a Flemish community facility as a measure of last resort, which is only taken when other steps have failed and where there appears to be no alternative. In 1986, juvenile court magistrates were asked what factors they take into consideration when placing a young person in a Flemish community facility[5]. This revealed that magistrates regard the case for such placements as self-evident for those who have committed many or serious offences, or when other measures have failed, or when there are no places available in appropriate private facilities.

6

Unlike private provisions, the Flemish community's facilities are not at liberty to pursue their own policies with regard to criteria for the admission of young people. Rather, they are obliged to accommodate any youngster sent by the juvenile court. It is therefore not uncommon for young people who have been refused admission elsewhere to end up in a Flemish community facility, and young people with psychiatric problems are sometimes admitted to community facilities.

As a consequence of their role as places of last resort in the child welfare system, the Flemish community's facilities accommodate many young people who are difficult to help. Their behaviour is often challenging to a degree that other facilities are unable to cope with, and is frequently characterised by aggression, delinquency, and absconding; many exercise a negative influence on their peers and are generally uncooperative.

The Flemish community's facilities reflect the strain between welfare and justice. The by-laws concerning special youth assistance stipulate that pedagogical measures must be taken in the 'child's interest' even when the latter has committed an offence. These measures are often perceived as a form of punishment by the child, and they are sometimes intended as such. It is known that some group workers, welfare officers and committing authorities use the threat of committal to a Flemish community facility as a means of securing the cooperation of an unruly youngster. In this ambiguous context, it is often very difficult to develop a helping relationship with the child (Vereecke, 1990).

However, Flemish community facilities are no longer exclusively seen as the 'terminus' of the child welfare system. They are increasingly being ascribed a 'turn-table' role, whereby the goal is either to return youngsters to their families or to place them in the less restrictive environment of a private facility (Gryspeerdt, 1987). This shift has increased the demands placed on residential staff. One of the major problems currently besetting the Flemish community's facilities is that they do not have sufficient qualified personnel.

Private homes The Flemish government's decree of May 22 1991 concerning the conditions for the authorisation and financial subsidy of private homes, refers to the following types of facilities.

- Provisions for children from 3 to 14 years, in which there must be at least one group worker for every ten youngsters.
- Provisions for adolescents under 20 that may also supervise youngsters who live independently following a period in residential care.

7

- Foster homes, which offer family life to young people. The person responsible for the home must reside there, and the maximum number of children permitted in each foster home is ten.
- Centres for relief and orientation, where young people can stay for temporary periods (e.g. while awaiting transfer to another facility). The treatment provided must be of a short-term nature, and there must be at least one group worker to every five youngsters at each home.
- Centres for observation, accommodating children who require assessment. A psychiatrist is responsible for a care team consisting of a psychologist or an orthopedagogue, a social worker and, depending on the age of the youngsters, a paediatrician.
- Provisions for children from 0 to 3 years, in which there must be at least one group worker for every ten children.

As can be seen, the facilities listed have been classified according to the age of the young people accommodated or the type of service offered. The categories are not related to specific problem groups. There is, for instance, no category for young people with conduct disorders. In practice, therefore, there is no differentiation of provisions according to the problems of the children looked after (Hellinckx and De Munter, 1990)[6].

We will now consider the geographical spread of services, the issue of small-scale residential provision, the process of professionalisation and the children's characteristics.

Recent research shows that the geographical distribution of facilities over the different provinces and administrative and judicial districts is very uneven (Bestuur Bijzondere Jeugdbijstand, 1992). The number of facilities varies greatly from region to region. Moreover, in some regions, there were high numbers of vacant places in certain types of facilities, whereas for other types there were no places available. This conflicts with the goal of 'regionalisation', that is : on ensuring that target groups in each region are adequately served by the full range of services, so that youngsters do not have to be placed away from their home localities. In order to realise the ideal of residential care near home, there should be a sufficient number of different facilities in the regions to meet the needs of children and young people for whom residential care is considered to be desirable.

Since the 1970s, efforts have been made to organise residential care into small, autonomous, units accommodating a maximum of 10 young people per facility (or self-contained living unit within larger establishments). In Flanders, only about one third of residential homes were found to meet this criterion[7].

Turning to the issue of professionalisation, recent years have seen growing recognition of the key role performed by group workers in social care. In addition to a deepening of their educational task, which entails a greater emphasis on their emotional relationships with children, group workers have been given more responsibility. As well as attending to the day-to-day needs of children, group workers must liaise with children's birth families, schools, referring authorities, and other group workers and staff members (Klomp, 1985). Consequently, there is a need not only for more, but also for better qualified group workers.

Between 1978 and 1990, the number of group workers employed in Flanders rose by almost 33 per cent (Hellinckx and De Munter, 1990; Lammertyn and Antoons, 1990). This trend has been accompanied by improved professional training and a significant rise in the numbers holding professional qualifications. From 1976 to 1990, the proportion of group workers holding the highest qualification almost tripled. In the same period, the proportion of group workers possessing only the most basic qualification decreased sharply (Lammertyn and Antoons, 1990).

Another indication of increased professionalism in residential care is the growth of other professional staff (i.e. psychologists, orthopedagogues[8], paramedics and social workers), who act as advisors or consultants with regard to pedagogical methods and policy, or provide direct help to young people. Research shows that on 1 January, 1990, more than half of the total number of such staff were social workers[9] (Lammertyn and Antoons, 1990). Pedagogues and psychologists, on the other hand, represented less than one quarter of the total number of professionally qualified staff.

Although there has been an increase in the number of professionally qualified staff, as recently as 1986 there were no such staff in roughly 40 per cent of residential facilities (Hellinckx and De Munter, 1990). The shortage of professional staff is particularly acute in smaller units. This is a consequence of the legal regulations which make the number of staff employed in each setting dependent on the number of children accommodated.

Whilst evidence of increasing professionalisation can also be found in the management of residential homes, research carried out in 1986 showed that no more than one fifth of residential establishments were managed by a director holding a university diploma (Hellinckx and De Munter, 1990).

Boys comprise an estimated 60 per cent of the residential population[10]. Over half of the young people (56 per cent) are aged from 13 to 18. One-third are in the range of borderline intellectual functioning or are mentally handicapped, and over half have stayed down a class at least once. The average length of stay at a single residential facility is markedly long : three years and four months. About two-thirds of the young people in residential care have experienced at least one previous residential placement. Fostering breakdowns are increasing, and account for some 15 per cent of current admissions to residential care.

Over 25 per cent of young people in residential care have no behavioural problems. 'Problem behaviour' denotes behaviour which hampers the child's development and/or creates real problems for others. This ranges from behaviour problems such as bed wetting to serious problems such as addiction and absconding.

However, when examining the group of children with behavioural difficulties, we observe that the nature of their problems are often serious. Moreover, more than half of the children who manifest behaviour problems commit one or more offences during their stay in residential care; that is, behaviour which leads to direct contact with the police or with the court. Almost all children whose behaviour is difficult manifest a cluster of presenting problems.

Most children in residential care are from problematic family backgrounds. Although there are very few orphans in residential care, about two-thirds of residential children come from broken homes. The family backgrounds of these children are often multiply disadvantaged, which includes problems concerning relationships, mental and physical health, and financial and housing difficulties. These problems are reflected in serious parenting problems. Three-quarters of children in residential care are the victims of inadequate or inconsistent parenting, and about half have exprienced neglect or rejection.

In most cases, it is problems within families and not in the children themselves which lead to placement in residential care.

Foster care In Flanders, foster care placements can be arranged by any service, which may continue to be responsible for the child's welfare following placement. The juvenile court and the committee of special youth assistance, for example, have an associated social welfare service to which children may be referred for placement with foster families. However, the agencies that are best suited to this kind of task are the 'foster care referral services'. The role of these specialised services includes recruiting foster parents, selecting children for foster placement, providing foster families with advice, practical help and financial remuneration, and encouraging cooperation between children's birth and foster families.

There has been a recent shift from direct placement with a foster family by the juvenile court or the committee for special youth assistance to placements arranged by the foster care services. In 1991, however, no referral was made to the foster services in more than one-third of cases (Bestuur Bijzondere Jeugdbijstand, 1991).

Parents who find themselves temporarily unable to care for their children will sometimes seek to place them with alternative families. In many cases, this will involve placing children with relatives or friends. In other cases of social emergency, professional help is sought. Such placements are referred to as private foster placements. By not applying to have their child committed to care via either the juvenile court or the committee of special youth assistance, the parents who initiate private foster care arrangements hope to remain more involved in decision making about their child than would otherwise be the case. Some parents contribute towards the costs of private foster placements.

In 1990, about 270 private placements were arranged by the foster services (Zwysen, 1992).

A large proportion of those seeking private foster homes for their children are single parents, who are unable to turn to relatives for support. In the large cities, particulary Brussels, immigrant parents are over-represented among those applying to have their children fostered. In most cases, there is an understanding between parents and child that they will be re-united as soon as the crisis has abated.

Sometimes a foster family is required for a lengthy period. Such cases frequently involve young mothers whose relationships with their spouses have broken down, and who need support in adjusting to the changes in lifestyle brought about by child birth.

The following range of foster care placements may be distinguished, based on the characteristics of the child looked after and the duration of placement.

- foster-family - a family that provides long-term care for a child.
- host-family - a family that offers a long-term home for an adolescent or an adult.
- weekend-family - a family which the child visits at weekends and during the school holidays.
- relief-family - a family which provides the child with short-term care.
- a room with supervision - a family which provides a room and appropriate guidance for a young person.
- orientation-family - a family that accommodates a child at short notice, and for a specific period, in order to assess and prepare the child for future long-term placement. These tasks are either undertaken by the foster parents themselves (who, in most cases, will

have received (ortho)pedagogical training) or by an observation service.

therapeutic foster family - a family which offers therapy to the child (again, most of the foster parents involved will have received (ortho)pedagogical training); the foster parents and the child may be given intensive help by the referral service.

The classification presented above is not an official one. By contrast with private residential care services, no attempt has been made by government to categorise foster care services.

In practice, the development of the various types of foster care referred to has been uneven. For example, therapeutic foster families of the kind which exist in Germany and the Netherlands for very difficult children, and where the foster parents are professionals who receive enhanced fees and have special pedagogical expertise, have yet to be introduced in Flanders. Although foster family services do exist which offer very intensive counselling for children whose problems are severe, orientation-families have not developed to a degree whereby the foster parents may be regarded as 'professionals'. The other types of foster care mentioned are fairly common.

Almost all foster care services now place younger children with surrogate families for longer periods than was formerly the case. The number of foster families available for younger children exceeds actual demand for placements. The opposite applies to 'host-families' for older children. There is a shortage of suitable families for adolescents, not least because families generally prefer to take in younger children.

A study of the pedagogical functioning of foster care services in Flanders suggests that almost half of all new cases referred to the services[11] involve children under five years of age (Schils, 1990). When we compare this finding with data from Hellinckx and De Munter (1990) on the population of children in residential care in 1987, it is clear that more younger children (toddlers and children of primary school age) than adolescents are placed in foster care. By contrast, adolescents are disproportionately represented in the residential care population.

Following discharge from their foster placements, some 25 per cent of children move on to another foster family; only around 25 per cent return to their birth families (Schils, 1990).

At one time, foster care was the only alternative to residential care. The decreasing capacity of instititions has not, however, been accompanied by a significant rise in foster care placements. Between 1981 and 1991, foster placements remained at around 30 per cent of the total number of placements for young people living away from home in Flanders as a result of intervention by the special youth care services (Lammertyn and Antoons, 1990; Bestuur Bijzondere Jeugdbijstand, 1991; Vademecum Pleegzorg, 1991).

Expenditure on residential and foster care[12]

Annual expenditure on special youth assistance in the Flemish community amounts to approximately £70 million, which represents about 9.3 per cent of the total spent on social welfare (De Standaard, 1992).

Private provisions The private institutions, authorised and subsidised by the government, receive a daily allowance for each child to cover maintenance and education. The sums paid to private institutions depend on a variety of factors.

The daily charge may be separated into two parts : one that is calculated (the costs of staff), and one that is fixed (covering other expenses). The fixed part covers the costs of a child's stay and the costs of the buildings. The daily costs of a child's stay are determined by age and are set out below[13]

- 0-2 years : £6.
- 3-11 years : £6.7
- 12 years and over : £7.8.

There is a fixed amount for accommodation costs.

As indicated, staffing forms part of the calculated costs. For each institution, there is a maximum number of staff on which the amount of subsidy is based. This number depends on the number of the children accommodated.

Some - for example, the Acknowledgement Commission, 1992 - consider that the occupancy rate should not be an absolute criterion for subsidy. It has been argued that the occupancy rate should be weighted against other criteria such as the nature of the target group; in particular, the severity of the problems presented by the children looked after.

Residential institutions can, subject to meeting certain requirements, receive an extra allowance for special costs. These may include the costs of medical care, instruction, education, and travel (Lammertyn and Antoons, 1990).

Foster care Foster families receive an allowance irrespective of whether placement was direct or occurred via the mediation of one of the foster care services. There are, however, placements that are not subsidised by the Flemish community. These mainly involve placements with members of the family.

Foster parents usually receive a daily allowance. If placement was by private arrangement, and did not result from special youth assistance, an allowance is provided by an organisation called Child and Family.

This is a government agency commissioned by Decree to take care of the health and welfare of families with young children in the Flemish community. One of its tasks is to subsidise foster families with young children, on condition that the children concerned have been placed by authorised foster care services.

The allowance paid to foster families by Child and Family is identical to that associated with youth protection. When a foster placement has been arranged through the mediation of services authorised by Child and Family, the birth parents are required to make a contribution towards the costs of the placement based on their income.

Daily allowances are linked to the age of foster children. The following daily allowances are paid to cover current expenses for food and maintenance.

- 0-3 years : £7.5.
- 4-11 : £8.
- 12 years and over : £8.5.

As with residential care, an allowance can be paid to cover additional costs, the so-called special costs, such as the costs of medical treatment, schooling, holidays, visits to birth parents. The foster parents must submit a special application in order to obtain these allowances.

In addition to the daily allowances which they pay to foster parents, the foster care referral services can receive funds to cover their operational costs, including staff costs (Vademecum Pleegzorg, 1991; Dossier Private Gezinsplaatsing, 1990).

Research on residential and foster care

In recent years, research on residential and foster care in Flanders has been stimulated by government, umbrella organisations (of which the services often form a part) and universities. University based research is carried out by departments of Orthopedagogics, Sociology, Psychology, and Criminology, depending on the subject of investigation.

Emphasis is increasingly placed on the collection of systematic data about young people in care and their families, the referring agencies and the care facilities. This is necessary in order to ensure that the supply of facilities is geared to the needs of children and families (Hellinckx and De Munter, 1990).

Since 1969, a longitudinal study sponsored by the National Fund for Scientific Research has been undertaken on juvenile delinquents. In the first phase of the study, male and female juvenile delinquents accommodated in institutions of the Flemish community[14] were interviewed about their attitudes towards marriage and family life. Seven years on, the same persons were questioned. Those adolescents whose prospects appeared poor at the time of the first study, were later found to have made greater progress with regard to personal and social development than was originally expected and predicted by care workers. The progress made by the most difficult to manage group was particularly impressive. These very positive results, which contrast sharply with much of the European literature on the outcome of residential care, appear to validate the principles of dialectical developmental psychology (Riegel, 1979). This perspective views the experience of conflict or opposition as a necessary, though not sufficient, condition for the process of development. To further test and explore this proposition, a new follow-up study was set up over a period of eight years with a broader representative sample of non-delinquent adolescents (Verhofstadt-Denève, 1981; Verhofstadt-Denève, Schittekatte and Braet, 1990). Another follow-up project concerning delinquent youngsters was established in 1987 (Vandevelde E., Faculty of Psychology, University of Brussels, under supervision of Prof. Dr. Ponjaert). This project is monitoring the development of 100 young delinquents. The variables under study include personality, family background and type and severity of delinquency.

Over the past decade, the following major projects were commissioned by the government.

Demeulemeester (1983) attempted to examine how care workers in special youth care perceived their roles. The study comprised, first, a historical and theoretical study of ideological and structural roles and role-conflicts among care workers. A combination of quantitative and qualitative methods were used in the design of questionnaires and the analysis of data.

In 1986 Hellinckx and De Munter (1990) examined the pedagogical functioning of 188 private Flemish institutions under special youth care. A number of services for independent living under supervision and day centres were also evaluated. In order to study the population of young people in care, 439 youngsters were included in an investigation carried out in 1987.

15

In addition to a pedagogical evaluation of residential care, the finance and organisation of the residential sector was also investigated (Andersen et al., 1988).

Lammertyn and Antoons' (1990) study forms part of a larger research project that has examined all aspects of special youth care and special youth assistance. Following the constitutional changes of 1980 and 1988, responsibility for special youth care was transferred to the communities and a new framework of by-laws was introduced. Lammertyn and Antoons' (1990) studied the implementation of the new decrees and collected statistics on the macro-organisation of the services comprising special youth assistance.

Walgrave and Poels (1991) have looked at the regime of a controversial Flemish community institution. In response to an increasing rate of absconding, a regime was introduced based on 'aversive deprivation' and the principles of 'token economy'. The study set out to evaluate the operation of the new regime.

In Flanders, an experimental scheme was recently established to provide an intensive form of residential care for young people who are particularly difficult to manage. The Research Group on Juvenile Delinquency is currently carrying out research on the the decision making process which results in placement into residential care. The group further intends to delineate treatment procedures in residential care and to evaluate the long-term effects of such treatment.

In addition to research sponsored by the National Fund for Scientific Research and government funded research projects, small-scale, descriptive, studies have been undertaken for academic theses. These include projects on the population in residential care, and the pedagogical functioning of residential institutions. Research has also been completed on the supervision of group workers (Hellinckx, Martens and Punter, 1985), and the history of residential care (e.g. D'hoker et al., 1986). The latter has concentrated on the ideas that informed residential care in the past and their impact on the current organisation of services.

However, as yet no large scale, systematic, research has been undertaken on the population of children in foster care and the activities of the foster care referral services. Academic theses have, however, been written on the support offered to foster families, the problems experienced by birth parents in coming to terms with their child's placement in a foster family, the problems encountered by foster families, and the pedagogical functioning of foster care services.

There is a striking lack of long-term outcome studies on residential and foster care. This owes much to the fact that policy makers are more interested in short-term, immediately relevant, studies.

Moreover, no comparative research has been carried out in which residential care is evaluated in conjunction with the major alternatives. Finally, there is also a need for studies focusing on the perspective of service users.

Part III: Residential and foster care in the French-speaking Community of Belgium[1]

The nature of residential and foster care provision

At present, child welfare services in French-speaking Belgium are provided under two pieces of legislation : the law of 8 April 1965, which concerns the protection of young people (protection de la jeunesse), and the decree of 4 March 1991 covering aid for young people (aide à la jeunesse).

These laws have their origin in quite different political contexts. While the 1965 law is national in scope, the 1991 decree was produced by the Executive of the French-speaking community following the institutional reforms of 1988, which allowed the different linguistic communities to manage various aspects of their own affairs.

After 1988, responsibility for the whole sector of social aid in Belgium, and aid for young people in particular, passed to the community authorities. That which follows thus refers to the present organisation of aid and protection for young people in Belgium's French-speaking community. Matters pertaining to the penal and civil codes (notably with respect to the delinquency of minors) remain under the national authority of the Minister of Justice. Consequently, the 1965 law on the protection of young people continues to apply throughout Belgium to young people who have committed offences.

As far as aid to young people is concerned, the French-speaking community is still very much in the experimental stage with regard to implementing the 1991 decree. The new structures which have been set up - *Services de Protection Judiciaire* (Legal Protection Services), *Services de l'Aide à la Jeunesse* (Youth Aid Services), together with the *Conseils d'Arrondissements de l'Aide à la Jeunesse* (Borough Councils for Youth Aid) - are right at the very start of the process of identifying organisational partners, and defining areas of responsibility.

The main objective in setting up the new institutional structures is to prevent cases which involve problems of a primarily psycho-social order from coming before the courts, and to separate aid to young people, where policy is essentially preventive, from restrictive and repressive

17

intervention in a legal context. The principles of decriminalisation, prevention and keeping the young person in his or her environment, thus justify the existence of two distinct services.

Below are a number of tables illustrating the recently introduced administrative structure :

Table 1.1
Direction de l'administration de l'aide à la jeunesse (DAAJ)[2]
(Directorate of administration for aid to young people)

1. Missions

Legal bases :
1. The law of 8 April 1965 concerning the protection of young people.
2. Decree of 4 March 1991 concerning aid to young people.

Purpose :
General prevention.
Specialised aid to young people in difficulty or danger.
Specialised aid to young people who have committed offences.
The search for abandoned children.

2. The means

                    organised by the DAAJ = Public
Institutional
                    approved and subsidized by the DAAJ = Private

The total annual budget for 1992 is approximately £81,650,000, which represents some 2.7 per cent of the overall budget of Belgium's French-speaking community.

Public sector

For the Wallonia and Brussels Capital Regions, the public institutions for the protection of young people (IPPJ) offer the following services :

 - residential = 186 places + 2 emergency places
 - non-residential (accompaniment) = 22 places

The public sector is assisted by two advisory councils : the *Conseil Communautaire d'Aide à la Jeunesse* (community council for youth aid) and the *Commission d'Agrément* (approval committee).

Private sector

Table 1.2
Services and capacity of the private sector

	Number	Assisted capacity	Take-up (on 03/92) private + public sector
Different types of residential services	178	4,085	3,785
including :			
2 initial reception centres			
2 observation and orientation centres			
Services organising family houses	2		84
Family placement services	15		1,364
Foster homes, not supported	840		919
Services approved by other authorities (Office de la Naissance et de l'Enfance; Medico-Pedagogical Institutes; Hospitals, Residential schools; etc.)			473
Total			6,541

Other means of action are available to the private sector, namely non-residential services. These are the *Centres d'Orientation Educative* (educational orientation services), the *Services de Prestations Educatives et Philanthropiques* (educational performance and philanthropic

19

services), the *Services de protutelle* (acting guardian services) and, finally, various preventative services (Open Environment Action).

The tables presented above show that approximately 4,000 minors are placed in residential institutions which are controlled by the *Administration de l'Aide à la Jeunesse*.

Decisions to place children and young people in residential care are taken by judges sitting in the juvenile court, by the aid services for young people, and by *Centres Publics d'Aide Sociale* (public social services which are administered by the local authorities or 'communes').

In the first case, the judge takes control of the situation and makes a court order for the child's placement in care which is then acted upon by the *Service de la Protection Judiciare* (Legal Protection Department). In the other two cases, the placement is negotiated with the young person and his or her family. The length of the placement is re-negotiable between the parties concerned and must be re-examined every six months.

The choice of residential placement is made on the basis of criteria linked to the character and ethos of the establishment in question, taking into account such matters as whether or not it is co-educational, the availability of places, and the age, personality, and educational level of the child, etc.

Each establishment lays down its own criteria and procedures for admission. On the young persons entry to an establishment, a care or treatment plan will be formulated by the various parties concerned : the young person, the family, the institution, and the referring authority.

When we look at graphs showing the distribution of young people placed in residential institutions on the basis of age, we see that the population can be broken down into three groups : young children (under fives), children of primary school age and adolescents. There is, therefore, a basic differentiation of residential establishments according to the age of the children and young people accommodated. The placement of children in the first two age groups is the responsibility of the protective services of *Aide à la Jeunesse*. These services intervene in families where the welfare of children is jeopardised by unfavourable socio-economic circumstances.

With regard to adolescents, protection may become confused with punishment and constraints linked to acts of delinquency which are not always described as such. This is often combined with a hardening of behavioural attitudes among the youngsters concerned. It is customary to speak of 'difficult adolescents' as a group which requires special forms of residential help and a greater number of qualified supervisory staff.

Every private residential facility is free to decide on the target population which it will serve, and the style of help it will provide. It is, however, clear that present trends in aid to young people reflect a preference for keeping individuals in their familiar environment as much as possible, and thus for short-term residential placements.

Public residential institutions (IPPJ) are exclusively reserved for young delinquents, and have two primary tasks : first, to promote the social reintegration of young people; second, to help them acquire a positive self-image. This implies the need to help young people come to terms with their own responsibility for the process of exclusion they are experiencing, and to motivate and support them towards reintegration into society. However, public institutions are not permitted to refuse admission to any young person except on the grounds of a lack of space. This means that they are obliged to accept young people with serious psycho-social difficulties, and who may be extremely difficult to manage.

The staff structure in establishments approved by the youth aid authorities (administration de l'aide à la jeunesse) is based on formal standards of support and supervision. For example, there must be one instructor for every three children and one chief instructor for every 12 children. The financial budget to cover staff salaries is allocated on a lump sum basis (on condition that the establishment is full to 80 per cent of capacity on an annual basis), which allows for flexible management.

The 'price per day', that is the estimated cost of one day's placement, varies according to the type of service offered, the establishment's capacity, the age of the children, and the qualifications and seniority of the staff. Institutions which have been approved to undertake specialist tasks, such as the treatment of difficult adolescents, may receive additional resources.

Nevertheless, in 1991 the authorities calculated an average price per day which came to £43.6 (roughly 62 Ecus). This estimate includes the costs of personnel, fixed overheads, variable costs and a set average of so-called special costs. The latter include the costs of 'buying in' the services of outside experts, such as medical practitioners, physiotherapists, orthopaedists, etc., in so far as these costs cannot be covered by health insurance.

Research on residential and foster care

The overall level of funding allocated for research on child welfare is relatively low; it is also difficult to estimate as budgets for research on aid to young people are divided between two different ministries.

The *Centre d'Information, de Formation et de Perfectionnement* (Information, Training and Further Training Centre) of the *Administration de l'Aide à la Jeunesse* (youth aid authority) is presently undertaking a census of recent or current research into specialised forms of aid and legal protection for young people.

This involves contacting the ministries concerned, together with the universities and the various colleges which train social workers, psychology assistants, etc. It is too soon to offer a definitive account of their findings, but it appears that an extremely wide range of research topics are being investigated. This includes studies by those working in a variety of disciplines : psychology, education, medicine, law, criminology, town planning, economy and sociology.

We will close this section with a brief review of a number of important research studies.

Between 1985 and 1990, a research project was carried out by the University Faculties of Notre-Dame de la Paix in Namur (Meunier, 1989), entitled 'Analysis of the efficiency and effectiveness of the protection services for young people'. Efficiency was defined with reference to a comparison of the costs of services and their effectiveness in terms of one or more performance indicators.

A large part of this work involved comparing the relative costs and outcomes of placements in institutions and foster homes. The average length of stay, approximately 5 years, did not differ between one type of placement and another, while the costs of institutional placements were 2.4 times higher than placements in supervised foster homes.

One of the most significant findings of this study was that after the age of 12, the most difficult youngsters are to be found in institutions - usually large institutions with between 61 and 89 beds. The study also highlights the need to increase the number of foster homes for younger children, and to improve the support given to foster parents. It is suggested that additional help might be offered to institutions so that they can respond to the individual needs of the diversity of young people accommodated.

The latter proposal is supported by Detraux and Mercier (1990), who carried out research on the criteria to be applied when planning the take-up capacity of establishments and services specialising in the treatment of young people with disabilities in Belgium's French-speaking community. Part of this research focuses on children with emotional and behavioural disorders (Courtois, 1990) who appear to represent half of the population of children in care with learning disabilities. Some 7 per cent of such youngsters are placed by the *Administration de l'Aide à la Jeunesse.* The young people concerned manifest personality disorders, antagonistic symptoms and aggressive and/or depressive behaviour. Institutions which look after such youngsters must offer psychological, medical and socio-educational help which, rather than being exclusively centred on the child alone, embraces the child's family environment.

Delogne (1990), in his work on the re-organisation of residential institutions (IPPJ) run by the *Administration de l'Aide à la Jeunesse,* also stresses the importance of working with children's families, not least because over half of all young people placed in IPPJ institutions return to their families at the end of their stay.

The ultimate goal of residential institutions is to adapt to the needs of young people and their families, while at the same time providing specialised, high quality, services which are effective in meeting their socio-educational responsibilities. In conjunction with external services, residential care performs a valuable role in helping to meet the varying needs of vulnerable young people and their families.

Research on residential care depends heavily on personal initiatives, professional associations and the federation of children's homes; it can also originate within the context of action-research as in the case of Felinne (Pain, 1987), which led to the publication of a joint 7 year study on the care careers of 60 children aged between 3 and 18 in a rural environment.

Also worthy of mention is an assessment study carried out in 1985 at one residential educational establishment (Bonami and Vanthurnhout, 1985). The objective of this research was to identify an assessment model for use in residential institutions. The study also resulted in the development of a number of analytical tools.

Other topics have provided the subject matter of psycho-educational theses. For example, studies coordinated by Lepot-Froment (1990) have concerned matters such as the observation of the private behaviour of children educated in residential institutions, and symbolic games for underprivileged children.

Institutions which accommodate very young children are interested in parenting methods (Pourtois, 1979; Pourtois et al., 1984). The location of the residential institution often determines the line of research. For instance, residential institutions situated in the urban environment of Brussels have provided the venues for research concerned with the needs of young people from different ethinic backgrounds (Bastenier, 1991).

Finally, it is essential to ensure that research findings are disseminated to practitioners. Therefore, it is encouraging to note that a number of residential institutions have programmes which involve a system of in-service training whereby research informs practice (Hayez et al., to be published).

Part IV : Residential and foster care in Luxembourg[17]

Prior to 1960, there were two main types of residential child care institutions in Luxembourg : those run by the government, and private children homes - usually administered by convents.

Although residential institutions were strongly criticised during the 1950s and 1960s, little change occurred in the care system. However, at the beginning of the 1970s, the Ministry of Family Affairs initiated a programme of reform, and within 13 years the financial resources allocated to residential care had increased by six-fold. The goals of the reformers were to create small units of between 10 and 12 children ('foyers') and to improve the training provided for residential staff. Alternatives to residential care - particularly foster care - were also expanded. Some 800 children and young people aged under 18 years are placed away from home in Luxembourg. About 67 per cent are placed in institutions, and 33 per cent live with foster families. Roughly 25 per cent of children in residential care are accommodated in public provisions, the remainder (75 per cent) are looked after in private institutions (Ministry of Family, 1991). About half of all placements in public institutions are in 'reform schools' (*centres socio-éducatifs*), while the other half belong to institutions which have the same function as private institutions (Ministry of Family, 1991). The residential child care task in Luxembourg is, first, to ensure that children are integrated into social life; second, where possible, to re-integrate them with their birth families (Soisson, 1991, p.207).

Children are placed away from home under the law on youth protection passed in 1971. The Ministry for Family Affairs is responsible for all such children. Children can be placed away from home by the judge or by other services such as medical social services (*Centres Médico-Sociaux*). All placements are arranged by a special agency (*Commission National de l'Arbitrage de Placements*).

Private institutions are not regulated by law. However, contractual relations do exist between these institutions and the government. The government's contribution to the finances of private establishments is fixed by an agreement or 'convention' between the Ministry of Family Affairs and the institutions.

24

There is little specialisation of services. For instance, institutions for therapeutic treatment do not exist. As a consequence, many troubled children from Luxembourg are placed in special institutions in Belgium and Germany. However, short-term placements for children and families in crisis were recently introduced.

The ammount of money which the private institutions receive from government does not depend on the number of children actually present, but rather on the staff structure and the number of designated places.

Two services are responsible for the provision of foster family care : the *'Service de Placement Familial'* and *'CARITAS-Fir Ons Kanner'*. The role of these services involves assessing the needs of individual children, finding appropriate foster families, and maintaining contacts with the children, their families of origin and their foster families.

No systematic research has been carried out on foster and residential care in Luxembourg. This is partly because there are no universities in Luxembourg.

Conclusions

It is difficult to make direct comparisons between the three regions examined in this chapter. Nevertheless, despite administrative differences, recent developments in residential and foster care have been very similar in each region.

There has been a significant reduction in the numbers of young people placed in residential settings in the past two decades. However, the fall in numbers of children in residential care has not led to a sharp rise in the number of children in foster care. In all three regions, there are still more children in residential care than in foster care. The ratio of children placed in residential care to children placed in foster care is 6:4 in the Flemish community of Belgium. In the French-speaking community this ratio is even higher : almost three-quarters of children in care are placed in residential settings. In Luxembourg, the ratio of children placed in residential care to children in foster care is roughly 7:3.

Nevertheless, the decline in residential placements has been accompanied by a growth in other community based services. In the Flemish community of Belgium, in particular, we can observe the development of day-centres, independent living under supervision and home based treatment.

Day centres provide children and young people in problematic parenting situations with place to go after school. As such, day centres

25

are the link between residential and field work services, and carry out valuable preventative work with children and young people. Treatment programmes involve children, their families and their schools. In Flanders, the first day centre was opened in 1979. Since then, day centres have received official approval from government. They may take the form of autonomous centres, or be part of pre-existing residential homes.

A young person who is living independently under supervision, lives autonomously but with support from a central service. This type of help has been available in Flanders since the early 1980s, was approved by the government in 1984, and may assume one of two forms. The first entails young people living on their own with support from staff who are based at residential homes. With regard to the other, young people are supported by services that have been specifically established for this purpose. Both forms involve the young person living alone or in a small group of up to 3 young people.

The opposite end of the care continuum to residential care involves home-based treatment, whereby families of vulnerable youngsters are offered intensive, pedagogical, practical, material and social support. The first such services were approved in 1991. This kind of help is provided by specially created autonomous services, or by staff from centres which provide lodgings and support for young people.

Despite steady growth, the provision of alternatives to residential care remains fairly limited. Home-based treatment exists only in the Flemish Community. Independent living under supervision is more common and can be found in all three regions. Day-centres also exist in each of the three regions, but there is only one day-centre in Luxembourg. Whilst the Flemish community has led the way in community alternatives to residential institutions, at the end of 1991 only 10 per cent of children in care were using such services (Bestuur Bijzondere Jeugdbijstand, 1991).

Although a generally positive reception has been given to the growth of community alternatives, concern has been expressed that the decline in residential provisions means that young people with the most serious problems do not always receive appropriate help. As yet, with the exception of a very small number of experimental projects, there are no specialist facilities for this group of young people. This is partly due to the fact that the classification of services in the three regions is not linked to specific groups of children and young people. Moreover, the funding of services does not depend on the characteristics of the youngsters accommodated. This means that homes which are prepared to admit the most challenging young people do not receive the additional resources which they require.

An obvious trend in all three regions is the move towards small-scale residential homes. In Luxembourg, large institutions have been completely abolished. Currently, one of the key objectives of residential homes is to facilitate the child's reintegration with his or her natural environment. Residential practice is becoming more sensitive to the needs of children's families and the surrounding community.

The quality of residential care has improved in recent years. Not only have more and better qualified staff been recruited, but residential practitioners are also increasingly adopting a more methodical approach, which includes the use of theoretical 'decision making models'. This is evidenced in improved admission and discharge procedures and care and treatment plans. However, research in the Flemish community of Belgium suggests that there are shortcomings in residential practices in relation to the following[18]

- Admission

Requests for admission are not always supported by adequate information, which makes it difficult to assess whether admission is appropriate. Moreover, a sizeable minority of services (18 per cent) still fail to involve young people in decisions about admission.

Written admission criteria are often vague and unspecific, and criteria for rejection are enormous.

- Care and treatment plans

A large number of services (40 per cent) operate without such plans. Services that do work to plans tend to be those employing professionally qualified staff, who act as advisers or consultants with regard to pedagogical methods and policy, or provide direct help to youngsters. Some 40 per cent of services in Flanders do not employ such staff.

- Family-oriented action

All institutions are aware of the fact that residential care can only be effective when it is part of a package aimed at helping the family as a whole and where parents are involved in all aspects of the care process. However, intensive treatment programmes geared to helping parents are not yet common. In Flanders, less than 20 per cent of files examined in a study of young people in residential care contained evidence of intensive family-oriented care.

- After care

The provision of after care is by no means universal. Although over 80 per cent of services claim to offer after care, only half of these were found to offer help 'systematically' and 'always'.

On a more positive note, the Flemish government (via the Flemish Executive's Decree of May 22, 1991) has made certain aspects of good practice, such as the use of care plans in residential care, obligatory. However, the government has failed to allocate the additional resources that are required in order to implement this policy.

Research on the population of children in care shows that such children mainly come from families with multiple problems. The question arises as to whether alternative forms of help might have prevented the separation of at least some of the children from their families. A decision to place a child in care should only be made when the parents, in spite of all kinds of support and counselling, are no longer able to bear the responsibility of looking after their child (Hellinckx and De Munter, 1990). A large number of parents of children in care are willing to look after their children at home but are unable to do so because of various socio-economic or relationship problems which jeopardise the welfare of their children. The load carried by such parents, which may include bad housing, unsatisfactory work conditions, long periods of unemployment, poor relationships within the family, etc., is so crushing that they have neither the time nor the energy to devote to caring for their children. The most appropriate approach in such cases is not placement in care but, rather, real help that encompasses all aspects of life : better housing and conditions of employment; and practical help in the home, including help with housekeeping, and guidance and support for parents in undertaking their child care roles (De Ruyter, 1983, p.162).

Notes

1. In 1988 the German-speaking people represented about 0.7% of the population of Belgian (Nationaal Instituut voor Statistiek, 1991).
2. This part was written by Walter Hellinckx and Benedikte Van den Bruel.
3. The Flemish community became responsible for the 'reform schools' in 1989. Since then, these institutions have been referred to as 'facilities of the Flemish community'.
4. The data on the population in the community's facilities are borrowed from Vereecke (1990).
5. This inquiry was instigated by the Administration for Youth Care (*Dienst voor Jeugdbescherming*) in cooperation with the National Federation of Youth Judges (*Nationale Federatie van Jeugdmagistraten*).

6. On 1 December, 1991, however, a project was initiated with a view to offering intensive residential help to especially troubled young people (Onderzoeksgroep Jeugdcriminologie, 1992). These facilities have not yet been classified as a separate category of provision.
7. This study was carried out in 1986, is reported in Hellinckx and De Munter (1990), and preceded the study undertaken in 1987 on the characteristics of children in private residential care.
8. 'Orthopedagogue' is a qualification awarded by Flemish and Dutch universities. The task of the orthopedagogue is to supervise group workers and to coordinate pedagogical activities.
9. In estimating the total number of staff members only psychologists, pedagogues and social workers were included.
10. The data on children's characteristics have been taken from research carried out in 1987 (Hellinckx and De Munter, 1990).
11. These cases do not fall exclusively within the domain of special youth assistance.
12. The way in which the Flemish community's institutions are financed is not dealt with here. Because the Flemish community takes full responsiblity for the management of its institutions, the latter receive authorisation and financial subsidies without first having to meet stipulated requirements.
13. The sums mentioned here are those that were paid in May 1992. They were calculated from the sums mentioned in the Flemish Community's Decree of May 22, 1991.
14. At the time of the study (1969-1976) these institutions were still under national authority and were called 'state reform schools'.
15. This part was written by Christine Vander Borght.
16. The Direction d'administration de l'aide à la jeunesse provided useful information for this section.
17. This part of the text was written by Walter Hellinckx and Benedikte Van den Bruel, and is based on work by Soisson (1991) and information from the following agencies: *maisons d'enfants de l'état* (Schifflange), the Ministry for Family and the National Commission for Mediation in Placements (*Commission National de l'Arbitrage de Placements*).
18. The data are from Hellinckx & De Munter (1990).

References

Arthur Andersen and co (1988), *Doorlichting van de sektor bijzondere Jeugdbijstand. Finaal Rapport*, Arthur Andersen and co, Brussel.

Bastenier, A. (1991), 'Recherche : immigration et délinquence - Belgique', *Youth Horizons*, n° 3, Ed. Aide à la Jeunesse et Protection de la Jeunesse.

Bestuur Bijzondere Jeugdbijstand, 31/12/91 (personal communication).

Bonami and Vanturnhout, A. (1985), *Méthodologie pour l'évaluation d'institutions éducatives*, Report on research into assessment procedures carried out in 85 - 86 at la Goudinière - 7542 Mont St Aubert.

Bowlby, J. (1951), *Maternal care and mental health*, WHO, Geneva.

Courtois, A. (1990), *Approche de la population caractérielle. Aperçu théorique sur la question*, Under the supervision of J.J. Detraux, Fascicule n° 4.

Delogne, R. (1990), *Study on the restructuring of 'Institutions Publiques de la Protection de la Jeunesse de la Communauté Française'*, CRIDIS.

Demeulemeester, C. (1983), *De opvoeder in de Jeugdbescherming*, K.U. Leuven, Onderzoeksgroep Jeugdcriminologie, Leuven.

Demographic Yearbook 1990, (1992), United Nations, New York.

De Ruyter, P.A. (1983), 'Inrichtingsopvoeding? Nee. Residentiële hulp verlening? Ja, mits', in R. De Groot and J. Van Weelden (Eds.), *Onvoltooid of onbegonnen. Hulpvragende kinderen. Antropologische uitgangspunten*, Wolters-Noordhoff, Groningen, pp. 151-166.

Detraux, J.J. and Mercier, M. (1990), *Recherche relative aux critères devant présider à la programmation de la cpacité d'accueil des établissements et services spécialisés dans le traitement des personnes handicapeés de la Communauté Française*, Final report, Université Libre de Bruxelles/University Faculties of Notre-Dame de la Paix - Namur.

D'hoker, M. et al. (1986), *Het kind in de inrichting. 150 jaar residentiële zorg voor kinderen met psychosociale problemen*, K.U. Leuven, Faculteit der Psychologie en Pedagogische Wetenschappen, Afdelingen Historische Pedagogiek en Orthopedagogiek, Leuven.

Dinnage, R. and Pringle, M. (1967), *Residential child care : facts and fallacies*, Longman, London.

Dupont, L. and Vander Auwera, C. (1988), *Het nieuwe jeugdrecht van de Vlaamse Gemeenschap. Teksten met inleidende commentaar*, Acco, Leuven/Amersfoort.

Erkenningscommissie (1990). *Advies m.b.t. een vernieuwd voorzieningenbeleid in de bijzondere jeugdbijstand.*

Federatie Gezinsplaatsing v.z.w. (1990), *Dossier kennismaking met de private gezinsplaatsing in Vlaanderen.*

Geukens, M. (1989), 'Opvang van moeilijk opvoedbare jongeren in Rijksinstellingen', Debatlunch te Brussel op 27 januari 1989, *Contact*, 2.

Goffman, E. (1961), *Asylums. Essays on the social situation of mental patients and other inmates*, Penguin, Harmonsworth.

Grote Winkler Prins. Jaarboek. Een encyclopedisch verslag van het jaar 1991, (1992), Elsevier, Amsterdam/Antwerpen.

Gryspeerdt, I. (1987), 'De rol en de functie van de R.O.O.T.', *Contactblad van de Dienst voor Jeugdbescherming*, 2.

Hayez, J.Y., Boutsen, H., Kinoo, P., Meynckens, M. and Vander Borght, C., *L'institution comme médiateur thérapeutique*, to be published, 'Institutions' Group - 1200 Brussels.

Hellinckx W. et al. (1989), 'Hulpverlening aan minderjarigen in het kader van de bijzondere jeugdzorg. In residentiële voorzieningen, dagcentra en diensten voor begeleid zelfstandig wonen', in *Welzijnsgids* (Organisatie II.A.3.1, afl.43, januari), Van Loghum Slaterus, Antwerpen, Hel.1-Hel.33.

Hellinckx W. et al. (Eds) (1991), *Innovations in Residential Care*, Acco, Leuven.

Hellinckx, W. and De Munter, A. (1990), *Voorzieningen voor jongeren met psychosociale problemen. Onderzoek naar residentiële voorzieningen, diensten voor begeleid zelfstandig wonen en dagcentra*, Acco, Leuven/Amersfoort.

King, R.D., Raynes, N.V., and Tizard, J. (1971), *Patterns of residential care. Sociological studies in institutions for handicapped children.* Routledge and Kegan Paul, London.

Klomp, M. (1985), 'Teambegeleiding : begeleiden van een samenwerkingsproces vanuit orthopedagogische doelstellingen', in J.F.W. Kok and M. Klomp (Eds), *Ambulante en residentiële hulp. Regionalisatie en integratie in de geestelijke gezondheidszorg*, Acco, Leuven, pp. 65-84.

Knorth, E.J. and Smit, M. (Eds) (1990), *Residentiële jeugdhulpverlening. Mogelijkheden voor planmatig werken*, Garant, Leuven/Apeldoorn.

Lammertyn, F. and Antoons, P. (1990), *De welzijnszorg in de Vlaamse Gemeenschap. Voorzieningen en overheidsbeleid. De bijzondere jeugdbijstand*, Sociologisch Onderzoeksinstituut, Departement Sociologie K.U.L., Leuven.

Lepot-Froment, C. (1990), *Orthopedagogie*, UCL, Louvain-La-Neuve.

Meunier (1989), *Analyse de l'efficience et de l'efficacité des services de Protection de la Jeunesse*, Faculty of Economic and Social Sciences, Faculty of Law, Fac. Univ. Notre-Dame de la Paix, Namur.

Nationaal Instituut voor Statistiek (1991), *Bevolkingsstatistieken*, Ministerie van Economische Zaken, Brussel.

Pain, J. (1987), *Placés, vous avez dit? : Méthodes actives et practique institutionelle en maison d'enfants*, GRAPHI,Ed. Matrice, Paris.

Pourtois, J.P. (1979), *Comment les mères enseignent à leur enfant (5-6 years)*, PUF, Paris.

Pourtois, J.P. et al. (1984), *Eduquer les parents ou comment stimuler la compétence en education*, LABOR, Bruxelles.

Pringle, M.L. and Bossio, V. (1960), 'Early prolonged separations and emotional adjustement', *Child Psychology and Psychiatry*, 1, pp. 37-48.

Riegel, K.F. (1979), *Foundations of Dialectical Psychology*, Academic Press, New York.

Schils, K. (1990), *Het pedagogisch functioneren van gezinsplaatsingsdiensten van de bijzondere jeugdbijstand : Een descriptief onderzoek*, K.U. Leuven, Afdeling Orthopedagogiek, Leuven (unpublished dissertation).

Soisson, R. (1991), 'Residential care in Luxembourg', in M. Gottesman, (Ed.), *Residential Care. An International Reader*, Fice International, London, pp. 214-221.

Statistical Yearbook (1991), Unesco, Paris.

The New Encyclopaedia Britannica. Vol. 23. Macropaedia. Knowledge in depth (1986), Encyclopaedia Britannica, Chicago.

Vereecke, J. (1990), 'Extreem moeilijk te begeleiden jongeren in de Rijksgestichten voor Observatie en Opvoeding onder Toezicht', in W. Vandamme (Ed.), *Extreem moeilijk te begeleiden jongeren*, Acco, Leuven, pp. 93-105.

Verhofstadt-Denève, L. (1981), 'Adolescentiecrisis en jonge volwassenheid tegen de achtergrond van een dialectisch ontwikkelingsmodel', in F.J. Mönks et al. (Eds), *Psychologie van jeugdjaren en adolescentie. Nieuwe ontwikkelingen en bevindingen*, Dekker and Van de Vegt, Nijmegen, pp. 122-165.

Verhofstadt-Denève, L., Schittekatte, M. and Braet C. (1990), 'Van adolescentie naar jonge volwassenheid. Een follow-up onderzoek vanuit een dialectische visie', *Nederlands tijdschrift voor de psychologie*, 45, pp. 259-269.

Vlaamse Vereniging Pleegzorg en Federatie Gezinsplaatsing (1991), *Vademecum Pleegzorg*.

Walgrave, L and Poels, V. (1991), *Bijzondere Jeugdbewaking? Een studie over de praktische en ethische aspecten van het regime in sectie A van de Gemeenschapsinstelling De Hutten te Mol*, K.U. Leuven, Onderzoeksgroep Jeugdcriminologie, Leuven.

Ysebaert, C. (1989), *Politiek Zakboekje. Onze politieke structuren na de vijfde grondwetsherziening*, Kluwer, Antwerpen.

Zwysen, E. (1992), *Private gezinsplaatsing. Enkele elementen ter discussie*, Beleidsdenkdag van 22 mei 1992 georganiseerd door de

Federatie Gezinsplaatsing en Verbond van Instellingen voor Welzijnswerk rond de positie van de private gezinsplaatsing 'Gedreven tussen drie dekreten'.

2 Denmark

J. Melhbye

Recent political history : Following a long period of government by the social democratic party, a conservative party has been in power for some 10 years. In common with other EC countries, Denmark has quite a high rate of unemployment (10% of the work force). Young people have particular difficulty in obtaining work. Despite efforts to reduce unemployment through special programmes, the number of people out of work is increasing. In a referendum held earlier this year, the Danish people voted against the Maastricht treaty. It is anticipated that certain 'opt-out' conditions will have to be agreed with other member states of the EC before Denmark accepts the treaty.

Geographical Size : 43,093.37 Km².

Principal industries : Manufacture of beverages, food and tobacco, fabricated metal products, and machinery.

Date of EC membership : 1973.

Total number of inhabitants (01.01.1992) : 5,162,126.

Age of majority : 18 years.

Number of people under the age of majority (01.01.1992) : 874,945.

Number of children and young people (31.12.91) :

in residential care :	3,600
in foster care :	5,613
other placements :	4,891.

The nature of residential and foster care provision

The Danish child care system comprises various types of provision for children placed outside home. Choice of placement for the individual child is usually determined by the child's age, and the nature of the presenting problem; that is, by the kind of help the child requires.

34

The most common type of placement is foster care. Typically, foster families consist of a married or cohabiting couple, who usually have children of their own living with them. Some foster parents work, or have previously worked, with children on a professional basis (e.g. as psychologists, social workers, or teachers). Others have employment experience in residential or day-care institutions. However, many foster parents are 'ordinary' people whose occupational backgrounds are unrelated to child welfare work. Some foster parents, mainly those with just one or two foster children, continue to work outside the home, whilst others put all their energy into caring for their foster child(ren). Whether foster parents are able to remain in outside employment often depends on the seriousness of the foster child(ren)'s problems.

Foster children usually attend ordinary schools, where they may receive special help; for example, an extra teacher may be assigned to the foster child's class, specifically in order to support the foster child. Children with severe emotional or behavioural problems tend to be placed with foster parents who have received professional training. Finally, it should be noted that foster care is usually a privately organised provision.

In addition to foster care, there are various kinds of residential provision for children of different ages and with different problems. In recent years, however, there has been a tendency to reduce the degree of variation between residential homes and to standardise residential provision. Most residential homes accommodate between 20 and 30 children. On average, the adult/child ratio is about 1:2.

The first major type of residential placement is the 'Children's Home', which usually accommodates youngsters without behavioural problems, or whose difficulties in this respect are not severe. As with foster children, the children placed in such homes attend ordinary schools. Second, there are 'Community Homes', where children attend school on site. These institutions accommodate youngsters with serious educational problems. Third, we have 'Treatment Homes' for children with severe behavioural and educational problems. Such institutions also have schools attached. Each class consists of about three to five pupils. An intensive treatment programme is formulated for every child, and the ratio of adults to children is higher than the average for residential homes.

In addition, there are residential 'homes for infants'. Young children may be placed in such homes with or without their mothers, either for observation prior to adoption or with the aim of teaching the mother how to care for her child. These institutions are quite similar in some respects to 'Family Care Homes', where families are able to remain together while the parents receive guidance about how to look after their children and cope with their own problems. There are also a relatively small number of 'Assessment Centres', which accommodate children of all ages for short periods, usually with the aim of observing the child's behaviour to ascertain what sort of help is required.

The types of residential provision so far referred to are usually publically administered. However, there are also privately run establishments, such as the 'Collective Care' homes. These accommodate between six and eight youngsters. The caregivers often have professional backgrounds as psychologists, social workers, or teachers. Children and adults live together in ordinary houses in the community. Collective homes tend to specialise in the care of older children and young people with quite severe emotional and behavioural problems, and who have usually experienced several previous placements outside home without beneficial effect. Consequently, the financial costs incurred by local authorities who place youngsters in such facilities are high by comparison with other forms of residential care.

A further form of residential provision are the 'Ship Projects'. The youngsters associated with these schemes live and work on small ships. Like collective care, most of the projects are privately run. 'Boarding Schools' represent another residential care option. This kind of provision is mainly used in cases where the prime reason for placing the child outside home is parental illness, or where the nature of the parent-child relationship is adversely affecting the child's development. Children may also be placed away from home in 'Continuation Schools', which accommodate youngsters who have tired of ordinary school or whose relationships with their parents are poor. Finally, there are the 'Youth Dens' and 'Youth Boards' or apartments, where young people stay with or without adult supervision.

Expenditure on residential and foster care

The costs of a residential care placement depend on the numbers and range of personnel employed at the insititution, and whether children attend school on site. With regard to foster care, placement costs are determined by the seriousness of children's problems, and by whether or not the foster parents are professionals.

The amount spent on a foster placement ranges from about 68 kr. or approximately £5 to 800 kr. or approximately £76 per day. Thus, although foster care is the cheapest form of provision, it can be quite expensive. A children's home placement costs about 1,000 kr. per day or approximately £95, whereas placement in a treatment facility costs around 2,500 kr. or approximately £238 per day. Collective care and ship project placements also tend to be rather expensive. The costs of placing children outside home are divided equally between the municipality and the county.

Numbers of children in residential and foster care

Every year since 1976, between 15,000 and 17,000 children and young people have been placed outside home. This represents around 1 per cent of the population under 20 years of age.

Young people between 15 and 17 years, particularly boys, are more likely than other age groups to be placed outside home. Almost 3 per cent of all young people in the 15-17 age group are placed outside home. However, one third of this number are placed at boarding schools and continuation schools. Most of these youngsters are placed outside home because they were unhappy at their ordinary day school, or because they were in conflict with their parents.

The proportion of youngsters aged between 12 and 14 years placed outside home is also quite high, representing roughly 1.5 per cent of all 12-14 year olds. The reasons for many such placements relate to fairly serious family problems. About half of the children concerned are placed in foster homes.

As table 2.1 shows, approximately 40 per cent of all children and young people living away from home are placed in foster care; it can also be seen that just over 25 per cent are accommodated in residential homes, with a little under 20 per cent placed in boarding schools. Table 2.1 further reveals that only around 7 per cent of children in care are placed in alternative forms of provision, such as collective care and the ship projects.

Table 2.1
Numbers of children and young people placed outside home
under laws §33,1,3;§123 and §127
on 1 January, 1990, according to type of placement and age

Age	0-6	7-11	12-14	5-17	18-19	+20	Total
Percentage of population	0.4	0.8	1.4	2.6	1.0	-	0.9
Total number	1,517	2,358	2,871	5,635	1,481	848	14,710

Of this, percentage placed in :

	0-6	7-11	12-14	5-17	18-19	+20	Total
Foster care	70.7	66.2	46.2	27.1	28.3	36.2	42.2
Residential homes	27.6	29.7	31.3	24.5	26.5	26.2	27.3
Boarding schools	0.2	2.4	18.5	32.7	14.4	4.8	18.3
Collective care	1.4	1.5	3.8	6.3	11.1	27.1	5.9
Ship projects	-	-	0.1	1.4	0.9	0.7	0.7
Own room	-	-	0.1	7.9	18.7	10.3	5.5
Hospital	0.1	0.3	-	0.1	-	0.1	0.1

Source : Bistand dèl børn og ünge (1991)

Moreover, the majority (71 per cent) of young children aged from birth to 6 years are placed in foster homes. Collective care with professionals tends to be reserved for older youngsters aged between 15 and 19 years. Some young people are also placed in 'their own room', which denotes youth dens and apartments. These youngsters are often supervised by adult child welfare workers, and have usually previously been in care at some point during their childhoods.

As mentioned earlier, the number of children and young people placed outside home has remained fairly stable over the past 15 years, with between 15,000 and 17,000 youngsters placed outside home each year. However, since 1989, the number of children in care has been decreasing annually. This trend is expected to continue in view of the current policy of reducing the number of children and young people in care. Emphasis is now placed on preventing the separation of children from their birth parents.

About 4 per cent of children in care are compulsorily placed outside home against the wishes of their parents. The majority of such children are under 11 years of age.

Historical antecedents of services

In the 17th century, destitute children were regarded as a cheap source of labour. 'Children's Houses' were established for those who were healthy enough to work. Conditions in these institutions were harsh in order to deter all but the most needy. Little change appears to have occurred until the early years of the 19th century, when public authorities and private organisations began to place children and young people with foster families in the country, rather than accommodating them in orphanages located in large towns and cities. Nevertheless, children boarded out in this manner were still expected to work and earn their keep, and many orphanages were established from private funds and by charitable organisations. Throughout the 19th century, the prevailing view was that the care of neglected and delinquent children and young people was the task of charitable organisations.

However, by the turn of the 20th century, there was increasing recognition that private and charitable initiatives were an inadequate response to the needs of such children. A law was passed in 1905 which regulated the philanthropic system of institutions, and enabled the public authorities to meet the costs of maintaining needy children.

In 1933, a statute was introduced transferring responsibility for the care of maltreated and delinquent children to the Ministry of Social Affairs. This task had previously been carried out by the Ministry of Justice, Education and Church. The term 'orphanage' gave way to a more elaborate classification of different types of provision, and the problems experienced by children in care began to be viewed as worthy of the attention of psychologists and psychiatrists.

A new Child Care Law was passed in 1958 which further increased the role of the state in supervising and paying for the care of children placed outside home, and a formal system of educating and training child care workers was established.

In 1964, legislation differentiated child care institutions according to the age of the children and their behaviour problems. Henceforth, institutions were seen as therapeutic establishments with pedagogical functions. Work and training were not to be considered ends in themselves, but rather as means by which to facilitate children's development. The importance of play for the child's development was also acknowledged. In the 1960's, although most institutions were privately run, they nevertheless received substantial grants from the state. Moreover, by this period responsibility for children placed outside home resided with the state's Directorate for Child and Youth Care.

During the 1970s the number of children placed outside home increased. At the same time, foster care was given priority over residential care, in response to research findings indicating that children derived little, if any, benefit from the latter; indeed, it was found that some children may be adversely affected by residential care.

By contrast with earlier measures, the Social Security Act of 1976 sought to reduce differences between residential homes, and required them to admit children regardless of age and presenting problem. The 1976 Act also made county authorities responsible for supervising residential homes. Furthermore, the new law stressed that children should be placed near to where their parents lived, in recognition of the importance to children of familiar surroundings and contact with their birth families. The Act identified foster care as the preferred form of substitute care, and defined the purpose of placement outside home as that of providing the child with the opportunity to live an independent life outside an institution. Finally, the Act said nothing about training the child or young person for the labour market. This omission marked a significant break with former policy and practice.

It may be noted that the goal of reducing differences within the residential sector has not been achieved; also, throughout the 1980s much criticism was directed towards residential homes, which were said to be ineffective and to serve merely as 'warehouses' for children until foster families were found for them. Some have argued that residential homes should only be used as a last resort when other options have been exhausted.

The 1980's were also characterised by a growth in privately initiated alternatives to traditional foster and residential care, such as collective care and the ship projects. The Social Security Act of 1985 removed the priority which had formerly been given to foster care, and identified three important types of provision : foster care, residential homes and 'domiciles' for children and young people. The latter comprise alternatives to traditional foster and residential care.

Legal and administrative framework of services

The Social Security Act 1985 increased state supervision of child care provision, and laid down new rules concerning the placement of children and young people outside home. The county authorities are responsible for providing the requisite number of residential places. Each county consists of several municipalities. The task of finding placements for children is shared by the municipal and county social services.

The costs of placing children outside home are also shared between the municipalities and the counties. Individual institutions may belong to the county or to the municipality, or they may be privately run and accommodate children under contract from a county. The political committees of the municipalities and the county councils have overall responsibility for children placed outside home and for the residential homes. The municipal authorities have a duty to ensure that children placed away from home maintain contact their birth families.

The Social Security Act 1985 makes it unlawful for foster parents to receive children under 14 years of age without first obtaining permission from the local social services. Further, under the 1985 Act, foster families are only permitted to accommodate a maximum of 4 children. The Act also states that foster parents should be couples who have lived together for a period of over three years. Finally, the foster parents must not be too old, i.e. there should not be more than 40 years between the foster parents' ages and that of their foster child(ren).

The Social Security Act 1985 covers the following 5 types of placement :

1. 'Domiciles' which accommodate up to 4 children or young persons. These include foster families, and also youth dens in which young people have their own, self contained, living space.
2. 'Domiciles' which accommodate more than 4 persons - for example, collective care provisions.
3. 'Domiciles' such as boarding- and continuation schools administered by the Ministry of Education.
4. Ship projects accommodating up to 3 youngsters, and those with between 4 and 10 youngsters on board.
5. Residential homes.

Under the 1985 Act, the social welfare authorities are permitted to place children outside home against the wishes of their parents. In such cases, the parents must be offered the services of a lawyer, and must be informed of their right to read the case files maintained on their child by the social welfare authorities. Before a decision is taken to remove a child without the parents consent, the parents, the child, the lawyer, and sometimes an independent assessor, must be given the opportunity to discuss the case with the social committee of the municipality. The Town Court Judge and a consultant educational psychologist nominated by the County Council must also participate in such meetings, albeit without voting rights or a decision making role. Where such meetings are not possible prior to placement (e.g. emergency cases), the parents must be provided with a written report within 24 hours explaining why the decision to place the child against their wishes was taken. The social committee has to be notified about such decisions within 7 days. The parents, accompanied by their lawyer, must then be given the opportunity to discuss their case with the social committee.

Recent innovations and trends in residential and foster care

Children placed outside home in Denmark are currently the subject of a nationwide debate embracing both child welfare professionals and lay members of the public. This centres on whether the number of children placed outside home is increasing or decreasing, whether it is right to place children away from home, and whether children benefit from such placements. There is also much discussion about the costs of placing children outside home, what can be done to prevent children entering care, and the respective strengths and weaknesses of foster and residential care.

In 1990, the Graverson committee published its report on child welfare law (Graversen, 1990). The committee's task was to critically examine the law concerning procedures for helping vulnerable children, young people and their parents. The Graverson report argues that (i) steps must be taken to safeguard the rights of both children and their parents; (ii) the goals of social welfare intervention, and the means by which they are to be achieved, should be formulated more precisely; (iii) comprehensive assessment of the needs of children and their families is essential if they are to be offered appropriate help; (iv) children over 12 years of age should be given the opportunity to express their views before decisions which affect their lives are taken.

The Graverson report has raised awareness of the need for a general improvement in the quality of the case work undertaken by social welfare agencies; more specifically, the report succeeded in highlighting the importance of assessment and planning in helping children and their families.

The work of the Graverson committee recently resulted in legislative change (Lov om andning at lov ..., 1992). Local authorities are now required to formulate treatment programmes for all children placed outside home, setting out the purpose of the placement, specific arrangements for the child's care, treatment, education, and so on, together with measures for supporting the family during the child's placement and the period following the child's return home. Moreover, the consent of young people aged 15 years and over must be obtained prior to decisions being taken to place them outside home.

As a reaction against institutionally-oriented care practice, and in response to the relatively high costs of residential care, the past few years have seen a good deal of innovation with regard to prevention and alternatives to residential care. This trend has been further encouraged by the Ministry of Social Welfare, which initiated a scheme whereby municipalities can receive grants for innovations in social care. During the last three years the Ministry of Social Welfare has awarded grants totalling 350 million kr. or approximately £34.5 million for this purpose.

A number of these schemes are concerned with improving inter-agency cooperation. This includes, for example, cooperation between (i) social welfare services and day-care institutions; (ii) schools and social welfare offices; and, (iii) education, social welfare, and the police.

Innovations have also included attempts to establish small, neighbourhood, welfare offices, which provide advice and counselling for children and their families. Moreover, efforts have been made to set up small-scale, flexible, residential homes in local areas which are able to accommodate and provide help for the whole family, or provide help for children on a day basis.

Schemes have also been introduced which provide a range of social activities for children, young people and their families in districts with high rates of social problems. This is done in cooperation with local leisure services and organisations. The aim is to strengthen the social networks of vulnerable families.

To this, we may add the efforts made to develop alternatives to traditional foster and residential care in the form of collective care. It may also be noted that residential homes are increasingly offering help to children on a day-care basis. Along with the other innovations reported, this development is encouraging in view of the research which shows that placement away from home is not always conducive to the child's welfare.

Research on residential and foster care

Over the last 10 years, an estimated 7-8 million kr. or approximately £690,000-£790,000 has been spent on research into residential and foster care. This work is mainly funded by the state (the Ministry of Social Affairs), but private foundations, counties and municipalities also sponsor research.

Research is carried out by a variety of agencies, which include the Local Government Research Institute, the Institute of Social Research and the Universities. Professionals such as psychologists, employed by social welfare agencies, also carry out research.

Review of recent research findings

Children and young people in collective care (Gustafsson, 1981)
Gustafsson's study involved 262 children and young people who left 12 different collective care institutions in April 1977. Not surprisingly, it was found that 70 per cent of those placed in collective care are boys. Around 30 per cent of the children were below 14 years of age, and 10 per cent were aged over 22 years. Almost half of the children and young people had earlier been placed in residential care, and 20 per cent had lived away from home for more than 5 years. Over 80 per cent of the youngsters appeared to have been adversely effected by their previous experiences in residential care.

The average length of stay in collective care was around 11 months. However, some of the youngsters had been placed in collective care for over five years. On leaving collective care, about two-thirds of the children and young people either returned to their parents or moved to their own dwelling. Only a small number of youngsters were placed directly into foster care or treatment homes on discharge from collective care.

However, the study also revealed that about one third of the children and young people who had left collective care were later placed outside home once more. This included about two-thirds of those younger boys with serious problems. On the other hand, only 10 per cent of young women, older boys and boys with minor problems re-entered care.

Thus, it was concluded that collective care is 'successful' in relation to 50 per cent of the most 'problematic' children and young people, and eighty per cent of youngsters whose problems are not severe.

Children growing up outside home (Boolsen, Mehlbye and Sparre, 1986)
Boolsen, Mehlbye and Sparre (1986) studied 107 children and young people who were placed outside home in 1980. The children were monitored through their case files over a five year period from 1980 to 1985. Eighteen young people over the age of 18 years were interviewed about their experiences during their childhood, with particular reference to their lives in care. In addition, 35 social workers from the three social welfare offices in Copenhagen participating in the study were interviewed.

The investigation addressed three major questions. First, why are children placed outside home? Second, what kinds of help are offered to children and their parents? And, third, how do the children manage later on?

The study shows that those placed outside home are often emotionally neglected children from families with severe economic, social and psychological problems. Most parents (who are usually single mothers) of children placed outside home are financially supported by public aid, have often been out of work for several years, are likely to be depressed and socially isolated, frequently have marital problems and physical ailments, and may be addicted to drugs and alcohol. Two-thirds of children raised in such families manifest severe behavioural problems and fail to attend school regularly. When they do go to school, these children tend to be anti-social and aggressive, and are restless and disruptive in the classroom; they have problems in communicating with other children as well as adults, experience serious learning difficulties, and may show psychosomatic symptoms.

Approximately half of the children in the study had received help from the local social welfare office before being placed outside home. However, such help, which may have involved an advisor visiting the family for a couple of hours 2-4 times a month, often proved inadequate. The social workers responsible for helping the children and their families complained that they did not have sufficient time to devote to their task. At the same time, they found it difficult to persuade the political committee dealing with social services to allocate funds for the provision of more intensive forms of help. The latter may, for instance, involve a worker staying with the family for several days a week to help them manage their daily problems.

The study further revealed that many placements of children outside home are requested by parents. However, little information about children and their parents is collected and placed on file prior to placement. Moreover, very few files contained written goals for the child's placement outside home. Thus, preparations for placements are unsatisfactory. Consequently, all too often children returned home prematurely, and the problems which led to the child's entry to care quickly re-established themselves. Some 75 per cent of the children were away from their parents less than a year. On average, the children had experienced 2 previous placements in care. Only 25 per cent of the children had not been previously placed outside home. A major problem in the case work undertaken by the social welfare offices was that treatment typically concentrated on the children rather than on their parents. This goes a long way to accounting for the fact that many of the children seemed to go in and out of care on a sort of revolving door basis. Only about one-third of the parents had received help or treatment during their child's placement outside home.

However, the study found that some success was achieved in relation to helping children. Whilst two-thirds of the children were reported as having problems in 1980, this figure had fallen to around one-third by 1985. The most favourable outcomes were obtained for children placed outside home between 4 and 11 years of age. One third of the children were still placed outside home in 1985.

The interviews with young people placed outside home during childhood showed that they felt rejected as children and unloved by their mothers and fathers. However, when placed outside home they missed their parents, and felt stigmatised as a result of being in residential care; they also tended to have rather low self-esteem, and easily gave up if they encountered difficulties at work or at school. Predictably, therefore, many were unemployed.

Boolsen et al's (1986) study, together with the following investigation by Jørgensen, Gamst and Boolsen (1989), has played an important role in informing discussion about how best to help vulnerable children and young people.

Child care cases in the municipalities (Jørgensen, Gamst, Boolsen, 1989)
Jørgensen et al. (1989) evaluated child care practice in seven municipal social welfare offices. Between five and seven cases were studied at each office. This included interviews with social workers, and others who had contact with the families concerned.

Like Boolsen et al. (1986), Jørgensen et al. (1989) found that children placed outside home come from families characterised by problems such as unemployment, marital discord and poor parenting skills. It was clear from interviews with the social workers that had help been offered to the families sooner, the removal from home of many of the children could have been prevented. The problems experienced by many of the families studied were of long-standing. Further, whilst such families may receive various kinds of help, this is seldom co-ordinated and rarely includes the services of a psychologist. Prevention is difficult to achieve, and demands an intensive and long lasting commitment to the family. However, the study also suggests that seeking to prevent the child's removal from home is not always appropriate. Sometimes placement away from home is the only viable means of safeguarding the child's welfare.

The investigation demonstrates that some local authorities have more children placed outside home than others. For example, in Copenhagen between 2.5 to 3 per cent of children and young people are placed outside home. By contrast, in rural areas less than 0.5 per cent of youngsters are placed outside home. These differences reflect the relatively high concentration of families with problems in the municipalities, together with different child care policies. Some local authorities try to avoid placing children outside home. However, many such authorities do so without attempting to find new, and more effective, ways by which to deal with the underlying problems. Other local authorities are more innovative and, although they continue to place children outside home, they also stress the importance of prevention and are active in seeking to develop alternatives to care. A third group of authorities adopt a traditional approach. They operate according to long established policies and procedures, and make little, if indeed any, attempt to innovate.

The course of placements (Andersen, 1989) Andersen (1989) examined data on children who were placed outside home between 1977 and 1986. One third of the children concerned had experienced more than one placement outside home. However, a small decrease in the number of such placements was observed over the period in question.

Foster care (Christoffersen, 1988) Research by Christoffersen (1988) addressed the following questions : what qualifications do foster parents hold? What contact takes place between the foster family and the social welfare office, on the one hand, and between the foster parents and the child's birth parents, on the other? The investigation was based on a representative sample of foster parents.

Some 40 per cent of the foster parents had been trained as social workers, teachers, psychologists, or allied professionals, and half had previously worked with children. The study also indicates that the preparations made for foster placements are often inadequate. Foster parents reported that they are typically given insufficient information about the child and his or her family. Further, it was found that programmes containing goals for the child's stay and arrangements for contact between the child and his or her birth parents are seldom formulated. Only one third of the children visited their mothers at least once a fortnight. With regard to the supervision of foster parents, no more than half of the foster families in the study were visited by a supervisor every 3 months.

Compulsory placement of children outside home (Caspersen, 1988) A study undertaken by Caspersen (1988) looked at the cases of 50 children in the north of Jutland who had been placed outside home against their parents' wishes between 1975 and 1985. The children were followed up until April 1987. Most of the parents were single mothers. Many of the children had lost contact with their fathers. The majority of youngsters in the study were aged under 11 years. A good number of them had asked to be placed outside home. This was particularly true of the older ones. The children's mothers were poorly educated, many were unemployed, and their circumstances did not improve during time that their children were living away from home. However, the problems manifested by the children tended to diminish over the course of their placement. Yet, it remained to be seen whether such progress would continue after the children returned home.

Outside home (Hansen, 1989) In studying 293 child care cases from several municipalities in the south of Jutland, Hansen (1989) observed that the parents of children placed outside home may be divided into four categories : (i) those who are deceased, (ii) drug addicts, (iii) immature parents, and (iv) parents who are divorced or have severe marital problems.

It is further suggested that such characteristics contribute to the placement of children outside home. However, in a fifth group of cases, the cause of placement was conflict between parents and youngsters aged 13 years and over. The investigation stresses the importance of preventative measures, particularly in relation to children's leisure activities and guidance to parents; it also emphasises the need for initiatives aimed at improving the self-confidence, self-esteem, and social skills of parents and enlarging their social support networks. Such an approach is premised on the notion that improving the quality of life for parents will, in turn, result in benefits for their children.

Placements at boarding- and continuation schools according to the Social Security Act - an analysis of 210 children and young people from Copenhagen placed at boarding- and continuation schools (Ydebo, 1990) A research project carried out by Ydebo (1990) was published in the report of the Graversen Committee on the law concerning the provision of help to children and young people. The main purpose of Ydebo's (1990) study was to ascertain whether there were fundamental differences between placements at boarding- and continuation schools and 'ordinary' placements outside home in residential and foster care. The investigation included all children and young people from Copenhagen who were placed outside home at boarding- and continuation schools in April and May of 1989. This involved some 210 pupils at 13 boarding-schools and 50 continuation schools.

Data on the 210 youngsters were compared with data from the study referred to above by Boolsen et al. (1986). From this, it is evident that placement away from home in boarding- and continuation schools tends to be reserved for children whose problems are less serious than those of children placed in residential and foster homes. The problems experienced by parents of boarding- and continuation school children also appear less serious than those of parents whose children are placed in residential and foster care.

Comparisons were also made between the boarding- and continuation schools. This showed that personal and social problems were more prevalent among parents of the boarding-school children than among parents of the children placed at the continuation schools. Equally, the boarding-school children manifested higher overall levels of anti-social and disruptive behaviour than their continuation school counterparts. However, whilst the behaviour of the boarding-school children is similar in some respects to that of youngsters placed in residential and foster homes, the latter are more likely to present serious, and multiple, problems.

Thus, it was concluded that boarding- and continuation school pupils placed away from home under the Social Security Act have fewer and less serious problems than youngsters placed in foster and residential care.

It was also found that the class work of the youngsters placed away from home at boarding- and continuation schools was usually of a comparable standard to that produced by other children at such schools. Also worth noting is the finding that social welfare workers were seldom responsible for arranging placements at boarding- and continuation schools. In most cases, placements were initiated either by the parents or by the children themselves.

Finally, given the clear differences between the boarding- and continuation schools, on the one hand, and residential and foster homes, on the other, the study raises the question as to whether placements outside home in boarding- and continuation schools should continue to be funded by the social welfare services.

Family education (Mehlbye, 1990) A project called 'Home is Best' was initiated in five municipalities as an alternative to placing children and young people outside home. The project offered families intensive counselling for 6 weeks in their own homes. Mehlbye (1990) evaluated the short- and long-term effects of the initiative. This included interviews with 41 families, and counsellors and social workers from the five local social welfare offices which participated in the scheme. In addition, a comparison group was studied comprising 50 families of children placed outside home and 14 families who had received traditional counselling at home.

The evaluation showed that the 'family education' initiative achieved little success in preventing placement outside home. Although counselling proved helpful during the period in which it was provided, its impact was shortlived. In most cases, little benefit could be observed 12 months after counselling had ceased.

With regard to the comparison group, the evaluation showed that more than half of such youngsters were still living away from home 12 months after they had originally been placed. Some 25 per cent of the children spent less than 6 months away from their families. The problems of half of the comparison group had been significantly reduced after 12 months in placement, whereas no significant progress had been made by the other half. Children who had only been placed outside home for a very short time had made the least progress.

Mehlbye (1990) concludes that family education is most beneficial with families whose problems are of a relatively minor nature. When family problems are serious and of long-standing, placing the child outside home is often the only feasible option. The study further suggests that in such cases, placements should be of sufficient duration to facilitate progress. Finally, Mehlbye (1990) argues that for family education to be effective, counselling must be extended over a considerably longer period than the 6 weeks offered in the scheme which she evaluated.

Future research on foster and residential care

Research currently being undertaken in Denmark centres on prevention. This includes treatment at day centres for children and parents with problems, and intensive counselling at home.

However, whilst increased emphasis on preventive measures is welcome, future research should also include attempts to compare different types of residential and foster care, in order to make good the current dearth of such studies. For example, we need to know more about the content and quality of foster and residential care practices, including interactions and relationships between children and their caregivers. Such studies are vital if we are to offer a comprehensive range of services to vulnerable children and their families.

References

Andersen, B.J. (1989), *Anbringelsesforløb - en registrerundersøgelse af børn og unge anbragt uden for hjemmet*, (The Courses of Placements), København, Socialforskningsinstituttet (Rappord Socialforsknings- instituttet, 89:2).

Bistand til børn og unge 1988 (1990), *Danmarks Statistik*, Social sikring og retsvasen (Statistike efterretninger) nr.3, København.

Bistand til børn og unge 1989 (1991), *Danmarks Statistik*, Social sikring og retsvasen (Statistike efterretninger) nr.1, København.

Bistandsloven (Lov om socialbistand), Lov nr. 333 af 19 juni 1974, med senere ændringer.

Boolsen, M.W., Mehlbye, J. and Sparre, L. (1986), *Børns opvækst uden for hjemmet*, (Children Growing up Outside Home), AKF Forlaget, Amternes og Kommunernes Forskningsinstitut, København.

Børneforsorgsloven af 1905.

Børneforsorgsloven af 1933.

Caspersen, E. (1988), *Tvangsfjernelse af børn*, (Compulsory Placement of Children Outside Home), Aalborg Kommune.

Christoffersen, M.N. (1988), *Familieplejen*, (Foster Care), Socialforskningsinstituttet, København (Rappord Socialforsknings- instituttet, 88-11).

Graversen-betænkning (1990), *Betænkning om de retlige rammer for indsatsen over for børn og unge,* Statens Informationstjeneste, (Betænkning, nr. 1212), København.

Gustafsson, Jeppe (1981), *Børn og unge i Miljøerne - nogle erfaringer*, (Children and Young People in Collective Care), Aalborg Universitetscenter, Aalborg.

Hansen, C.Y. (1989), *Uden for eget hjem* (Outside Home), Aabenraa, Institut for Grænseregionsforskning.

Jørgensen, P.S., Gamst B. and Boolsen, M.W. (1989), *Kommunernes børnesager*, (Child Care Cases in the Municipalities), Socialforsknings- instituttet, København (Rappord Socialforskningsinstituttet,1989;1).

Lov om andring af lov om social bistand og lov om styrelse af sociale og visse sundhedsmassige anliggender samt lov om påligningen af indkomst - og formÜlskelt dil staten m m (Andring af reglerne om foranstaltninger for børn og unge, herunder reglerne om tvangsmassig gennemførelse af foranstaltninger), Lov nr. 501 af 24 juni 1992.

Melhbye, J. (1990), *Forældreuddannelse - en evaluering af projekt 'Hjemme er bedst' i Vejle Amt*, (Family Education), AKF Forlaget, Amternes og Kommunernes Forskningsinstitut, København.

Nielsen, B.G. (1986), *Anstaltbørn og børneanstalter gennem 400 år*, (Children of institution and institutions of children through 400 years), SCOPOL, Holte.

Ydebo, I. (1990), *Anbringelse i kost-og efterskole med hjemmel i bistandslovens kap. 8 set i i relation til lovens anbringelsesbegreb. Analyse af 210 københavnske kost-efter-skoleanbringelser,* (Placement and boarding- and continuation schools according to the Social Security Act - an analysis of 210 children and young People from Copenhagen placed at boarding- and continuation schools), I: Graversen-betænkning.

3 France

M. Corbillon

Recent political history : The 1980s were characterised by changes in the French political system. There was a shift in traditional voting patterns, and a weakening of the long-standing ideological differences between the major political parties. This was accompanied by the decline of the 'Jacobian' planned state economy, and the decentralisation of power to local government. For administrative purposes, France is divided into 22 regions, and also into 95 'départements'.

Geographical Size : 549,000 Km².

Principal industries : food, armaments, civil aviation, engineering, tourism and cultural activities.

Date of EC membership : 1957.

Total number of inhabitants (05.03.1990) : 56,625,000.

Age of majority : 18 years.

Number of people under the age of majority (05.03.1990) : 13,203,000.

Number of children and young people (31.12.90) :　　　in residential care :　　60,800
　　　　　　　　　　　　　　　　　　　　　　　　　in foster care :　　66,100.

The nature of residential and foster care provisions

In France, responsibility for children and adolescents in residential and foster care is shared by several services - youth welfare (social, and legal/judicial), child welfare and those for young people with behavioural problems. Services for children and young people with disabilities are beyond the scope of this chapter, which will focus on services provided for youngsters whose difficulties are of a psycho-social nature.

Administrative structures

Two ministries are primarily responsible for the administration of the services : the Ministry of Justice and the Ministry for Social Affairs. The role of the latter has, however, been significantly reduced by decentralisation of responsibility to local government - the 'départements'. Moreover, although the Ministry of Education is involved in the education of troubled children, it plays little part in the placement of children in residential and foster care. The various authorities ('département' or state) entrust the care of young people either to services funded by the public purse or to private, non-profit making, organisations.

Historical antecedents of services

The history of child placement is part of the broader history of child welfare, which often entailed efforts to protect society against 'dangerous' children.

In France, the first residential homes for children were founded as early as the 5th century. However, several centuries passed before such provisions were widespread. The Order of the Holy Spirit of Montpellier is generally credited as having taken a leading role in the development of care for abandoned children. Founded during the 12th century, the Order first received children into its local institution (up to 600 children were admitted), and went on to create similar institutions throughout Europe with the support of the Catholic Church.

For several decades after the Middle Ages, the circumstances of foundlings seems to have deteriorated. War and starvation were obstacles to the development of charitable work. Abandoned babies were left under the porches of churches. Trading in children was common and the child mortality rate was very high. 'At 'La Couche' (an institution for foundlings created in Paris in 1570), children were sold to beggars, acrobats or magicians for 10 sols. The mortality rate was horrendous, reaching 100 per cent in some homes' (Cayet, 1953).

This was the context in which Saint Vincent Paul began his work, which represents the beginning of 'modern' substitute child care. With the help of charitable bodies, he sought to change attitudes and practices towards abandoned - in particular, illegitimate - children, and established the first foundling homes in 1638 (Dupoux, 1958). Fundamental improvements in care practices were achieved. For example, nurses were supervised, children were fed cow's milk and increased attention was generally given to their physical health, social development and future employment.

The 18th century was marked by a sharp increase in the number of abandoned children. Factors underlying this growth included higher numbers of illegitimate births, and the unintended consequences of improved conditions for children in institutions. As a result, admissions to the Foundling Home in Paris, for example, increased from 372 in 1640 to 1,733 in 1700. By 1772, the number had risen to 7,676.

Bianco and Lamy (1980) offer the following description of the life-cycle of foundlings at the end of the 'Old Régime' : '...on the eve of the Revolution, the destiny of a foundling is theoretically as follows : 0 to 6 years old : mothering period by a paid nurse; 6 to 12 years old : placed with a paid family; 12 plus : professional training period; the teacher is not paid and recovers his money through the free services that the child must provide until about 25'... Given the high mortality rate among abandoned children, few actually survived long enough to complete the cycle.

The revolution of 1789 resulted in the secularisation of child welfare services, which had previously been organised by the church. Child welfare became the state's responsibility, and the provision of accommodation for abandoned children was conceived as an act of social justice. The legislature compelled local authorities to make provision for abandoned children, and to take steps to ensure that families who were able and willing to care for their children had the means to do so. Although these measures were never fully implemented, the work undertaken by the revolutionaries was of great importance and set the course for future legislation and practice.

The 19th century was characterised by increased spending on child welfare, innovations in the provision of services, and the rationalisation of administrative frameworks. The Napoleonic decree of 19 January 1811 was an important point in the development of child welfare provision; it stipulated the eligibility criteria for admission to public institutions, the standards of care which had to be provided, and arrangements for the funding of institutions. The decree also initiated the inspection of institutions, and special commissioners were recruited to undertake this task (these were replaced in 1870 by the 'Inspectors of Assisted Children').

The 'police and security law' passed on 27 June 1904, classified needy children according to a number of categories, which remained more or less unaltered until 1986. These included : 'children who are being helped', 'children in custody', 'children who are supervised' and 'wards'. The early 20th century saw the beginning of preventive action, and the separation of abandoned or 'deficient' children from other categories of deprived children. Thereafter, increasingly sophisticated methods of prevention and care were developed.

Recent legislation

Child welfare   On 22 July, 1983, a law was passed delegating administrative responsibility for child welfare services to the 'départements'. This was accompanied by the transfer of funds to enable the latter to discharge their new duties. Whilst central government retained legislative and regulatory power, the County Council assumed responsibility for the organisation of child welfare services, including personnel management, the creation and funding of institutions, and charging for services.

Between 1984 and 1986 additional laws and decrees were passed to fine-tune this transfer. These statutes followed in the wake of two major reports reflecting the evolution of child welfare services over the last twenty years (the Dupont-Fauville report, 1973, and the Bianco/Lamy report, 1981), and an important ministerial circular of January, 1981.

The statutes referred to, which included the Children's Act of 6 June 1984, set out a number of key principles for child care practice. First, children should remain with their own families whenever possible. Second, parents of children in care should retain responsibility for their children. To this end, parents should be fully informed of their rights and duties, and participate in the decision making process. Third, the circumstances of children in care should be regularly re-assessed, and case reviews should be held at least once a year.

Judicial youth welfare   Youth welfare services are provided under an ordinance passed on 2 February, 1945, which is currently being reviewed to ensure that services are attuned to contemporary needs and comply with the 1989 United Nations Convention on the Rights of the Child, ratified by France on July 7th, 1990. The 1945 statute established the juvenile court; it also recognised the psycho-social factors underlying delinquency, and promoted treatment and re-education for offenders in place of condemnation and punishment (Pandele, 1987). Further, under article 375 of the Civil Code, judges are empowered to intervene in the lives of youngsters in order to prevent offending behaviour. It is worth highlighting that the responsibilities of the Ministry of Justice and the 'départements' sometimes overlap : measures decided on by the judges must be implemented by the 'départements'.

Children in care

Two major routes into care may be distinguished. First, where temporary difficulties make it impossible for a child to remain with his or her family, an administrative decision will be taken to receive the child into care. In such cases, admission should be requested by the family. Second, where a child is at risk of abuse or neglect, or is on the verge of delinquency, judicial steps will be taken which will result in the child being compulsorily committed to care by the court. Recent years have seen an increase in the number of children entering care by this route[1].

Categories and numbers of children in child welfare In France, child welfare provision is the responsibility of the youth welfare service, which has its origins in public assistance. The term 'youth welfare' first appeared in a decree passed in 1953. Originally concerned with the care of abandoned children, the role of the service has expanded considerably since it was founded. Children or adolescents whose parents are temporarily or permanently unable to take care of them continue to be accommodated in residential settings or placed with foster families. However, the youth welfare service has also established preventive programmes for young people and their families. This includes the provision of financial help to families, and the supervision of children within their own families.

The youth welfare service currently intervenes in the lives of some 450,000 children, or just under 3 per cent of the population under 20 years of age in France. Alternative methods of intervention have evolved over the course of this century, and especially during the last few years. Today, less than 120,000 children are in care. Whereas in 1973, children in care constituted the majority of youth welfare's clientele, they now represent less than 25 per cent of the total number of youngsters served. Currently, less than 1 young person per 100 under the age of 20 is in care. Financial help to children in need and their families has increased sharply over recent years. The families of some 260,000 children presently receive such help. The number of children served has tended to fluctuate, rising from 37,000 in 1955 to 156,000 by 1973, and falling to around 100,000 since then.

Whilst the number of children in care may represent only one-quarter of the total number of children receiving support, it should not be forgotten that entry to care may have far reaching, and adverse, consequences for children and their families. The financial costs of care are also high.

Four major categories of children in care can be identified. First, 'state wards'; that is, orphans or children who have been abandoned or whose parents have forfeited their parental rights. Today less than 1 per cent of children in care fall into this category. Second, children placed 'under supervision' by the court because of risk to their health, safety or morality. Currently, 50 per cent of children in care belong to this category, which represents the largest group of children in care. Third, children 'in temporary care', who entered at the request of their parents because of short-term incapacity on the part of the latter (e.g. because of illness or financial difficulties, etc). Finally, young people under 21 who requested admission or, more often, who have asked to remain in care, because their families are unable to provide for their needs.

Attention should be drawn to geographical disparities in the number of children in care and the quality of care provided. These differences existed prior to decentralisation, but have since increased.

Categories and numbers of children in judicial youth welfare About 3,000 young people are cared for directly by the public welfare service of the Ministry of Justice, which constitutes a relatively small proportion of the total number of children in care. The number of young people in prison is falling and this trend is expected to continue. On 1 January, 1989, an estimated 493 young people under 18 years of age were in prison. Some 392 of these were in 'preventive detention' awaiting trial, and 101 had been given a custodial sentence by the court.

Changes in the child welfare population Between 1984 and 1988, a study was carried out on the evolution of the child welfare population[2]. This involved a national sample of 7,422 children and young people from 47 French 'départements'. A number of important conclusions were drawn from the study. First, changes in the population of children served and methods of care reflect a series of historical transitions, which include shifts from : public assistance to youth welfare; from the provision of care for children without families to helping families in difficulties; from long-term care to the provision of temporary accommodation; and, from the severence of links between children and their families to practices aimed at maintaining such ties. The central factor underlying these changes is the decreasing frequency of abandonment as the reason for entry to care. Whilst at the beginning of the century, two in three Public Assistance children had been abandoned by their parents, such children now represent only one in ten children in care, or one in fifty of the total child welfare population.

Second, improvements in child welfare services, and the increasing diversity in the types of placement available, mirror a child care literature which emphasises the importance of stability, and the adverse effects of separation, for children's development. Such ideas have stimulated attempts to rehabilitate increasing numbers of children in care with their birth families, and have promoted the growth of two kinds of placement : (i) adoption, and (ii) stable or 'permanent' long-term placements for children who cannot be adopted.

Third, the study also highlighted the parallel evolution of vulnerable families and French society. Although the clientele of child welfare services may manifest characteristics that serve to distinguish them from the general population, the changing nature of the former is shaped by forces in the wider society.

Fourth, and despite the tendency towards parallel development referred to above, it was found that families of children in need have maintained a higher than average birth rate over time. Following a 'baby boom' in the 1950's and 1960's, birthrates among the general population in France followed a downward curve before levelling off in the late 1970's. By contrast, birth rates among the families of children in need have remained remarkably stable. On average, such families contain four children.

Fifth, a trend towards what might be termed the 'psychologisation' of social work was identified. This is evidenced in the concepts used to characterise children and parents, judgements made about the personalities and relationships of service users, and the nature of social work interventions.

Sixth, there is increasing recognition of the interdepency between the child's development and his or her environment.

The nature of the services

Public services and private associations In addition to the public sector, numerous, and in some cases, very powerful private associations devote themselves to social action. These have been described as 'the promotors and managers of a considerable patrimony' (Thévenet, 1986). The child welfare services of the 'départements' are responsible for children in care. Such children may be accommodated in one of several types of placement. These include : institutions administered by the departemental child welfare agencies, such as children's homes (in law, one such home per 'département' must be provided to offer temporary shelter, or long-term care, or to prepare children for a subsequent long-term placement), day-care centres, maternity homes, judicial Youth Welfare centres (these are relatively few in number), privately run institutions (e.g. children's homes providing social care to some 3,000 youngsters), boarding-schools, hostels for young workers, institutions for handicapped children, children's villages, and foster family care (which accounts for roughly half of the total number of placements for children in care). It should be noted that privately run residential establishments and associations play a vital role in child care at both the national and local level in France (Ceccaldi, 1989).

Co-ordination of services Following the relatively anarchic development of private initiatives, attempts are being made to rationalise the provision of services. This is reflected in a number of measures taken by the state, such as the unification in 1969 of child welfare, mother and child welfare, and the maladjusted youth and school health services into a single agency, and current efforts to co-ordinate the work of the 'départements' in order to ensure a coherant framework of services. The relationship between local authorities and private institutions was clarified and regulated by legislation passed in the 1970's and 1980's (Children Acts 30.06.75 and 6.02.86). Closer liaison between judicial services and child welfare is also essential given that they largely serve the same children and families. Without such co-operation, conflicts will inevitably result that will undermine the quality of services offered.

Personnel The personnel employed in the field of substitute child care include mother's helpers in foster care, and professional staff in residential care. The former must obtain a permit to practice from the child and mother welfare service and may make use of optional training courses. The size of the foster care sector has remained relatively stable since the middle of the 1970's. Some 57 per cent of children in care are placed with foster families (SESI, 1989).

The professionals employed in residential child care comprise several categories of 'educator's' (social workers in residential care) : (i) 'special educators' (3 years training after secondary school), (ii) 'monitor-educators' (2 years training), (iii) 'monitors of young children' (2 years training), (iv) 'educators in supervised education' (2 years training), and (v) 'vocational trainers'. Although different forms of training have been developed over the last 20 years, the turnover rate for unqualified personnel is very high. Such workers are often young people whose employment situation might be described as precarious[3]. Additional categories of personnel include management and personnel officers, other administrative and general services staff, welfare officers, psychologists, and medical officers.

Finance In general, substitute child care services, irrespective of whether they belong to the state or to the private sector, are funded from the public purse. Usually, funding is based on the number of days for which accommodation is provided for the individual child. This method of allocating resources produces unintended consequences in that a child may be kept at a placement simply as a means of increasing revenue, and innovative projects are restricted. Clearly, alternative funding arrangements are required.

For some years now controlling or reducing social expenditure has been a goal of central government. However, such efforts have been hampered by decentralisation, which means that the overall cost of welfare services reflects the spending of local authorities (the 'départements'). Efforts to cut social expenditure has fuelled debate about the comparative merits of foster and residential care. Although the respective financial costs of each form of provision must be taken into account, this should not be the determining factor in the choice of placement for a child. Rather, in selecting the appropriate placement, the child's welfare must be the paramount consideration.

Average spending on child welfare represents over 40 per cent of annual social expenditure by the 'départements'[4]. In 1986, spending on child welfare totalled 16.5 billion francs (roughly £1.65 billion) (Boisguerin, 1990). Expenditure grew steadily until 1983 (e.g. a 14 per cent increase occurred between 1980 and 1983), since when, however, it has decreased; for example, spending fell by some 4 per cent between 1983 and 1985.

Ideas that have shaped service provision

A wide range of ideas and theories influence the approach of residential workers, reflecting the multi-disciplinary training of the various groups of 'educators'. The 'special educator', a prominent figure among residential workers in France, may best be described as a general practitioner (Ginger, 1980). The knowledge base of residential child care is derived from several academic disciplines, including psychology, social policy and sociology. After the second world war, social welfare in France was shaped by psychiatry (Chauvière, 1980). A little later on, the training of social workers and their practice bore the influence of psychoanalysis : thus, it was said that the child counsellor had become the ground level operator of the psychoanalyst (Faucheur, s.n.). However, the social unrest of 1968 and the acknowledgement of a new social and economic context represent a watershed in the evolution of social welfare, and new approaches to residential practice were developed[5]. More recently, systems theory has informed the activities of residential educators. The law on social welfare work with children and families has also been given greater emphasis in training courses, together with the skills involved in the organisation and management of social care, and alternative methods of social work intervention (Ladsous, 1991).

Recent innovations

For some ten years now, the activities of child welfare professionals have been informed by the notion that it is impossible to offer effective help to children without taking account of their origins, family networks and cultural environments. This has led to important changes in child care practice and the organisation of services. With regard to practice, greater emphasis is currently placed on allowing parents to exercise their rights and responsibilities without undue restriction, and parents are encouraged to share in decisions made about their children. Further, increasing effort is given to ensuring that children remain with their parents. Where this is not possible, stress is placed on maintaining links between children in care and their families. In relation to the organisation of services, attempts have been made to bring services closer to users. This entails the decentralisation of services and the development of small scale provisions in urban areas.

Critical issues in child care

On an organisational level, there is considerable debate about the geographical variation in child care policy and practice; the need to develop closer cooperation between youth welfare services and the courts; and, the increasing role of courts in the field of child welfare. Indeed, aside from its regulatory function, it is unclear whether the state will maintain a significant future role in child welfare.

At the level of practice, the challenges faced by those responsible for the provision of foster and residential care include finding ways to : (i) promote residential and foster care as complementary, rather than rival, approaches to helping children and their families (David, 1989); (ii) improve the status and training of mothers' helpers in foster care; (iii) develop alternatives to the inappropriate incarceration of young people; (iv) improve educational opportunities for young people in care; (v) make the idea of 'partnership' work in practice (which includes partnership between families and child welfare professionals, and between the birth parents and foster parents of children in foster care); (vi) improve residential services for mothers and their young children; and, (vii) ensure that children and young people participate in decisions made in their 'best interests'.

In addition, increasing attention is being given to the consequences of intervention. This includes attempts to monitor the immediate effects of the latter, and evaluative research on the medium- and long-term outcomes of alternative forms of care. Ultimately, the question remains as to how 'residential care' should be designated. Some would like to abolish the term altogether, and replace it with one that has less restrictive, and more positive, connotations.

Research on residential and foster care

Surprisingly little evaluative research has been undertaken on the care of separated children. Studies carried out according to scientific criteria are particularly rare. At a recent UNESCO colloquium concerning research on children in care held in Paris in 1989, there were no more than 30 contributions from French researchers, and half of these involved innovations in practice rather than evaluative research (Corbillon, 1989). Moreover, whilst the 1989 yearbook on social research lists some 328 researchers and 97 research units, only 8 researchers and 1 unit are classified under 'residential care' or 'foster care'.

The reasons for the paucity of research on children in care and, indeed, on social welfare work in France more generally, are diverse, but not least embrace the fact that social work training usually takes place outside the university system. Because social work is not taught in universities, major research programmes in this field are scarce.

A further structural reason for the paucity of evaluative studies relates to the lack of an integrated research policy on the part of the Ministry of Social Affairs (Chauvière, 1989). There is no national planning bureau attached to the latter equivalent, say, to the National Children's Bureau in Britain. Nor are there any regional social research units of the kind that exist in the field of health. The situation is somewhat different in relation to the Ministry of Justice which does have a research centre - the CRIV (Interdisciplinary Research Centre of Vaucresson) - and which has carried out evaluative research on the services provided by the Judicial Youth Welfare agency and the Ministry of Justice. However, substitute child care is marginal to the activities of the Centre.

Unfortunately, the care of separated children is a subject accorded only secondary import, despite the indispensible role performed by residential and foster care in French society. So far, the structures and means required to promote adequate research on substitute child care have been decidedly lacking (Chauvière, 1989). Moreover, research is currently funded on an ad hoc basis. This approach falls a long way short of that which is necessary to develop a sound knowledge base (Soulet, 1987).

However, some progress has been made over the last few years. This includes the creation of an inter-ministerial research task group (MIRE) in 1982 and the Childhood and Family Institute (IDEF) in 1983, initiatives taken by a number of universities (such as the introduction of a Master's degree in applied social sciences and a higher certificate in social work), and the development of research services in social work training centres.

Nevertheless, progress is slow. Research on social welfare failed to benefit from the renewal of scientific research which occurred in the 1960's and 1970's (Chauvière, 1989); it also missed the boat in the 1980's. Traditional antagonism between pure and applied research is partly to blame for this. The number of action-research programmes and studies lacking methodological rigor has multiplied in recent years. However, it should be noted that one of the objectives of the MIRE is to support exchanges between applied and pure research.

The agencies which initiate and fund research include the following : the Ministry of Social Affairs (through organisations such as MIRE); the Ministry of Justice (through CIRV); large research institutions such as INSERM (National Health and Medical Research Institute) and CNRS (National Centre for Scientific Research); the CNAF (National Fund for Family Allowances); those responsible in the 'départements' for social action; training institutes; and a small number of large associations in the private sector (especially, Childhood and Youth Protection).

These agencies promote problem-centred research which is directly related to practice[6]. Funding for research is often provided by organisations which are responsible for the provision of services. This serves to limit both the subject matter of research and the independence of researchers.

Research may be carried out by university staff, by the employees of research institutes (e.g. INSERM or CNRS), by members of research associations, and by the staff of quasi-governmental organisations such as CTNERHI (National Technical Centre for Studies and Research on Handicap and Maladjustment) and the CREAI (Regional Centres for Maladjusted Children and Youth). However, research is also undertaken by residential practitioners and field social workers. The SCORE report on social welfare research, which is based on data collected in 1986, notes that 23 per cent of such research was carried out by CNRS and INSERM, 36 per cent by universities and other public agencies, and 39 per cent by 'associated and independent' researchers (Chauvière, 1989). The community of social welfare researchers mainly comprises psychologists, sociologists and educationalists[7].

Having outlined the organisational framework of research, reference will now be made to a number of important recent studies[8]. These may be separated into the following three categories : historical studies, general analyses, and thematic approaches[9].

Historical studies

The period between the end of the Middle Ages and the Revolution has been considered by Capul (1984) in his work entitled, *Internat et internements sous l'Ancien Régime*. Capul shows that a double or ambivalent image was held of destitute and abandoned children : the negative one of the pauper - a condition which was attributed to laziness, immorality, and heresy; and that of the innocent child. The abandoned child was represented as both 'corrupt and innocent', as both 'dangerous and attractive'.

Marmier's (1969) thesis *Sociologie de l'adoption* tackles past conceptions of adoption from a socio-juridical viewpoint. Studies on the history of residential institutions have also been completed (e.g. Dessertine, 1990). An association was also recently established to promote research about the history of judicial youth welfare[10]. Mention should also be made here of the writings of modern historians whose work has served to highlight changing conceptions of childhood and child care, including care for abandoned children (Ariès, 1973; Badinter, 1980; Donzelot, 1977; Foucault, 1972; Gelis et al., 1978; Rollet-Echalier, 1990).

General analyses

Studies have been carried out on the process of child placement from a variety of theoretical and methodological perspectives. A number of studies have examined the trauma experienced by separated children. This approach, which is now well established, developed in the 1970s and was pioneered by writers such as Soule and Noël, Leibovici, Dolto, Mannoni, David, and Appell. Many recent works have been undertaken in a similar vein.

Some researchers have attempted psycho-social analyses of institutions or evaluations of practices using an approach similar to that of action-research. Many little known studies of this kind have been completed. These include work by the following : Dutrenit (1989), who adopted a 'social audit' perspective; Lepoultier (1990), who examined the aims of care; Durning (1986, 1988, 1989) who attempted to understand the relationship between the organisational dimensions of care and the educative task with the children. Durning discusses the processes of care in terms of the notion of socio-economic climate (C.S.E.).

Epidemiological and statistical studies on the population of children placed away from home have been carried out by Bianco and Lamy (1980), Corbillon et al. (1990), Mignacca (1989), Fenet and Sagot-Duvauroux (1987), and the statistical departments of the Ministry of Justice and the Ministry of Social Affairs.

Finally, a small number of socio-economic studies (Fenet, 1989; Joël and Charvet-Protat, 1992) and ethnological studies (Cadoret, 1991; Lallemand, awaiting publication) have been carried out on separated children.

Thematic approaches

Research has been undertaken on various aspects of foster care practice such as the recruitment, training and status of foster parents, and relations between foster and birth families. The organisational dimension of foster care has been considered, along with the professional relationships between the different categories of care workers involved in fostering. David (1989) has published an important work on these issues. In addition, a national study is being carried out with the purpose of evaluating foster care practice in France (IFREP, Cebula).

Several studies have addressed the issue of violence in residential institutions (Durning, 1992; Duyme, 1987; Tomkiewicz and Vivet, 1991; Tomkiewicz, 1992), and a number of studies have been carried out on adoption. One such project collected statistical data on adopted children and attempted to evaluate adoption services (IDEF, Corbillon and Duyme). Moreover, investigators have sought to examine the long-term effects of placement away from home by studying adults who grew up in care (Cadoret, 1989; Corbillon et al., 1990; Dumaret and Duyme, 1982; Loutre de Pasquier, 1981). The development of young children placed away from home has also been investigated (Waysand, 1989).

Research findings are disseminated through seminars organised by public authorities, research organisations and welfare associations, and via in-service training courses for residential workers and other social welfare practitioners. In addition, research findings are published in books, reports and journals. Here it is worth remarking that there is no research journal specifically concerned with the care of separated children.

In closing, attention is drawn to the following topics, which require immediate investigation : the medium- and long-term effects of different styles of care; the criteria for entry to care; and the abuse of children in residential care settings.

Notes

1. Admission to care may be the result of behaviour problems manifested by a child, and reported by the school, the family or by a doctor (each département has a special education commission, CDES, which determines whether or not a child is handicapped and the type of residential care he or she requires.

2. The methodology and techniques applied in this study are described in a work published in the Documentation française: Corbillon, Assaily & Duyme (1990), *L'enfant placé, de l'Assistance publique à l'Aide sociale à l'enfance*. The sample was based on two main criteria: (i) year of admission; three years (1950, 1965, 1980) were chosen in order to evaluate changes over time; and, (ii) category of admission: 'wards', children placed under 'supervision' of the court and children in 'temporary care' were included in the sample.

3. A study carried out by the CREAI of Orléans found that, in the central region (6 departements), one-fifth of posts were held by unqualified staff. Whilst high, this figure represents a distinct improvement on the situation ten years earlier when more than one-third of staff were unqualified (CREAI Centre, 1985).

4. In the Northern departement, the French departement with the largest population, spending on child welfare represents 20 per cent of the annual budget (Fenet, 1989).

5. For example, the work carried out by GRAPI (Research and action group in residential pedagogy), (see Pain, 1987).

6. Soulet (1987) has noted that research is not planned in a way that promotes the accumulation of a coherant body of knowledge, but rather is driven by increasing welfare problems and the policies designed to tackle them, or by urgency.

7. Noteworthy works in this respect are those by Duyme (1981 and 1987) and the Laboratoire 'Education et formation' of the Educational Sciences Department of Paris X University - in particular, research undertaken by Durning (1988) and his colleagues within the framework of family education.

8. Information about these studies can be obtained from the following organisations: CTNERHI (Centre Technique National d'Etudes et de Recherches sur les Handicaps et les Inadaptations, 2 Rue Auguste Comte, 92170 Vanvas), IDEF (Institut de l'Enfance et de la Famille, 3 Rue du Coq-Héron, 75001 Paris), CEDIAS-Musée Social (5 Rue Las-Cases, 75007 Paris).

9. This typology was inspired by P. Durning's intervention during the conference *'L'enfant placé, actualité de la recherche française et internationale'* (UNESCO, Paris, 1989). A report on this conference has been published by CTNERHI (1989).

10. This association is entitled : *'Association pour l'histoire de l' éducation surveillée et de la protection judiciaire des mineurs'* (54 Rue de Garches, 92420 Vaucresson).

References

Annuaire de la recherche sur le social, éd. CRTS, Caen, 1989.

Ariès, P (1973), *L'enfant et la vie familiale sous l'Ancien Régime*, Seuil, Paris.

Badinter, E (1980), *L'amour en plus*, Flammarion, Paris.

Bianco, J.M. and Lamy, P. (1980), *L'aide à l'enfance demain*, Ministère de la santé et de la sécurité sociale, Coll. 'Etudes et documents'.

Boisguerin, B. (1990), 'L'aide sociale en 1986', *Données sociales*, INSEE, Paris.

Cadoret, A. (1991), 'L'enfant d'ailleurs : enfant placé et famille morvandelle', *L'homme*.

Cadoret, A. (1989), *Le devenir des enfants placés dans la Nievre*, IRTS de Bretone, Rennes.

Capul, M. (1984), *Internat et internement sous l'Ancien régime*, Publications du CTNERHI (diffusion PUF), Vanves.

Cayet, R. (1953), *L'enfant sans foyer. Etude historique*, Imprimerie des orphelins de Guenange.

Ceccaldi, D. (1989), *Les institutions sanitaires et sociales*, Ed. Foucher, Paris.

Chauvière, M. (1980), *Enfance inadaptée : l'héritage de Vichy*, Editions ouvrières, Paris.

Chauvière, M. (1989), *La recherche en quête du social*, Ed. du CNRS, Paris.

Corbillon, M. (1989), *L'enfant placé, actualité de la recherche française et internationale*, CTNERHI et MIRE, Actes du Colloque UNESCO, diff. P.U.F., Paris.

Corbillon, M., Assailly, J.P. and Duyme, M. (1990), *L'enfant placé. De l'assistance publique à l'aide sociale à l'enfance*, Documentation française, 1990.

Corbillon, M., Duyme, M. and Auscher, T. (1991), 'Transmission intergénérationnelle des comportements : le placement', in G. Raimbault and M. Manciaux, *Enfance menacée*, INSERM, diff. La documentation française, Paris.

CREAI Centre (1985), *Etude sur les personnels éducatifs non-diplômés*, Publication du CREAI d'Orléans, Novembre 1985.

David, M. (1989), *Le placement familial, de la pratique à la théorie*, ESF, Paris.

Dessertine, D. (1990), *La société lyonnaise pour le Sauvetage de l'Enfance (1890-1960)*, Erès, Toulouse.

Donzelot, J. (1977), *La police des familles*, Ed. de Minuit, Paris.

Dumaret, A. and Duyme, M. (1982), 'Devenir scolaire et professionel de sujets placés en village d'enfants', *Revue internationale de psychologie appliquée*, 31, (4).

Dupont-Fauville, A. (1979), *Pour une réforme de l'ASE*, ESF, Paris.

Dupoux, A. (1958), 'Sur les pas de Monsieur Vincent. Trois cents ans d'histoire parisienne de l'enfance abandonnée', *Revue de l'Assistance publique*, Paris.

Durning, P. (1986), *Education et suppléance familiale : psycho-sociologie de l'internat spécialisé*, CTNERHI, diff. P.U.F..

Durning, P. (1988), *Education familiale, un panorama des recherches internationales*, Matrice, Vigneux.

Durning, P. (1989), 'Dimensions organisationnelles et tâche de suppléance familiale en internat', in M. Corbillon, *L'enfant placé, actualité de la recherche française et internationale*, CTNERHI et MIRE, Actes du Colloque UNESCO, Paris.

Durning, P. (1992), 'Conditions psycho-sociales de l'émergence des violences dans les institutions éducatives résidentielles', *Sauvegarde de l'enfance*, n° 3/4.

Dutrenit, J.M. (1989), *Gestion et évaluation des services sociaux*, Economica, Paris.

Duyme, M. (1981), *Les enfants abandonnés : rôle des familles adoptives et des assistantes maternelles*, CNRS, Paris, monographie n° 56.

Duyme, M., Chivot, M.C. et al. (1987), *Mauvais traitements institutionnels*, Science libre, Paris.

Faucheux, F. (s.d.), *Idéologie de la rééducation et formation des éducateurs*, texte dactylographié.

Favard-Drillaus, A.M. (1991), *L'evaluation clinique en action sociale*, Brès.

Fenet, F. and Sagot-Duvauroux (1987), *Enfants placés pourquoi? Une histoire de la protection sociale de l'enfance depuis 1945*, Ed par l'ADSEA du Nord, Lille.

Fenet, F. (1989), *L'aide sociale à l'enfance, stratégies et redéploiement*, publication du CTNERHI, Vanves.

Foucault, M. (1972), *Histoire de la folie à l'âge classique*, Gallimard, Paris.

Fraisse, J. Bonetti, J. and de Gaulejac, V. (1987), *L'évaluation dynamique des organisations publiques*, Les éditions d'organisation, Paris.

Gelis, J. et al. (1978), *Entrer dans la vie. Naissances et enfances dans la France traditionnelle*, Archives Gallimard Julliard, Paris.

Ginger, S. (1980), 'La profession d'éducateur spécialisé en France et dans le monde', *Action éducative spécialisée*, n° 85.

Joël, M.E. and Charvet-Protat, S. (1992), *Analyse économique de la Protection judiciaire de la jeunesse*, CTNERHI, diff. P.U.F., Paris.

Ladsous, J. (1991), 'Etre éducateur spécialisé aujourd'hui', *Soins psychiatriques*, Paris, n° 122/123, décembre 1990.

Lallemand, S., *L'ethnologie de l'adoption*, Harmattan, Paris (in preparation).

La lettre de l'IDEF (1991), 'Mise à jour de l'ordonnance du 2 février 1945 sur la jeunesse délinquante, n° 52, février 1991.

Le Poultier, F. (1990), *Recherches évaluatives en travail social*, Presses Universitaires de Grenoble, Grenoble.

Loutre de Pasquier, N. (1981), *Le devenir d'enfants abandonnés : le tissage et le lien*, P.U.F., Paris.

Marmier, M.P. (1969), *Sociologie de l'adoption*, LGDI.

Martin, C. (1985), *Les recherches actions sociales, miroir aux alouettes ou stratégie de qualification*, Documentation française, Paris.

Mignacca, G. (1989), 'Etude des processus de décision en matière de placement', in M. Corbillon, *L'enfant placé, actualité de la recherche française et internationale*, CTNERHI et MIRE, Actes du Colloque UNESCO, Paris.

Pain, J. (1987), *Placés vous avez dit? Méthodes actives et pratique institutionelle en maisons d'enfants*, Matrice, Vigneux.

Pandele, G. (1987), *La protection des jeunes par le juge des enfants*, ESF, Paris.

Rollet-Echalier, C. (1990), *La politique à l'égard de la petite enfance sous la IIIième république*, INED, diff. P.U.F., Paris

Soulet, M.H. (1987), *La recherche sociale en miettes*, CTNERHI, Vanves.

Thévenet, A. (1986), *Les institutions sanitaires et sociales de la France*, PUF, Paris.

Thévenet, A. (1989), *L'aide sociale aujourd'hui*, ESF, Paris.

Tomkiewicz, S. and Vivet, P. (1991), *Aimer mal, châtier bien*, Le Seuil, Paris.

Tomkiewicz, S. (1992), 'Violences en institution : les causes' in E. Corbet, *Violences en institution*, 1, CREAI Rhône Alpes, Lyon.

Verdier, P. , *L'enfant en miettes. L'ASE bilan et perspectives d'avenir*, Privat, Toulouse.

Waysand, E. WAYSAND (1989), 'Les difficultés scolaires des enfants de l'ASE placés en institution', in M. Corbillon, *L'enfant placé, actualité de la recherche française et internationale*, CTNERHI et MIRE, Actes du Colloque UNESCO, Paris.

4 Germany

H. Colla-Müller

Recent political history : End of World War I : Collapse of the German Empire and the establishment of the Weimar Republic -> 1933 : Beginning of Nazi-dictatorship/ World War II -> 1949 : Establishment of the Federal Republic of Germany and the German Democratic Republic -> 1989 : Collapse of the GDR -> 1990 Treaty for a common Germany.
Geographical Size : 356,957.44 Km².
Principal industries : Manufacture of automobiles, chemicals, steel, mechanical engineering.
Date of EC membership : 1958.
Total number of inhabitants (01.01.1990) : 79,112,831.
Age of majority : 18 years.
Number of people under the age of majority (01.01.1990) : 10,459,049.
Number of children and young people (01.01.1991) :   in residential care :   56,468
in foster care :   41,392.

The nature of residential and foster care provision

The kind of residential care discussed in this chapter involves youth-welfare (*Jugendhilfe*) provision.   This excludes boarding school education (*Internatserziehung*) and forms of help involving medical or psychiatric treatment.

An estimated 200,000 children and young people live apart from their families of origin in residential homes, foster-homes, special institutions for handicapped young people, psychiatric units, boarding schools and homes for apprentices (1.6 per cent of the population below the age of majority).   About 60,000 young people are placed in residential child care institutions (this does not include the figure for the former GDR), which amounts to 3.9 per thousand of the child population. A total of 37,000 children and young people are placed in foster homes, some 2,200 of which return to their birth families at weekends, with 26,000 fostered on a day care basis. Approximately 140,000 young people in public care live with their grandparents or other relatives.

Types of provision

Residential care in the Federal Republic of Germany (FGR) comprises one element of youth welfare and may be understood as a socio-pedagogically legitimised institution for socialisation.

In the FRG there are various forms of residential care, based on differences such as geographical location, the physical size of institutions, numbers of children and young people accommodated, staff working hours, division of labour among staff, the organisation of educational and vocational training, and the age and problems of the children and young people. The adults responsible for the children's education differ according to their professional qualifications, age, attitudes and experience. Further, the concepts informing residential practice vary. The material resources, equipment and staff deployed in residential care have distinctly improved in both quantity and quality in recent years.

The number of youngsters living in individual residential establishments ranges between 3 and 400. Table 4.1 shows the varying size of residential homes in more detail.

Table 4.1
Numbers accomodated

% of institutions	N places	
30	up to	10
19		20
10		30
10		40
7.5		50
7		60
13		100
4.5	over	100

Usually, residential establishments contain one or more living groups, comprising between 6 and 15 youngsters of both genders and various ages. The staff/child ratio ranges between 1:10 and 15:10. The cost of maintaining a child or young person in residential care, excluding special items such as holidays, clothes, and individual therapy, amounts to approximately 3,000 DM or £1,300 per month, with homes for the handicapped and orthopedagogical institutions charging up to 6,000 DM or £2,600. Between 70 and 75 per cent of the residential care budget is spent on staffing. Altogether, around 7,5 million DM or £3.2 million is spent on residential care each year. This is a very high figure given the relatively small number of youngsters involved. Indeed, the sum quoted represents about 25 per cent of the whole youth service budget, and raises questions about the balance between residential and fieldwork services. The professionalisation of social welfare work and the extension of university education and training for social pedagogic/social work in Germany during the last twenty years means that most residential practitioners are qualified. Due to the 'unsocial hours' worked by staff, residential care is not such a popular choice of career for younger social workers who tend to opt for field social work or employment in child guidance centres.

Residential care is mainly used for older children and young people. About 40 per cent of youngsters who enter residential care do so after the age of 15. Only 15 per cent enter before the age of 6. Recent years have seen a major growth in a form of residential care termed *Wohngemeinschaften* (commune). Currently, some 150 such settings provide accommodation for around 1,100 young people.

The reasons underlying admission to residential care include family problems such as an extremely low level of education on the part of parents, alcohol-abuse by parents, violence against mothers and their children, conflict between parents and children (which often involves step-parent and -child relationships), and child abuse and neglect.

The following table shows the proportions of children who manifested various sorts of behavioural problems prior to entering residential care.

Table 4.2

Behavioural problems manifested by children and young people prior to admission to residential care

under 10 years

girls	1. maladjusted behaviour	15.4 %
	2. school problems	7.7 %
	3. educational problems	7.7 %

boys	1. maladjusted behaviour	25.0 %
	2. school problems	25.0 %
	3. educational problems	14.0 %
	4. psychological problems	13.7 %
	5. runaways/tramp	6.8 %
	6. delinquency	6.8 %

10-15 years

girls	1. school problems	56.2 %
	2. education problems	50.0 %
	3. runaways/tramp	40.6 %
	4. sexual instability	28.1 %
	5. delinquency	21.9 %
	6. behavioural problems	15.6 %
	7. psychological problems	12.5 %
boys	1. school problems	67.3 %
	2. educational problems	57.1 %
	3. delinquency	55.1 %
	4. runaways/tramp	24.5 %
	5. behavioural problems	22.4 %
	6. psychological problems	10.2 %
	7. sexual instability	4.1 %

over 15 years

girls	1. runaways/tramp	55.9 %
	2. school/training problems	55.9 %
	3. educational problems	47.1 %
	4. sexual instability	35.3 %
	5. delinquency	14.7 %
	6. psychological problems	2.9 %
boys	1. delinquency	46.9 %
	2. runaways/tramp	34.4 %
	3. school/training problems	31.2 %
	4. educational problems	25.0 %
	5. behavioural problems	9.4 %
	6. sexual instability	9.4 %
	7. psychological problems	6.3 %

Source : Blandow et al., 1986.

Residential care is provided in purpose-built facilities, in former castles, hospitals, farmhouses, children's villages, rented houses, and in smaller family-sized houses. The care environment is predominently middle-class. An attempt is made to provide an educogenic milieu. It is recognised that the size of the institution and its physical amenities help to shape the quality of care provided.

Residential care is organised by local and regional authorities (177 institutions), large social welfare organisations and philanthropists (1,019 institutions), and other public interest societies (303 institutions).

Foster care In Germany, foster care involves the placement of children with a substitute family (*Familienpflege*) on a full-time or day-care basis. Exceptionally, children may be placed with single adults. Foster care may also entail placement with relatives (*Verwandtenpflege*). The youth authority (*Jugendamt*) is responsible for the administration of fostering services. This includes the licensing and supervision of foster parents, and the payment of their fees.

In addition to ordinary fostering, short-term foster care is offered if parents are unable to care for their children due to ill-health or other forms of family crisis (e.g. financial difficulties or problems associated with marital relationships), or where child abuse has occurred. Children may be fostered on a week-day basis and return to their birth parents at weekends. This type of care is mainly offered in cases where single mothers work 'unsociable hours', and where there is nobody to look after the child. Large foster families comprise up to six children. Therapeutic Pedagogical Foster Care (*Sozialpädagogische Pflegestelle, Erziehungsstelle*) is a professional service based on therapeutic residential child care institutions. At least one of the foster parents will have received professional training in either social work or psychology or an allied discipline. Therapeutic Pedagogical Foster Care is reserved for children with severe emotional or behavioural problems or for disabled children.

All foster families receive an allowance for food, clothing, rent, holidays, remedial lessons, and sometimes for additional household furniture. However, Therapeutic Pedagogical Foster Care Parents receive an additional payment of between 100 and 2,200 DM or between £42 and £930 per month depending on the *Bundesland* and the problems and age of the children.

There is on-going debate about special payments to foster parents. Some foster parents feel that special fees are unethical and refuse to accept them. Others regard their task as a professional service which should be adequately rewarded. However, it should be noted that only 3-5 per cent of special foster parents receive additional fees. Foster care is less expensive than residential care. The monthly costs of foster care ranges from about about 450 DM to 2,400 DM or £190 to £1,015 (including the special payment).

The average length of stay in foster care is 3.6 years. Some 27 per cent of children placed in foster care are less than 1 year old, 50 per cent are under 3 years and 15 per cent are over 10 years of age. Half of all youngsters placed with foster families had previously lived in one or more residential institutions. Despite a declining birth rate, the number of foster placements has increased at a constant rate over recent years. Unemployment and 'new poverty' have increased the strain on vulnerable families. Households headed by single mothers are particularly susceptible to break-up.

The criteria for foster placement, as distinct from admission to residential care, vary so widely between agencies as to defy classification.

Advocates of de-institutionalisation have, since 1968, argued for a reduction in the number of children placed in large residential facilities. This has increased demand for foster care placements, small scale residential units, and provision for individual living (*betreutes Einzelwohnen*).

Historical antecedents

The historical development of care and education in institutions and foster-homes is rooted in the social history of childhood, changing social needs and associated social welfare policies.

Prior to the middle ages, Germanic legal practice and the precept of doing 'works of Christian love' meant that responsibility for the care of orphans was assumed by wealthy families, the clergy, secular communities, knightorders and professional guilds. In addition to foster care, foundling-homes were established from the 11th century. Hospitals of the Holy Ghost Order also took in parentless children. However, educators (social workers in residential care) played no part in the care of such children.

With the beginning of modern times (*Neuzeit*) and increasing economic productivity, attempts were made to rationalise daily life. Education became necessary in order to impart the knowledge, skills, values and discipline necessary for work and a rationally ordered life. Poverty came to be viewed as self-incurred; as the result of individual idleness and fecklessness. In the 17th century, special work-houses for the correction of the poor were founded. Destitute children were among the inhabitants of these institutions.

At this time, conditions in foundling homes were appalling. Between 50 and 70 per cent of the small children placed in such establishments died from infectious diseases and inadequate care. It was not until the end of the 17th century that institutions specifically designed for children and juveniles were founded. Francke (1663-1727) was a prominent figure in this social reform movement. In his *Hallischen Waisenhäusern* (Orphanages of Halle, founded 1697), Francke attempted to bring up as many as 2,300 neglected children. His aim was to produce diligent and God-fearing adults through training that involved a constant round of work and prayer. Play was forbidden.

Francke's orphanages provided the model for institutions established during the 18th century. However, the latter served economic purposes and provided a source of income for the state. The goal was not so much that of ensuring the healthy development of residents as the pursuit of profit. Children were little more than factory hands, badly nourished and cared for by unqualified overseers.

By the second half of the 18th century awful conditions and high mortality rates resulted in the so-called *Waisenhaus-Streit* (Orphanage dispute). Pestalozzi (1746-1827) and philanthropists such as Salzmann (1744-1811) made public the brutal work-discipline and greed for profit of the directors of such institutions. They argued for more appropriate forms of care and education in foster homes situated in rural areas. Pedagogical and economic use of rural foster families was advocated. It was held that by means of communal work in the fresh air children would learn to be hard working and diligent. One side-effect of the toil of such children was a growth in rural trades in general, and farming in particular. Moreover, accommodating children in rural foster families proved to be much cheaper than the cost of institutional care.

Pedagogical reforms of the late 18th century endured a serious set-back in the 19th century. The War of Liberation (1813-1815) adversely effected the economy, and the industrial revolution increased social need and the privation of the lower classes. The state abdicated responsibility for the needy. This led private individuals and the churches to found institutions of education in the name of religion. The *Rettungshausbewegung* (Salvation House movement) was established. This movement marked itself off from the Pedagogics of the Age of Enlightenment by the creed : 'man is not good naturally but needs religious grooming'. Wichern (1808-1881), for example, employed the virtues of family discipline in his institutions. The Roman Catholic Church founded many religious orders, which worked on behalf of neglected children. In their eyes too, children were depraved and in need of a disciplined education similar to life in a monastery. The monopoly of the Christian churches in the field of institutional education in Germany can be traced back to this period (*Caritas, Diakonisches Werk*).

However, the ideas of the Salvation House movement proved unable to cope with the massive scale of social need found in the slums of the big industrial cities, and were replaced by the ideology of the sound patriarchal family. This went hand in hand with a growing religious and moral philosophy which held that social need was the product of individual failure. Institutional education became part of the domain of general social restoration and was submerged by the rising flood of needy children. Politically, there occurred a growing subjugation of everyday life under legal administration (Preussen: Fürsorge-erziehungsgesetz, 1900; finally the RJWG 1922/24).

The development of new disciplines such as social-pedagogics, psychology and psychoanalysis prompted the search for a conceptual foundation to education in institutions. In the 1920's three competing groups of reformers emerged : (i) the socialist pedagogues, who were associated with the Worker's Movement (Ruhle, Hoernle, Bernfeld); (ii) the theorists and practitioners of the Reform Movement (Nohl, Hermann, Bondy, Wilker); and (iii) residential educators of predominantly conservative persuasion. The ideas of the hermeneutic-pragmatic pedagogics and those who argued for socialist education, both of which were partially realised in practical alternatives to institutional education, did not survive the economic crises of the Weimar Republic. During National Socialist times, and by means of *Nazi Volkswohlfahrt*, coordination, unification and alignment occurred under a national, racial and military ideology of education. Republican, humanist and socialist pedagogics were systematically discredited, excluded and eliminated. A special system was established to supervise the murder of mentally and physically disabled children. *Schutzlager* were founded for the long-term incarceration of vulnerable young people in conditions similar to those in concentration camps. Release was not envisaged : transfer simply meant transportation to work-houses or concentration camps. Alongside such facilities were traditional, repressive, residential institutions.

From 1945 onwards a fundamental change occurred within institutional care in West Germany. At the end of the second world war, the needs of many of the 3 million institutionalised children and young people went totally unmet. Prior to the mid-1960's, three types of institution may be differentiated.

First, traditional, repressive, institutions, which were often run by medical authorities. Characteristic features of such establishments included : lining-up in the morning, the witholding of food or pocket-money, confinement to the quadrangle, incarceration as a means of punishment, the wearing of uniforms, censorship of mail, unqualified staff, the enforced separation of children's links with their past lives. Such features were particularly prevalent in institutions for girls.

Second, homes for babies and small children, which often entailed 15-30 children in one group, mass-dormitories, central kitchens, grouping according to age, and the strict separation of children from the outside world.

Third, a small number of institutions in which children were looked after in family-groups, together with the *Kinderdörfer* (Children's Villages). Both attempted to provide a family style of care. The adults (in most cases 'group-mothers') lived together with the children. Accommodation was often similar to that found in family households, and contact with the outside-world was encouraged (Widemann, 1991).

The post-war period of reconstruction in the FRG not only brought material affluence but also inter-generational conflict. In the 1960's, school pupils and university students engaged in a struggle against what they saw as the narrow minded pursuit of material security by their elders. Influenced by ideas on the theory of science developed by representatives of 'critical theory' (Horkheimer, Adorno, Marcuse) in the 1930's, the student avantgarde declared war on the establishment, on consumerism, and on the nuclear bourgeois family. The 'drop-outs' were discovered. Sociopedagogical practice was subject to critical analysis.

An important contribution to innovative practice was made by Thiersch (1967), who argued that the assessment or diagnosis of children's problems was not a value-free process; the idea that it was had led agencies of social control (school, youth welfare services, etc.) to a one-sided view of children's behaviour and development. In analysing life histories, too little attention had been given to the adverse social and environmental factors which hinder intellectual, emotional and social development. In view of such factors, it was clear that sociopedagogics had to work towards the amelioration of social deprivation. Moreover, psychic structure had to be viewed as a correlate of children's social experiences. Reformpedagogue Nohl's (1949; 1963) judgement that '... neglected youth is not a menace to society, ... (rather) ... society itself is menacing youth with neglect' was rediscovered. It was argued that sociopedagogical practice should conform to the principles of the constitution, the constitutional state and the welfare state, and that social exclusion should be replaced by participation in everyday life.

The analysis of 'residential care misery' by young left wingers, progressive residential practitioners and representatives of the scientific community was similar to the vehement criticism of institutional education articulated in the 1920's. These groups highlighted factors such as the inequality of educational opportunities, the lack of freedom of information, the setting aside of constitutional rights (e.g. through the censorship of children's letters), authoritarian educational practices, and the discontinuity experienced by children and young people as a consequence of frequent changes of placement. Attention was also drawn to the inadequate training, salaries and the poor working conditions of the educators, and the lack of co-operation between administrative authorities and residential establishments. In short, the care of separated children was acknowledged to be a social and political problem.

Then residential care discovered the 'therapeutic milieu', with a strong tendency to psychoanalytical models (Aichhorn, Bettelheim, Lennhof, Redl). However, the concept proved difficult to apply in practice. The euphoria with which the therapeutic milieu was greeted as a way out of the misery of residential care, was soon tempered by questions such as : was the change from talking to communication-training really a condition for the therapeutic re-learning process or was it more about making everyday actions a starting point for training and therapy, without alienating these everyday actions in therapeutic scenarios? In addition, the issue arose as to whether the call for a therapeutically orientated residential care was more an attempt by practitioners to gain in professional and social status, rather than a shift in thinking geared towards helping children overcome painful experiences.

Nevertheless, the application of therapeutic concepts enable some of the pitfalls of daily residential life to be avoided (Thiersch, 1977). However, one of the dangers associated with the therapeutic perspective is that residential care may become linked with medical treatment and social problems are thought of in psychiatric terms. Therapy can be defined as a specific form of intervention aimed at remedying dysfunctions, shortcomings, deficiencies and defects. By contrast, rather than focussing on pathology, residential care is concerned with helping the individual fulfill his or her potential. Giving up the socio-pedagogically justified everyday life in favour of making it therapeutic can, particularly in large institutions, lead to a problem-specific, technical, approach with young people. Small homes, on the other hand, through a mixture of Rousseauan utopia, a Seymourean feeling of 'We're going into the country' and Postmanean 'cloister-effect', are in danger of exaggerating their peripheral situation into a pedagogical and political principle.

Contemporary residential care

After 1968, and in the wake of the 'Second Residential Care Campaign', there was an initial willingness to discuss residential care publically. Bonhoeffer's (1967) criticism of its monopoly position in the system of youth welfare fell on fertile ground. In a great many cases, admission to residential care was replaced by counselling and guidance. The publicity that residential care received in this short period contributed to fundamental amelioration. Against the background of malpractice that had already come to light, social welfare agencies refrained from placing young children (3 to 6 year olds) in residential settings. An improved career structure and higher salaries were introduced for residential practitioners. Moreover, the so-called *Verselbständigungsgruppe* system (groups where one can reach independence) was developed within institutions. Such groups are based on foster family care. The aim is for young people and their carers to live as autonomously as possible whilst retaining the support of the institution. This new form of 'external living group' involves close contact with the community. Young people practice skills essential for independent living such as household budgeting, cookery, etc., and make decisions about how they spend their time and their lives more generally. A special form of residential care is the commune in which young people volunteer to live together, go to school or receive vocational training. Socio-pedagogues are available for counselling. This combination of independent living and supervision provides young people who, for various reasons, cannot be helped in a group home, with the chance to achieve independence.

The residential task may be defined as caring for children and young people who are temporarily or permanently separated from their families of origin. This aim is realised in a field of learning and experience, which can be supported by orthopedagogical or therapeutic help. All those reponsible for the provision of residential care would agree that children and young people with troubled life histories, require a nuturing environment, free from negative criticism and stigma.

An essential pre-requisite for successful residential care is an unburdened, but attractive living space, in which the children are given the opportunity to let themselves be helped through experiencing pedagogical meetings. Residential life should be structured in such a way as to offer children alternative models of appropriate behaviour, and guidance about how to make themselves understood and how to gain from experiences. In addition, the alternative models of behaviour should be related to the subjective way in which the children perceive their everyday lives. Moreover, children should be given the opportunity of experiencing themselves as persons who possess positive qualities, abilities and skills.

Currently, we have more than 6,000 places in so-called day-groups, which amounts to nearly 10 per cent of the capacity of residential child care institutions. After school the youngsters go to the children's home and engage in activities. It often appears to be easier to involve both school and family in an intervention programme when the youngster remains at home but spends supervised periods in an institution after school. The parents gain respite but maintain responsibility for the youngster.

The principle of regionalisation is considered to be very important. Residential establishments tend to accommodate children from a defined geographical region or area. Such areas are often quite small. In some towns the residential children's home is also the centre for community treatment. Most institutions have reduced their capacity over recent years and introduced a diverse range of programmes. Even large institutions have attempted to establish small autonomous living units and to integrate them into the community. Smaller institutions have formed themselves into networks in order to produce a variety of programmes which can be shared by youngsters from each institution in the network. This has produced worthwhile economies of scale with regard to programmes which would be too expensive for small institutions to provide alone.

Residential care in the former GDR

Since reunification in 1989, those responsible for social work and residential child care services have been confronted with the difficult problem of setting up a new system of social services and social institutions in the former GDR.

When the old GDR was founded, it was assumed that the creation of a socialist society would naturally lead to widespread sympathy toward persons in need. Consequently, the GDR did not attempt to develop child welfare services comparable to those in countries of Western Europe. In 1989, the government of the GDR employed as few as 1,536 trained people in child welfare services serving a population of some 16 million. By contrast, in the FRG more than 24,643 trained people worked for local government child care services (*Jugendamt, Landesjugendamt* etc.). Child welfare in the GDR was mainly provided for by private individuals or by so-called collectives based in small geographical areas, schools or factories. When non-professional approaches proved ineffective, the state offered residential child care in some 609 institutions with an overall capacity to accommodate around 34,000 youngsters. In addition, 28 institutions with 520 places were run by the churches. These establishments provided accommodation for handicaped youngsters.

The following system of child care institutions was set up in the GDR.

1. Ordinary institutions for children and young people who, for varying reasons, had been separated from their families.

Kind of institution	Population
* Pre-school homes	* pre-school children
* Children's homes	* pupils of forms 1-10, and sometimes pre-school children and apprentices
* Homes for children with learning difficulties	* retarded children
* Youth homes	* juveniles aged 13-19 years
* Homes for young people with learning difficulties who had previously been accommodated in special schools	

The criteria for admission to ordinary residential care included : loss of parents, extremely low level of education on the part of parents, and failure by parents to meet their parental responsibilities.

2. Special institutions for the re-education of deviant young people.

Kind of institution	Population
* Special children's homes	* pupils of forms 1-10
* Special homes for youngsters with learning difficulties	* retarded youngsters
* Homes (*Jugendwerke*) for young people from higher modern schools (*Oberschüler*)	* youth
* Homes for young people from schools for children with learning difficulties	* youth

The criterion for entry to a special institution was *Schwererziehbarkeit* (intractability). This included behaviour perceived to constitute a gross transgression of social discipline (e.g. intended flight from the Republic), and behavioural problems that could not be dealt with in the community. Intervention by youth welfare services was considered to be necessary where youngsters manifested behavioural problems at home, school, work and other public places (including sexual misconduct), or where youngsters committed criminal offences.

The task of special children's homes was that of 're-education' based on socialist ideology and pedagogics. The objective was to produce good citizens of the GDR.

The system of child care institutions in the GDR also comprised an additional tier of highly specialised facilities, which included
(i) special institutions for psycho-diagnostics and pedagogical-psychological therapy for children in residential care manifesting extreme behavioural problems, and (ii) institutions of transition, which provided short-term accommodation for homeless children or children at risk who had been removed from their families in cases of emergency.

Institutional education was usually undertaken on a collective or group basis. Groups contained between 8 and 15 children. The ratio of educators to children was between 1:2.7 and 1:3.5. Institutions were mainly co-educational, and groups contained youngsters of varying ages. In some cases, groups included children of pre-school age and young workers. Special institutions were single-sex establishments. Because such institutions had their own schools, living groups were usually based on school classes, and so youngsters were grouped according to age.

All residential institutions placed considerable emphasis on facilitating children's intellectual development. Contrary to attempts in the FRG to reduce the size of institutions over recent years, the size of institutions in the GDR increased from 1970 onwards. Some institutions in the GDR contained between 80 and 150 inmates.

In the GDR, the state proclaimed that it had the right to exercise power over the individual psyche. It is in this sense that we may define the GDR as a totalitarian State. The ideology underpinning residential child care was essentially fascist in that both Marxist-Leninism and fascist ideology involve a totalitarian claim on the personality (Bauer and Bösenberg, 1979). However, whilst child welfare services in the GDR were clearly based on the dogma of soviet pedagogics, the goals of a materialistic conception of education were seldom realised in practice. The GDR failed in its attempt to achieve a 'collective maturity', and to develop social solidarity by which to counter the de-humanisation of individuals.

Although increasing social solidarity was the main aim of practical (as opposed to purely theoretical) residential work in the GDR, how legal and political policies translate into practice must be assessed in the light of empirical evidence. However, so-called 'research' in the GDR was controlled by the communist party, and was published only in order to endorse the official doctrine. Wölfel and Unger (1990) point out that, as was the case in many areas of life in the former GDR, a marked contrast existed between official goals and actual social processes. In the period before 1989, this disparity was rarely questioned. Fearing damage to their careers, many residential educators failed to openly challenge the official general aims of education, but rather chose to quietly disregard them in practice.

Some directors of institutions introduced innovations in practice in an attempt to provide more individualised patterns of care for children and young people. However, such developments were based more on pragmatic intuition rather than on theoretical insight.

Theory of institutional education in the former GDR

Pedagogics in the GDR and, within this, residential child care services, were conceived as a means by which to create and support the socialist state. Alongside the obligatory study of Marxist-Leninism, the function of pedagogics was that of training educators or pedagogues for a leading role within the state. The task of educators was to further the cause of socialism. Residential child care institutions were factories designed to produce good socialists. Scientific principle (*Selbstverständnis*) was exclusively understood in normative terms. Western theories of education and research results had little impact on practice. This was because they were either completely forbidden or not available in the GDR due to lack of resources. Consequently, the quality of training received by educators fell below that of their counterparts in West Germany.

Universities and other institutions of learning and instruction were subject to tighter control than in West Germany. Moreover, the authority of professors was less subject to challenge and criticism. Academic personnel in the GDR were required to prove their merit in special examinations focussing on their 'reliability' in furthering the interests of the state.

Most pedagogues were members of the ruling political party, the SED. The Academy of Pedagogic Sciences, which comprised more than 800 trained instructors or pedagogues, and which was closely linked to the state, was responsible for the conceptionalisation, implementation and control of the socialist system of institutional care.

Professors at Humboldt University in East-Berlin and the Institute for Youth Aid Falkensee exercised a virtual monopoly over the production of ideas underpinning institutional care.

Since the 1950's institutional care in the GDR had been based on the ideas of the soviet writer, Makarenko (1968). Mannschatz (1975) notes that the latters' pedagogic novel, *Way into Life*, served as a kind of bible for residential educators '... It was a fundamental work which introduced us to the wealth of thought in soviet pedagogics. One can well say that this great pedagogue, with his books, has trained whole generations of directors of institutions and educators ... We developed our institutional pedagogics on the basis of doctrines of soviet pedagogics ...' (Mannschatz, 1975). Whereas Heimpel (1956), prompted critical discussion of Makarenko's work in West Germany, Soviet pedagogical theory went unquestioned in the GDR. Makarenko's view of institutional education emanated from the philosophy of Marxism-Leninism, and stressed the general and political norms of socialistic society : collectivism, patriotism, discipline and productivity. The uncritical reception of Makarenko in the GDR was accompanied by the suppression of other socialistic-psychoanalytical paradigms (e.g. Bernfeld). Moreover, the discipline of psychology was accorded only peripheral status in the field of institutional education. Ideas of reform-pedagogical hue were also discounted on the grounds that they were merely a manifestation of bourgeois ideology. In addition, the GDR isolated itself from international organisations such as FICE. As a consequence of all this, the GDR failed to develop the kinds of alternatives to institutional care and innovations in residential practice that have occurred in West Germany over recent years.

The public discussion of institutional education that took place in West Germany at the end of the sixties did not happen in the GDR. Whilst alternative models, such as that proposed by Schütze (1990), were discussed within a small circle of experts, these had little impact on practice because they went unpublished. Instructions for practice were published centrally by the department for teacher training of the 'Ministry for Public Education' (*Ministerium für Volksbildung*). Training and post-graduate instruction for educators within institutions were dominated by general topics of school and the party. Owing to lack of access to international literature, and to party-political censorship of the periodical *Jugendhilfe*, educators knew little about theoretical positions and practical examples of alternative forms of institutional education.

Between 80 and 90 per cent of pedagogical personnel in residential institutions in the GDR received 3 years of basic training. From 1969 onwards, educators were prepared for their professional work in one of six institutions specialising in the field of institutional education.

Training culminated in an examination of the student's proficiency in teaching. From 1966, reliable institutional directors and young *Nachwuchskader* (aspiring young educators), had the opportunity to gain the title of *Diplompädagoge* by undertaking a further 18 months of study at Humboldt University. The 'Institute for Youth Aid' in Falkensee also organised additional training for residential educators, and post-graduate study for *Jugendfürsorger* (youth social-workers).

Wölfel and Unger (1990) consider that the general public in the GDR held an ambivalent attitude towards institutional education. Whereas the plight of children separated from their families evoked public sympathy, the entry to care of deviant youngsters was seen as a 'just measure of punishment'. The demand for 'segregation' of difficult young people often came from hard-pressed parents and teachers.

Over the next few years, child welfare services in the old GDR will have to be integrated with those of the former FRG. In the first place, measures are required to ensure that the quality of provision in eastern Germany is raised to standards already attained in the west. This includes improving the training and professional status of residential workers in the east. Expectations must be realistic. Social pedagogics in the new *Länder* is not so much in need of a utopia, but rather a future which is relatively better than its past.

Legal aspects

The new child care law in Germany - KJHG, which was introduced in January, 1991, represents an attempt to improve and extend services to children and young people in need and their families. Under the KJHG, professionals should serve as advocates for the interests and concerns of children, young people and their parents (Part 1, para 3).

Residential care, which is covered in Part 34 of the KJHG, should promote the development of children and young people. Further, residential carers should contribute to attempts at rehabilitating youngsters with their birth families. If this is not possible, residential workers should help to prepare the child for placement with a foster family. Where appropriate, young people should be prepared for independent living. In exceptional cases, young people up to 27 years of age can receive such help.

Children's birth families must have received appropriate help and guidance before decisions are made to place children with foster families (part 36, para 1). The period of time a child will spend in a foster home must be agreed and specified in advance of the placement (part 36, para 2). Contact between the child and his or her natural family must be maintained, even in cases where the child cannot return to his or her birth family. Foster parents must also be provided with help and guidance (part 37, para 2).

During the last two years, higher than expected numbers of very young children were admitted to residential care. Moreover, fewer older youngsters were discharged from institutions. The former trend may indicate that increasing numbers of single mothers and fathers are over-stretched by their responsibilities and that help to vulnerable families is inadequate; it may also reflect increasing awareness and anxiety about child abuse. That older children are remaining longer in residential care appears to owe much to the difficulties associated with finding alternative supervised placements and indepedent living accommodation. More shared flats (*Wohngemeinschaften*) and hostels run by social workers are required. In big cities there is a need for crisis intervention centres. A number of excellent projects have been developed for drug addicts, runaways, young people with suicidal tendencies, and girls who have been sexually abused.

There is currently much discussion about residential care for girls. In Germany, social work reforms have traditionally been concerned with the problems of male children and adolescents. In this context, co-education in residential homes was a considerable achievement. Today, however, increasing emphasis is being given to residential care oriented towards the problems experienced by girls. Particularly attention is placed on helping sexually abused girls.

A further area of concern is the possibility that the working week will be reduced to 35 hours. Already, the operation of shift-systems disrupt relationships between children and their caregivers and the general continuity of daily care. Serious consideration obviously needs to be given to the question of how to mitigate such problems.

A recent Government report identified the poor cooperation which exists between child care and psychiatric services. The two services are informed by different theories and use different terminologies. Professionals in one field have little knowledge of the other. Consequently, a multi-disciplinary approach to helping children is often lacking.

A decline in the numbers of children and young people in residential and foster care has been forecast. By 2030 there will be only 7.3 million people under the age of 20 years in the region of the old FRG (there is no comparable data on the former GDR). Thus, a reduction of some 27,000 residential care places may be anticipated. However, it is difficult to make accurate predictions in view of the high level of immigration expected, particularly from eastern Europe. This will mean that residential child care services will increasingly be required to reflect the needs of a multi-cultural society.

Research on residential and foster care

Little interest has been shown in systematic research on residential care by government, child welfare agencies and professionals. It is estimated that as little as 0.3 per thousand of social expenditure is devoted to research. Most studies are undertaken in pursuit of academic qualifications. Despite this, the level of knowledge about residential and foster care has risen over recent years due to the increasing influence of the social sciences in the universities and the activities of social work students. Two main types of research may be distinguished. First, studies examining the causes of the problems experienced by social welfare users. Second, research which involves the analysis of institutions and practice concepts. Action research and project or development research predominate over empirical-analytical studies. Emphasis has been placed on examining the dysfunctional aspects of social welfare, and there has been a revival of interest in historical-biographical approaches to understanding the problems faced by clients. The latter entails reconstructing the life histories of individuals, groups and generations.

Research in Germany is pragmatic and geared to finding solutions to practical problems. The aim is to formulate action plans and strategies.

The Federal Government in Bonn (Ministry of Youth and Women; Ministry of Health) and the *Länder* (Ministry of Education and Cultural Affairs, Ministry of Health, Ministry of Justice) commission research by staff in universities, social work training institutions (Fachhochschulen), and private research institutions such as the *Institut für Sozialarbeit und Soziapädagogik*, Frankfurt. Private welfare organizations (*Diakonisches Werk, Caritas, Arbeiterwohlfart, Deutscher Paritätischer Wohlfahrtsverband, Deutsches Rotes Kreuz*) carry out their own research. Important publications on residential care are produced by the *Internationale Gesellschaft für Heimerziehung* (Section of the FICE) and *Arbeitsgemeinschaft für Erziehungshilfe* (AFET). The government has no research agencies of its own.

Flitner and Bittner brought the technique of participant observation to child welfare research in Germany. Under their guidance, Wenzel (1973) and Vollert (1970) carried out the first studies describing everyday life in institutions, and expounded arguments which contributed to subsequent reforms.

The action research approach was further developed by Schweitzer, Muhlenbrinck and Spath (1976). Of particular importance is the work of Munstermann (1981), who published economic data on one independent welfare association and interpreted this in the light of socio-pedagogic theory. Public awareness about the poor quality of life in large institutions grew as a result of the publication of the biographies of people who had grown up in care (Werner, 1969; Brosch, 1971) and, later on, by novels (e.g. Holzner, 1978). The grim descriptions of institutional life contained in such works (e.g. not being permitted to speak during work periods, incarceration, corporal punishment, and forced tonsuration after escapes) are similar to accounts published in the 1920's. In order to ensure therapeutic success, defined in terms of enhanced self-determination and self-control, Dalferth (1982) has advocated a more individualised approach to day-to-day care. Frischenschlager and Mayr (1982) examined daily routines in institutions. They found that the personalities of residential staff have an important bearing on the nature of care practice. Researchers at the *Deutsches Jugendinstitut*, Munich (Wolffersdorf and Sprau-Kuhlen, 1990) examined the problems of 'closed accommodation'. Their main finding was that the use of such facilities not so much reflects the needs of clients as structural deficiencies in child welfare services. Discontinuity in care careers, which includes frequent changes of care placements, helps to produce the youngsters that are considered especially problematic. Huesken (1976) showed that closed accommodation was widely used in institutional care up to 1975. Since then the number of youngsters in closed units has fallen. In 1987, some 350 young people were placed in such facilities, 123 of which were girls.

An analysis of 14 institutions by Project-Group Petra (Plannungsgruppe Petra, 1988) showed that the problems of institutional education often result from incompetent management, poor integration and out-moded practices and structures. Heum (1984) documents the biographies of children in institutions. He shows that, on average, they were in their 5th placement. Only 28 per cent of those interviewed felt 'at home' in the institution they were living in. Wedekind (1986) cites a number of weaknesses associated with institutional care, including : social distance between children and caregivers and bureaucratic controls which serve to undermine attempts to create child-centred social climates. Landenberger and Trost (1988) argue that the conditions of life within institutions produce a sub-culture which undercuts the formal aims of education.

A small number of studies have also been carried out on alternatives to institutional care. Wulf (1987) found that, in retrospect, youngsters who had been placed in cohabitational flats with socio-pedagogues tended to view their experiences positively. Some youngsters who had been transferred from a traditional institutional group to a cohabitational flat (in the same quadrangle), expressed satisfaction with the change.   Others, however, were disappointed by the transfer (Romanski-Sudhoff and Sudhoff, 1984).   In relation to difficult to manage youngsters, Freigang (1986) reports that even socio-therapeutic living-groups specifically designed to cope with young people expelled from other facilities have been obliged to exclude some youngsters.

Of the many library-based studies undertaken, the work of Kraft (1989) deserves mention.   In a critical analysis, the author describes changes within socio-pedagogics and institutional/residential education. Blandow (1986; 1989) has examined the socio-political aspects of residential education.   He views the reform of the seventies as essentially technocratic in nature.   Moreover, whilst residential care is, for many young people, a satisfactory way of living, the dynamics of the inter-personal relationships involved are often problematic.   He also notes that although residential education is extremely demanding, those who work in it have often not received adequate training.   Many of the problems which beset residential education result from the unfortunate clash between pedagogic theory and economics.   Although institutions like schools, hospitals, kindergardens, and so on, have social objectives, they are obliged to behave like industrial enterprises.   Consequently, quantity takes precedence over quality.

Colla and Karusseit (1990) analysed the attitudes of pedagogical personnel towards the question of how to deal with Aids.   Analysis revealed that because of the high level of stress associated with this issue, few could imagine themselves working permanently in residential education.   Issues such as how to cope with anxiety and risk, dying and death are not given adequate attention.   The subject of Aids is reduced to a medical-technical level.   Indeed, sex and sexuality are generally excluded from the agenda of residential life.

The first research on foster family care after the Second World War was undertaken by Dührssen (1958), who compared the development of foster children with that of children brought up in residential care. Blandow (1972) carried out the earliest empirical study of the factors contributing to fostering breakdown.   Schrapper et al. (1987) examined the processes of decision making in foster care.   The *Deutsches Jugendinstitut* carried out research on the effect of counselling as a means of helping to prevent fostering breakdown.   Several studies show that fostering breakdown is more likely where : (i) there is only a small difference between the age of the foster parents natural child(ren) and the foster child; (ii) the foster child is merely seen as a playmate for the natural child(ren); (iii) the foster parents are too young or too old; and, (iv) the style of parenting is inflexible (Blandow et al., 1980; Heum, 1984; Lausch, 1985; Salgo, 1987).

Currently, there is a theoretical debate between the psychoanalytical and systemic perspective; that is, between writers such as Goldstein et al., (1974; 1982), on the one hand, and Gudat (1987), on the other. This controversy revolves around issues such as the child's position in relation to his or her birth family and the new foster family, whether and to what extent the child should have contact with his or her original family, and whether or not the aim should be to seek the child's return to his or her family of origin. In addition, there are questions surrounding the legal status of foster parents. The new child care law in Germany - KJHG, tends to be informed by the psychoanalytic perspective.

References

Autorenkollektiv unter Leitung von Mannschatz, E. (1988), *Heimerziehung,* Berlin.

Bäuerle, W. and Markmann, J.C. (Hrsg.) (1974), *Reform der Heimerziehung,* Weinheim-Basel.

Bauer, R. and Bösenberg, C. (1979), *Heimerziehung in der DDR,* Frankfurt.

Bauer, H.G. and Nickolai, H. (1989), *Erlebnispädagogik in der sozialen Arbeit,* Lüneburg.

Birtsch, V. and Maelicke, B. (Hrsg.) (1986), *Geschlossene oder offene Heimerziehung - Bilanz der offenen Arbeitsansätze,* Frankfurt/M.

Blandow, J. (1972), *Rollendiskrepanzen in der Pflegefamilie,* München.

Blandow, J. and Frommknecht, B. (1980), *Adoption und Tagesbetreuung,* München.

Blandow, J. (1986), 'Heimerziehung und Politik. Anmerkungen zur Geschichte der Heimerziehung in der Bundesrepublik Deutschland', in R. Soisson (Hrsg.), *Aktuelle Probleme Jugendlicher in der Heimerziehung in Europa,* Zürich.

Blandow, J. et al. (1986), 'Erzieherische Hilfen' - Untersuchungen zu Geschlechtsrollen - Typisierungen in Einrichtungen und Diensten der Jugendhilfe', in W. Freigang and J. Blandow et al., *Mädchen in Einrichtungen der Jugendhilfe (Alltag und Biographie von Mädchen 15, hrsg. von der Sachverständigenkommission, Sechster Jugendbericht),* Opladen.

Blandow, J. (1989), 'Heimerziehung und Jugendwohngemeinschaften', in J. Blandow and J. Faltermeier (Hrsg.), *Erziehungshilfen in der Bundesrepublik Deutschland,* Frankfurt.

Bonhoeffer, M. (1967), 'Totale Heimerziehung oder Begleitende Erziehungshilfe. Kritik an einem ungerechtfertigten Monopol', in *Neue Sammlung*, Heft 5.

Brosch, P. (1971), *Fürsorgeerziehung - Heimterror und Gegenwehr*, Frankfurt/M.

Bundesminister für Jugend, Familie, Frauen und Gesundheit (Hrsg.) (1990), *8. Jugendbericht*, Bonn

Bürger, U. (1990), *Heimerziehung und soziale Teilnahmechancen*, Pfaffenweiler.

Colla, H.E. (1981), *Heimerziehung*, München.

Colla, H.E. and Karusseit, K.-H. (1990), *Jugend und Aids. Aids-Prävention und -Bewältigung in stationären Einrichtungen der Jugendhilfe*, Lüneburg.

Colla, H.E. (1991), 'Twenty years of innovation in residential care in the Federal Republic of Germany', in W. Hellinckx, E., Broekaert, A., Vanden Berge and M. Colton (Eds), *Innovation in Residential Care*, Leuven-Amersfoort.

Dalferth, M. (1982), *Erziehung im Jugendheim*, Weinheim - Basel.

Dalferth, M. (1982), *Erziehung im Jugendheim. Bausteine zur Veränderung der Praxis*, Weinheim.

Dührssen, A. (1958), *Heimkinder und Pflegekinder in ihrer Entwicklung*, Göttingen.

Freigang, W. (1986), *Verlegen und Abschieben. Zur Erziehungspraxis im Heim*, Weinheim - München.

Frischenschlager, U. and Mayr, W. (1982), *Erzieherpersönlichkeit und Handlungskompetenz im Alltag sozialpädagogischer Arbeitsfelder. Diss*, Tübingen.

Goffman, E. (1973), *Asyle*, Frankfurt/M. (Orig. Asylums, 1961).

Goldstein, J., Freud, A. and Solnit, A.J. (1974), *Jenseits des Kindeswohls*, Frankfurt/M.

Goldstein, J., Freud, A. and Solnit, A.J. (1982), *Diesseits des Kindeswohls*, Frankfurt/M.

Gudat, U. (1987), 'Entwicklungspsychologie der Eltern-Kind-Beziehung', in Deutsches Jugendinstitut (Hrsg.), *Handbuch Beratung im Pflegekinderbereich*, München.

Heimpel, E. (1956), *Das Jugendkollektiv A.S. Makarenkos*, Würzburg.

Heum, H.D. (1984), *Pflegekinder im Heim*, München (Deutsches Jugendinstitut).

Holzner, M. (1978), *Die Geschichte des Benjamin Holberg*, Hamburg.

Huesken, H. (1976), *Zur Situation 'öffentlicher Erziehung' in den Erziehungsheimen der Bundesrepublik Deutschland. Diss*, Münster.

Kraft, K. (1989), *Anpassung, Beteiligung, Selbstkontrolle. Heimerziehung in sozialintegrativer und therapeutischer Relevanz*, Weinheim.

Landenberger, G. and Trost, R. (1988), *Lebenserfahrungen im Erziehungsheim. Identität und Kultur im institutionellen Alltag*, Frankfurt/M.

Lausch, A. (1985), *Die Pflegeelternschaft - Erleben und Bewältigung*, Frankfurt/M.

Makarenko A.S. (1968), *Der Weg ins Leben, Ein pädagogisch Poem*, Berlin.

Mannschatz, E. (1970), *Entwurf zu einer Methodik der Kollektinerziehung*, Berlin (Ost).

Müller-Kohlenberg, H. (1972), *Berufsbild des Heimerziehers*, Weinheim.

Münder, J. (1981), 'Soziale Elternschaft - Erziehung ausserhalb der leiblichen Ursprungsfamilie', in *Zentralblatt Jug R*, Wohlf.

Münsterman, K. (1981), 'Untersuchung der den Diakonischen Werken angeschlossenen Heime für Kinder und Jugendliche in Westfalen und Lippe in ihrer strukturellen und qualitativen Entwicklung', in Müller-Kohlenberg, H. et al., *Die Unfähigkeit einer Institution. Geleistete und anstehende Reformen in der Heimerziehung*, Frankfurt/M. (GfH).

Nohl (1949), *Pädagogik aus 30 Jahren*, Frankfurt.

Nohl (1963), *Die ästhetische Wirklichkeit*, Frankfurt.

Planungsgruppe PETRA (1988), *Was leistet die Heimerziehung? Ergebnisse einer empirischen Untersuchung*, hrsg. von der IGfH, Frankfurt/M.

Peters, F. (Hrsg.) (1991), *Jenseits von Familie und Anstalt*, Bielefeld.

Röper, F.F. (1976), *Das verwaiste Kind in Anstalt und Heim*, Göttingen.

Romanski-Sudhoff, M. and Sudhoff, H. (1984), *Alltagswissen von Heimjugendlichen. Grundlagen für eine alltagsorientierte Nachbetreuung.* Frankfurt/M,

Salgo, L. (1987), *Pflegkindschaft und Staatsintervention*, Darmstadt.

Schrapper, C. et al. (1987), *Welche Hilfe ist die Richtige?*, Frankfurt/M.

Schütze, O. (1990), 'Wenn ich über due Heimerziehung nachdenke ...', *Jugendhilfe*, 5, Berlin.

Schweitzer, H., Mühlenbrinck, H., Späth, K.H. (1976), *Über die Schwierigkeit, soziale Institutionen zu verändern. Entwicklungsarbeit im sozialpädagogischen Feld 1*, Frankfurt/M.

Thiersch, H. (1967), 'Verwahrlosung', *Neue Sammlung*, 5.

Thiersch, H. (1977), *Kritik und Handeln*, Neuwied.

Vollert, M. (1970), *Erziehungsprobleme in Kinderdorf*, Stuttgart.

Wedekind, E. (1986), *Beziehungsarbeit. Zur Sozialpsychologie pädagogischer ind therapeutischer Institutionen*, Frankfurt/M.

Wenzel, H. (1973), *Fürsorgeheime in pädagogischer Kritik*, Stuttgart.

Werner, W. (1969), *Vom Waisenhaus ins Zuchthaus. Ein Sozialbericht*, Frankfurt/M.

Widemann, P. (1991), 'Erziehungshilfen-Fortschritt und Stillstand', in Deutsches Jugendinstitut (Eds), *Der Jugend eine zukunft sichern; Jugendhilfe im Nachkriegsdeutschland - Zwischen Anpassung und Parteilichkeit*, Münster.

Wölfel, I and Unger, C. (1990), *Heimerziehung in der ehemaligen DDR*, Typoskript, Neubrandenburg.

Wolffersdorf, C. and Sprau-Kuhlen, V. (1990), *Geschlossene Heimerziehung*, München-Weinheim.

Wulf, W. (1987), 'Sich-verantwortlich-Fühlen setzt Freiheit und Unterstützung voraus. überlegungen anläßlich van Gesprächen mit ehemaligen Bewohnern von Jugendwohngemeinschaften' in R. Berg et al. (Eds), *Jugendwohngemeinschaften. Eine Standortbestimmung*, München (AG SPAK).

5 Greece

H. Agathonos-Georgopoulou

Recent political history : Greece is at an intermediate stage of growth and development, trying to link the old with the new whilst addressing the future. Modern technological development and population trends such as urbanisation and migration, challenge traditional lifestyles and social and family values. Greece's recent political history has been marked by a series of devastating political events leaving the country and its population with economic, political and social scars. Two world wars, a civil war (1946-1949), the 1922 catastrophe of Asia Minor leading to the expulsion of 1.2 million Greeks to the mainland, an external migration wave of a further 1.2 million Greeks during the period 1955-1977, the seven year dictatorship (1967-1974), are some of the major historical landmarks which have hindered Greece's development. After the re-establishment of democracy in 1974, a national referendum led to the abolition of the monarchy. Since then, Greece has been a constitutional democracy. Over the past 2-3 years, Greece has received an increasing number of refugees. This has contributed to acute and delicate problems at the economic, social, cultural and political level.

Geographical Size : 131,944 Km².

Principal industries : Heavy industry includes cement, textiles, and steel; light industry centres on the production of clothing, shoes and other leather goods. The main agricultural products are olives and olive oil, wine, tobacco, and fruit. Greece also has one of the world's largest merchant fleets, sailing under both Greek and foreign flags.

Date of EC membership : 1979.

Total number of inhabitants (1991) : 10,120,000.

Age of majority : 18 years.

Number of people under the age of majority (1990) : 2,916,100.

Number of children and young people (December 1991): in residential care :

state, religious or philanthrophic child protection :	3,299
Ministry of Justice reformatories :	13,000
in foster care :	655

Nature of residential and foster care provision

In Greece, child welfare falls under the aegis of (a) the Ministry of Health and Welfare, (b) agencies such as 'PIKPA' (Patriotic Institution for Social Welfare) and the National Welfare Organisation, both of which are funded and supervised by the government, (c) the Greek Orthodox Church, and (d) private organisations operating mostly in large urban areas such as Athens and Thessaloniki.

Types of provision

Currently, the following types of residential care are provided by the various agencies :

a) 27 Centres for Child Care (former orphanages) run by the state in different geographical and administrative regions of the country;
b) 6 Children's Towns (*Pedopolis*) run by the National Welfare Organisation;
c) 47 institutions run by the church and by private organisations, many of which receive state funds (Ministry of Health, 1991).

The above facilities accommodate some 2811 children, aged from birth to 18 years.

Boarding schools represent a further category of residential living for children aged between 12 and 18 years, and often beyond. These accommodate children from villages which lack schools or where daily commuting to the nearest school is difficult. A good number of children (1012) live in boarding schools free of any tuition fees or other expenses. However, because of the educational orientation of this kind of care, they are not considered to be at risk or in need of protection.

Numbers of children in care

The number of children in residential care has decreased over recent years. Numbers of children accommodated in the various forms of residential care are as follows (Ministry of Health, 1991) :

1. State Centres for Child Care :	835	aged 5½-18 yrs
2. National Welfare Organisation 'Pedopolis' :	517	aged 2½-18 yrs
a. Living in :	(404)	
b. Home at night :	(113)	
3. Church and private organisations :	1274	
4. Babies' Centre 'METERA' :	105	aged 0-6 yrs
5. PIKPA's Temporary Shelter :	80	aged 0-18 yrs
Total	2811	

Foster care is currently provided by three main child welfare organisations: 'PIKPA', Babies' Centre 'Metera' and the National Welfare Organisation. The largest programme operates under 'PIKPA', which has the longest history of fostering. At present, some 500 children are fostered in 450 families. Babies' Centre 'Metera' provides care and protection to 80 children, aged 2-20 years, in 57 foster families, while the National Welfare Organisation, through its new foster care programme looks after 75 children in 48 families. It is important to mention that the number of children fostered by relatives exceeds those placed with non-relatives by a ratio of roughly 2:1.

The quality of residential and foster care provided by the different organisations varies. This is partly because the state does not stipulate basic standards or offer clear guidance as to the quality of care required. The most adequate staff-child ratio is that of Babies' Centre 'Metera' where 105 children, aged between 0 and 6 years, live in 8 detached houses and are cared for by 36 babies' nurses (all of whom hold a 3 year diploma) and 100 nurses' aids. Due to the operation of shift-systems and staff holiday's, the average staff-child ratio is about 1:3.

'Metera' also supervises the care of 80 children placed in 57 foster families. For the total of 185 children under its care, the corresponding professional staff comprises 12 social workers, 4 paediatricians, 4 psychologists and 1 part-time child psychiatrist.

'Metera' provides in-service training programmes for its staff and supports their participation in conferences and other forms of training in Greece and abroad. However, training is not provided on a systematic basis but as needs arise and conditions and time allow. Training for foster parents is limited to initial screening and on-going support on an individual basis.

The remainder of residential care provided in Greece presents a contrasting picture. The National Welfare Organisation in its 8 different Children's Towns (*Pedopolis*) currently cares for approximately 919 children : 517 in residential and semi-residential care, 98 in after school care, 120 in day care, 11 accommodated on a temporary basis, 140 in their families as 'long leave' from care, and 33 in foster families. Some 462 staff are employed for the different programmes and may be divided into the following categories : (a) administrative : 83 (18 per cent); (b) child care : 124 (27 per cent); (c) professional : 20 (4 per cent); (d) technical : 83 (18 per cent); (e) auxilliary : 96 (21 per cent); (f) health : 16 (3 per cent); (g) part-time educational : 40 (9 per cent).

It should be noted that only 31 per cent (categories (b) and (c) above) of staff work directly with the children.

With regard to staff training, in-service-programmes are provided on an ad-hoc basis, and professional staff are permitted to attend conferences offered by outside bodies. Aside from individual and family counselling, no training is provided for foster parents. Group training and counselling is included in the long range foster plan, but this has not yet been implemented.

Staffing in the 27 State Centres for Child Care is generally unsatisfactory. Exact numbers of staff employed cannot be provided here, because a large number of the posts described in the regulations have not been filled for several years due to economic recession and the low political priority given to child protection in Greece. There are no social workers in these Centres, each of which accommodates as many as 60 children. The staff responsible for the direct care of the children are high school graduates, who are referred to as 'pedagogues'.

Church supported residential care settings or those run on a private, non-profit making, basis tend to provide a different, non-institutional, 'care climate'. This owes a good deal to the fact that most staff live on the premises, and are extremely dedicated, often for a lifetime. Moreover, child-centred care often reflects progressive thinking on the part of a specific church region, or board of directors, or individual holding primary administrative responsibility.

Historical antecedents

In Greece, where wars and military occupation have marked the country's history, priority has been given to welfare policies geared to ensuring the survival of particularly vulnerable groups such as children. Historically, child protection has mainly involved the care of orphans, whose parents had died from infectious deseases, or from violence and hunger associated with war and ethnic strife. Such upheavals meant long periods of poverty for large numbers of families with young children. As an instrument of social policy, the traditional 'orphanage' was seen as the solution to child poverty and parental loss. In such circumstances, there was little, if any, need to work with the child's natural family with a view to the child's rehabilitation or return home. The orphanage served as the child's home and custodial parent. There seemed to be no necessity to develop alternative child protection schemes.

Residential care   The evolution of residential care for children in Greece can be divided into four major periods (Panopoulou-Maratos et al., 1988).

a) Post 1st World War Period (1922-1929). The First World War and its aftermath resulted in an ethnic crisis among the Greek population of Asia Minor, more than 1 million of whom returned to the mainland. The first large institutions were built by philanthropists during this period and these comprise 14 per cent of today's residential institutions.

b) Post 2nd World War and Greek Civil War Period (1947-1954). During this period, the State assumed a 'parenting role', providing food, shelter, clothing and education for children stricken by poverty and the loss of their fathers. Orphanages were built, primarily along the country's northern border, to act as a 'social fortification' against neighbouring communist countries.

c) Military Junta Period (1967-1974). The expansion of statism promoted by the dictatorship resulted in the building of a large number of residential units. These comprise 30 per cent of current establishments.

d) Restoration of Parliamentary Government (1974-present). The post-junta period has been marked by the restoration of parliamentary government and Greece's entry to the European Economic Community. The improvement of the country's economic status has acted as a 'buffer' towards the flow of children into residential care. Moreover, the absence of war has resulted in fewer children entering residential care as orphans. Social need during this period has been linked with unemployment, broken families, urbanisation and the gradual decline of extended-family networks of support, which has particularly effected young parents. The fall in the number of children in residential care has been accompanied by an increase in the demand for community alternatives to meet emerging needs. The decline in residential care is most evident in the case of babies and children up to 3 years of age.

Foster Care   The first foster care schemes were initiated by Foundling Homes and 'PIKPA'.   In 1858, The Municipal Foundling Home of Athens placed 35 children with foster families, who each received a monthly allowance of 20 drachmae or £6.74.   Much later in 1932, 'PIKPA' made an effort to reintroduce this scheme but it was not until 1952 that foster care was developed by the same organisation as a child protection measure.   The first such initiative involved a group of visiting nurses who placed 25 children with foster families.

A foster care scheme introduced shortly after World War II, and administered by governmental regional social welfare departments, slowly deteriorated.   Consequently, in 1970, it was decided that 'PIKPA', with its network of services around the country, should assume administrative responsibility for the scheme.   This decision, however, deprived many social workers of an essential 'tool' with which to help families in crisis and children in need, and thus further 'encouraged' social workers to resort to the use institutional care. Children were often placed very far from their families, which increased the strain on already very tenuous family ties.   Many children in care would undoubtedly have returned to their natural families or maintained close links with them had the foster care scheme not been abolished.

Foster care has since made little progress in helping to meet the needs of separated children.   A major reason for this is the extensive network of residential care settings around the country, which offer professionals a ready-made solution and inhibit efforts by the state to promote alternative forms of substitute child care.   Another factor militating against the development of foster care in Greece has been resistence on the part of residential workers who fear possible loss of employment and, indeed, any innovations in theory and practice which may alter their current conditions of work.   Finally, the absence of legislation promoting fostering as an alternative to institutional care has also obstructed the development of foster care (Triseliotis and Kousidou, 1989).

Legal framework of services

Few children enter care via routes set out in legislation.   There are two main reasons for this; first, it has only recently been accepted that the support provided by the extended family is gradually diminishing as a result of increasing urbanisation; second, preventive services for children in need and their families are inadequate.   A multi-disciplinary approach is generally lacking, and communication between health, welfare and legal services is poor.

Children mainly enter care with the consent of their parents. Consequently, parents may withdraw their children from care against the agency's wishes. In rare cases, the intervention of the Prosecutor for Minors is requested in order to prevent this and protect the child. Very few services (e.g. Babies' Centre 'Metera', the Society for the Protection of Minors, the Institute of Child Health - albeit in its research role - and quite recently, the National Welfare Organisation) use the legal process to both assume parental rights over children of dangerous or inadequate parents, and prevent such parents removing children from care.

The law (Civil Code) contains no provisions covering residential and foster care for children, in spite of a new and progressive Family Law (1329/1983) (New Family Law, 1983). Fostering is only indirectly mentioned in a general legal provision of 1961 concerning 'the prerequisites for support to children needing protection' which refers to financial support to children living with 'unrelated families' (The Government's Stationery Office, 1961).

Administrative framework

Administrative responsibility for residential and foster care services is shared among government, government supported, church and private, non-profit, agencies. Government, church and private agencies serve roughly equal numbers of children, with government supported organisations serving fewer children.

Expenditure

It is not possible to accurately estimate total expenditure on residential and foster care, since spending programmes often overlap the two forms of provision. In 1987, the Ministry of Health and Welfare's Department of Child Protection spent a total of 28,153,305,000 Greek drachmae or £83,540,964 on its various programmes, which include residential and foster care, day care for pre-school children, summer camps, residential care for severely handicapped children and boarding schools. The equivalent sum for church and private, non-profit, agencies is not known because individual agencies are responsible for their own fund raising, and information about such activities is not collected by central government.

The daily cost of residential care and monthly fostering allowances are listed below :

1. Babies' Centre 'Metera' (1988)
(a) Daily cost per child in residential care :   11,596 dr. or £34.40
(b) Average daily costs of residential care
    and fostering combined :   7,747 dr. or £23
(c) Current (1991) monthly allowances for foster care:
    1. Normal children   35,000 dr. or £104
    2. Children with special needs   50,000 dr. or £148
    3. Rare exceptions (child with Aids) 120,000 dr. or £356

With regard to foster care, additional expenses relating to clothing, health, education (private or special, if needed) are also met by the agency. Residential children's needs are usually met 'on site'. Where this is not possible, appropriate services are sought in the community.

2. National Welfare Organisation   The monthly allowances and additional sums for fostering are identical to those of Babies' Centre 'Metera'. In 1990, the average daily cost of residential care was 7,000 drachmae or £21 per child. The National Welfare Organisation is developing a large number of programmes with financial aid from the EEC. In 1990, this totalled 500,000,000 drachmae or £1,483,679.

3. State Centres for Child Care   In 1990, the average daily cost per child was 2,700 drachmas or £8. Where the Centre is unable to cover the child's additional needs (e.g. health and education) help is sought from community resources.

Major ideas underpinning service provision

As previously indicated, service delivery in the field of social welfare in Greece has primarily been based on the population's urgent needs and on programmes aimed at ameliorating problems such as widespread poverty, and the consequences of war and political vicissitudes. The sheer scale of social need could not be met by sophisticated theoretical approaches, resource books and other publications, but rather necessited immediate action to ensure the survival of the population. On the other hand, the government bureaucracy did nothing to promote the development of knowledge based on theoretical approaches and on empirical research data. As a result, traditional policy measures and institutional care seem out of step with contemporary needs. Although working groups and committees of experts have, from time to time, provided valuable proposals for improving services, these have had little practical effect.

For example, the 5-year plan (1988-1992) of the Ministry of Health and Welfare, (Ministry of Health and Social Services) introduced a policy of supporting the family and its members, regardless of age and presenting problem, through a system of multi-purpose welfare services in the community (Vorria and Denegri, 1991). To date, however, few services have been developed, and a great number of social work posts throughout Greece are empty due to economic constraints amd the low national priority placed on social welfare as opposed to health needs.

Recent innovations and trends

Under the pressure of newly emerging social needs and demands by the population, serious efforts are being made by both state, state supported, and private organisations, to develop a new approach to child protection and to re-orientate the state's role in child welfare.

The 1980's have been marked by the influence of research findings from abroad highlighting the negative impact of institutional life on children's development and competencies. Moreover, the introduction of family support policies by the Socialist government, as part of its efforts to create a Welfare State, have enabled many parents to keep their children at home.

It was soon realised that two objectives had to be pursued simultaneously : first, it was necessary to improve conditions in residential care; second, there was a need to develop alternative child care services to meet the range of current needs.

In 1984, a committee appointed by the Ministry of Health and Welfare studied the problem of child abuse and neglect in Greece, and suggested a policy response linking the newly established National Health Service with the welfare system, within a framework of decentralised services and a community approach centred on primary prevention.

More recently, in 1989, a working group appointed by the same Ministry was asked to study ways by which to improve residential care and to develop alternative approaches to child protection. A detailed report was produced a few months later, suggesting a variety of foster and residential care schemes aimed at addressing contemporary needs.

Irrespective of initiatives periodically undertaken by the state, little progress has actually been made. Care practices in the state's Centres for Child Care (*Kentra Pedikis Merimnas*) remain unsatisfactory. No social workers are employed in such Centres. Children are 'supervised' rather than 'cared for' by 'pedagogues' who, at best, are high school, rather than University trained, graduates.

In spite of this generally gloomy picture, however, serious efforts are being made to introduce innovative approaches based on new thinking about family and child care policy and the role of the state.

A Children's Village, set up by a private, non-profit, organisation along the lines of the Austrian model has been operating in Athens since 1979. A second is now being built in Thessaloniki. The public has supported this new scheme with generous donations. A major difficulty faced by the Children's Village concerns the recruitment of 'mothers' willing to devote a lifetime to the task. This difficulty may be associated with cultural issues relating to the role of women in Greek society. For most women, marriage and family life seems to be the ultimate goal, regardless of age. Further, widows and unmarried women are often supported by the wider family network and, therefore, many do not enter the employment market.

In 1984, the National Welfare Organisation, in collaboration with the Child Abuse Team of the Institute of Child Health (a research centre in Athens) opened a crisis unit. In the first 4 years of its operation, the unit, which had facilities for 12 children, took care of some 42 abused and neglected children, aged from birth to 4 years, who required temporary care until family crises had been resolved or an alternative placement, such as a foster or adoptive home, could be found. In 1988, however, the unit was closed following an administrative decision that took no account of the unit's success. Fortunately, Babies' Centre 'Metera' set up a child abuse programme, thereby filling the gap in provision left by the closure of the National Welfare Organisation's crisis unit.

The National Welfare Organisation is currently re-appraising its established programmes and introducing new initiatives (National Welfare Organisation, 1991). Such efforts include the following :

1. *The development of initiatives within residential settings (Pedopolis)* such as :

   (a) crisis units offering immediate protection to children aged 4-18 years;
   (b) intake units offering an adjustment period to children entering residential care;
   (c) a semi-residential hostel for older children leaving care and other youngsters;
   (d) opening the 'Pedopolis' to the community by offering study and recreational facilities to children whose parents work after school hours;

(e)   greater flexibility in admissions criteria, which includes accepting siblings regardless of sex and age differences;

(f)   geographical flexibility in order to keep children within their home regions and close to their families;

(g)   the abolition of 'single-sex' establishments;

(h)   efforts to link residential care with community resources to comprehensively meet children's health, education and recreational needs.

The National Welfare Organisation has employed new staff to implement such innovations. These are mainly social workers, but also include pedagogues and psychologists. In recruiting additional personnel, the National Welfare Organisation has introduced new selection criteria, and has improved the quality of supervision and training for staff. Attempts have also been made to improve staff-child ratios.

2. The development of new programmes in the community In Athens, three 'social apartments' have been opened for young men and women leaving the Pedopolis at 18 years of age, and who need a sheltered environment. Such apartments are also planned for Thessaloniki, Larissa, Volos and Ioannina.

3. Foster care In 1989, the National Welfare Organisation set up a pilot foster care project. More recently, it has incorporated fostering into its child protection services. This involves placing some children with relatives and boarding others out in medium-term foster placements (i.e. up to 2 years).

Two target groups of children may be distinguished. The first comprises children currently living in residential care. The second group consists of children for whom admission to care has been requested by their parents or by welfare agencies. Foster care in this case is used as a 'buffer' to residential care.

There are plans to extend foster care schemes to all provinces where the National Welfare Organisation operates (i.e. from Athens to the northern border of Greece).

Also worth mentioning is the transformation of a state residential institution for pre-school children in the Athenian community of Kallithea. Having operated as a traditional 'closed door' setting, the establishment now offers a day care programme for the community's children, a residential programme for 22 children, and a day care programme for 14 'high risk' children who return home in the evening.

A multi-disciplinary team works with the different target groups involved : natural families, children, staff, community agencies.

With regard to private initiatives, a voluntary Association for Foster Care has been set up in Athens which promotes fostering in various ways, including public awareness campaigns, fund-raising, and the recruitment of foster families to meet a range of needs from weekend accommodation and outings to long-term fostering.

The Association works in partnership with major child welfare organisations, and makes an important contribution to child care provision.

Substitute child care schemes in Greece have generally adopted a traditional model of separation from the community. A large number of the institutions built during the post-war period were set in isolated locations away from towns and communities, and functioned as self-sufficient units avoiding contact with the outside world. Although many services, such as education and health, are now provided by the community, children spend most of their leisure hours inside the institution. Further, most youngsters are unable to return home at weekends due to the distances involved and severed ties with their birth parents. Attempts to link children with families in the community have failed because of hostility to such policies on the part of residential caregivers and administrators. Moreover, the families approached were often unwilling to cooperate, and the children themselves often appeared to feel uncomfortable about participating in such schemes as a result of institutionalisation.

The National Welfare Organisation, in line with its new emphasis on improving the quality of life for socially and economically vulnerable groups, is attempting to develop a comprehensive framework of primary, secondary and tertiary prevention. Consequently, residential care is opening its doors, and institutions are being transformed into community centres. These are called Social Centres in rural areas, and Youth Centres or Neighbourhood Social Centres in urban areas.

As the number of foster care schemes is very limited, fostering plays a relatively minor role in the provision of social welfare for children and families. By contrast, residential care, because of the extensive number of placements it offers, and the fact that it is one of the few options available to social workers, meets a large part of the demand for family support services.

Greece's transition from a traditional agricultural country to an industrialised member of the European Community is reflected in its social welfare provisions. Current trends in residential care in Greece are very similar to those observed in more industrialised countries (Berridge, 1985), and include decreases in the number of children taken into care (particularly children under five years), the number of residential care settings, and the number of residential homes run by religious or voluntary organisations. In addition, there has been a corresponding increase in the demand for fostering and alternative forms of care, especially for crisis shelters.

Within this general framework, a number of important issues have emerged. First, how to adapt the residential sector to the task of providing temporary or 'crisis,' rather than long-term, care. Second, the problem of maintaining children's family links. Third, the difficulties experienced by young people leaving care. Fourth, the problem of achieving continuity and stability of care for children. Fifth, the need to develop fostering and residential care as complementary services, forming part of a comprehensive range of provisions for children in need.

The steadily decreasing population of children in residential care is welcomed by both administrators and professionals as a sign that the community is becoming better able to care for its vulnerable children. Although no doubt encouraging, the declining role of residential care must be seen in the wider context of social welfare provision in contemporary Greece. The dearth of community based family and child welfare services, and out-reach programmes, does not allow for proper assessment of the quality of the child's life. Children may be physically and sexually abused, or neglected, without any help being offered to them and to their families. District social welfare departments in urban areas, and regional departments in the provinces, act upon request by parents. This system excludes those disturbed and dysfunctional families who rarely seek help. Even if they do, the heavy caseloads of social workers only allows minimum help to be offered in the form of family and child allowances and, occasionally, residential care. For example, in the area of Athens and Piraeus, which has a population of approximately four million, there are only four District Social Welfare Departments. These operate under the Ministry of Health and Social Services and are staffed by an average of 13 social workers.

The need for crisis care, rather than long-term care, is reflected in the fact that although all residential care settings operate at only 20-60 per cent of their capacity, a temporary crisis unit run by 'PIKPA' operates to full capacity - in spite of offering poor quality care.

108

A major problem permeating residential care is the lack of awareness among decision makers that a sophisticated, multi-level, approach is required to address the complexity of children's needs, and which goes far beyond the mere provision of a physically safe environment offering food, shelter and schooling. Unfortunately, the main child protection services operate under a law passed as long ago as 1928, which could not have foreseen the current need for staff with therapeutic skills; although efforts are now being made at the governmental level to promote changes in the legal framework of services.

Innovative programmes established by the National Welfare Organisation require critical evaluation, particularly in relation to their administrative structure. The National Welfare Organisation is a large, bureaucratic, agency, with approximately 3000 employees, of whom only 4 per cent are professional staff. An estimated 80 per cent of its budget is spent on salaries and operating costs, and the services provided are not subject to systematic evaluation. Sectional interests and bureaucratic inertia tend to frustrate attempts to introduce innovative policies. The large size of many institutions, combined with the lack of supervision and systematic training for staff, and the excessive degree of bureaucratisation under which the whole system labours, results in policies which do not necessarily translate into clear improvements in the daily lives of the children themselves. Little Maria, as a consumer of the services, may never benefit from the changes ostensibly made in her 'best interests'.

Research on residential and foster care

The social, economic and political turmoil which has characterised Greece's recent history left little margin for research on child welfare. The limited research undertaken has primarily been linked with industrial development and, though to a lesser extent, with health. Research in the psychological, social and pedagogic fields has lagged far behind. Presently, only 0.35 per cent of public expenditure is devoted to research.

Major research funding agencies

The major source of research funding is the government, through its Ministries of Research and Technology, Education, Health, Welfare and Social Security, Industry, and Agriculture. The European Community has also funded a limited number of projects - mainly action-research in the fields of labour and health.

The private sector has so far shown no interest in promoting research. With the exception of a small number of philanthropists, who support private research centres or institutes, the private sector operates along traditional lines, which includes giving money to poor families, the sick and disabled, and funding residential homes - usually single-sex institutions for girls.

The Ministry of Health, Welfare and Social Security funds the Institute of Child Health, a private, non-profit, research centre in Athens, which for the last 25 years has been involved in various research activities concerning children and families. In 1990, its budget was 265 million drachmae or £786,350. Some 37 of the Institute's 77 employees are scientific staff, while the rest are laboratory technicians and administrative personnel. An estimated 44 million drachmae or £13,563.8 was spent on research into child protection. The Institute also seeks research grants from other sectors of government, the private sector, and international organisations, such as the European Economic Community and the World Health Organisation.

Research in the fields of child welfare and child protection is very limited. The research department at Babies' Centre 'Metera', which for many years had carried out research on residential care and the adoption of babies and young children, was recently closed. Moreover, 'PIKPA' has no research capability whatsoever, and the National Welfare Organisation's Department of Research and Planning limits itself to programme planning and the collection of annual statistics on populations served rather than carrying out methodologically sound evaluative studies of child protection services.

Who carries out research?

However, in the midst of this rather grim picture of an overall lack of interest in research on residential and foster care, the Institute of Child Health, through its departments of Social Psychiatry and Family Relations, has carried out a good deal of research on both residential care and child abuse and neglect. The professionals involved are full-time researchers representing disciplines such as psychology, social work, psychiatry, child psychiatry, paediatrics, sociology and law. Their educational qualifications range from a 3 year diploma in social work practice to doctoral degrees.

In Greece, salary levels for researchers vary according to employment setting. University staff primarily engage in teaching duties, and their opportunities to do research are limited. Researchers funded by the Ministry of Research and Technology undertake research on a full-time basis. The salaries of these workers are determined by academic status and years of experience, and are comparable with those of university staff. For example, a university associate professor and status B researcher in a government funded research institute both receive a monthly salary of approximately 200,000 drachmae or £593.47. Salary levels at the Institute of Child Health are lower, despite the fact that the latter is a designated research centre.

The occupational status of researchers is impossible to determine since most only engage in research on a part-time basis. Their primary responsibilities lie in clinical, administrative or academic work. However, because of the lack of priority given to research in Greece, especially research in the social field, the occupational status of researchers cannot be described as high. The small number of full-time researchers and research institutes is not conducive to the sort of professionalisation of the field that would lead to pressure for improvement.

Review of previous research

In Greece, no research has been carried out on foster care. This is because, despite its long existence, foster care has only recently begun to assume the status of a major alternative to residential care.

Over the past decade, research on residential care has mainly been associated with the Institute of Child Health. In the early 1980's the Ministry of Health and Welfare funded a joint-study by the Institute of Child Health and Babies' Centre 'Metera' evaluating residential care and its effect on children's psycho-social development (Panopoulou-Maratos et al., 1988). The study was carried out between 1979 and 1984, and included establishments for children with physical or mental handicaps. The sample comprised (a) 104 (36 per cent) orphanages for children aged 5-12 years, (b) 178 (61 per cent) hostels for children aged 12-19 years, who could not attend school in their villages beyond primary level because there was no high school or because of insurmountable difficulties in commuting to the nearest one, and (c) 8 (3 per cent) settings for pre-school children. Some 48 per cent of establishments accommodated boys only, 40 per cent girls only, and 12 per cent looked after both boys and girls. An estimated 54 per cent of establishments were 'small' in size (i.e. accommodated less than 40 children), 26 per cent were of 'average' size (41-99 children), and 20 per cent were large in scale (100 plus children). Most establishments were located in rural areas, 12 per cent were situated in the Attica region, and 35 per cent were located along the northern frontier regions of Macedonia and Epirus. Forty per cent of establishments were under government jurisdiction, 35 per cent under the Greek Orthodox church, and 25 per cent were privately run. The study revealed that many children from one parent families, or from broken homes caused by parental death or divorce, were admitted to care for economic reasons and could have remained at home if supported financially and supervised by a welfare agency.

The same study assessed the children's perceptions of institutional care. A total of 605 children from 72 institutions were interviewed. Significant differences were found between institutions run by the state and those run by private organisations or the church, between small (less than 60 children) and large scale settings, and between boys only and girls only establishments. Two major areas of concern identified by the children were their lack of adequate opportunity for personal development, and their need for an emotionally supportive social environment (Panopoulou-Maratos et al., 1988).

The effects of institutional care on the children's cognitive development and behaviour was also assessed using a group I.Q. test (Raven), Insel and Wilson's scale of conservativism vs. liberalism, and Rutter's questionnaire for teachers. Results showed that institutional life affects many aspects of a child's functioning. A consistent finding on all three measures was that the development of a number of children from each establishment was adversely affected. Moreover, feelings of alienation and abandonment were commonly expressed by children. The children also highlighted the lack of close interpersonal relations between themselves and their caregivers, and the rigidity of daily routines and strict rules governing institutional life (Panopoulou-Maratos et al., 1988).

A more recent study by the Institute of Child Health (Vorria, 1988) compared the behaviour and social relationships of 41 children, aged between 9 and 11 years, who had spent at least three years in institutions prior to the research, with that of a control group. The children's behaviour was observed both at school and in residential care. This showed that an institutional upbringing leads to deficits in social functioning and problems in interpersonal relationships. These results were confirmed by a follow-up study of the same children seven years later (Vorria, 1988).

A further study undertaken by the same researcher (Vorria, in press) compared the social behaviour of 48 residential children, aged 2½-5½ years, and 25 controls, matched for age and sex. The method used was that of 'naturalistic observation' during free play and formal activity sessions in class. The caretaker's opinion was obtained through the Richman and Graham questionnaire on the health and behaviour problems of pre-school children. It was found that the children living

112

in institutions did not play with other children as frequently as those living with their families. The residential children also tended to be disruptive and aggressive. No significant difference was found between the two groups in relation to their involvement in classroom activities. Overall, the children in residential care manifested higher levels of health and behavioural problems than the youngsters in the control group. Cluster analysis revealed that the children aged over 3½ years who had been admitted to care after the age of 2½ were generally less disturbed than children under 3½ years who had been in care almost from birth.

The social profile of mothers whose children had been admitted to institutional care has also been investigated (Vorria and Denegri, 1991). The study sample consisted of 76 mothers of children in residential care and 65 control mothers from intact families. Half of the first group were mothers of children aged 2½-5½ years who had been in institutional care for at least the previous six months, and half were mothers of children aged 15½-17½ years who had experienced institutional care for a period of 3 years or longer during their school years. The mean age of the first group of mothers was 27 years as compared with 42 years for the control group. All the mothers were interviewed using a semi-structured interview schedule. The mothers of children in residential care belonged to a lower social class than mothers comprising the control group, had experienced greater adversity in their own childhoods, had more health problems, left their parental homes at an earlier age, gave birth at a younger age, and faced more difficulties (e.g. financial, housing, marital, etc.). Differences were also found between the two sub-groups of mothers of residential children with regard to the reasons which compelled them to place their children in care, the experiences of their children before admission, and the frequency of contact with their children whilst the latter were in care. These results replicate findings of similar studies carried out in England. Moreover, differences were found between mothers of two generations in relation to the reasons underlying their children's entry to care. By contrast with older mothers, whose difficulties were associated with financial hardship, the problems faced by younger mothers appeared to result from lack of emotional support.

In 1984, a crisis-unit was opened by the National Welfare Organisation for 12 abused and neglected children aged from birth to 4 years in collaboration with the Institute of Child Health's Child Abuse Team, whose role was to evaluate the project. At the end of the first year, a study was carried out to assess the unit's operation (Agathonos, 1987). This entailed two sets of parameters : first, 'functional' parameters, which related to the staff-child ratio, socialisation (outings, social programme), creativity (stimulation, educational opportunities), nutrition, and visiting by parents and 'significant others'; second, 'objective' parameters, assessing the number of auxilliary staff, home appliances, and living conditions (safety, heating). Analysis revealed a clear correlation between staff-child ratio and level of functioning. Intervention at the objective-administrative level and a shift towards providing 'more care for the carer' significantly improved the unit's functioning. Questionnaires completed on each child by the 13 member staff team showed a high degree of consensus among staff about child-management issues pertaining to medical care and children's sleep, but less agreement about children's eating habits and bowel control behaviour. Another important finding was that, in general, staff objected to involvement by parents which they perceived as 'interference'. Staff behaved antagonistically towards parents, and showed little understanding of parents' needs and the factors which led parents to abuse or neglect their children. The reasons underlying such attitudes and behaviour on the part of staff appear to be related to their own upbringings. Most of the staff were raised in traditional, extended, families from small rural communities or semi-urban areas where a high degree of social stigma is attached to parenting failure. In addition, the training received by staff (1-2 years, after high school) was not sufficient to influence or alter long standing attitudes about child-rearing practice.

A further research project on residential care carried out by the Institute of Child Health (Paritsis et al., 1985) concerned a multi-level, systemic, method of intervention in a residential unit for girls and young women in Athens (Paritsis et al., 1989). The aim of the project was to reduce behavioural problems through an approach which viewed the institution as a system undergoing therapy. The unit comprised 27 girls and young women aged 3-21 years and 7 staff members. A number of tests were administered, before and after intervention, in order to measure behavioural change at both the individual and group level. Intervention included the following : (a) a 3-month analysis of the first set of data obtained through tests and observations followed by the formulation of the first hypothesis on how the system functioned; (b) two weeks of intense systems' oriented therapy on the 'natural' sub-groups to which individuals belonged (e.g. teachers, children's groups under supervision). The results show a statistically significant reduction of behavioural problems following intervention. This was accompanied by improved interpersonal and formal relations among members of the institution.

Because of the limited overall research interest in residential care and fostering, it is not possible to describe any current research trends. However, the Institute of Child Health plans to undertake two important research projects. The first concerns a study on the use of fostering by front-line social workers operating with families in crisis and children at risk of abuse. The study will be based on a systemic approach in which social workers are conceived as the consumers in the child welfare system. An attempt will be made to assess the relationship between the needs and wishes of families, social workers' understanding of requests for help by parents, and the system's response through its family and child protection services.

A second study will respond to a provincial town's demand for assistance in attempting to deal with a 'problem institution', which provides accommodation for some 54 boys, aged 5-18 years, some of whom are said to be exhibiting overt sexual behaviour which includes the sexual victimisation of younger boys by older ones.

In general, research on residential care and fostering is not initiated or supported by the large child protection agencies themselves, but rather is carried out on an ad hoc basis by researchers working primarily at the Institute of Child Health.

Information towards policy and practice

The extent to which policy and practice are informed by research findings is related to research ethics and the conduct of individual researchers, to adequate supervision, and to the administrative efficacy of executive boards. Often, research begun is not completed due to inadequate funding and supervision, other priorities, and a lack of pressure on researchers from the funding source which, in most cases, is the state. However, even where reports are submitted to the related Ministries or other agencies of social policy, they are mostly ignored. In Greece, as elsewhere, there is a yawning gap between research and social policy. This reflects poor communication between researchers and policy makers, and a tendency on the part of the latter to feel threatened by and, therefore, to ignore or mistrust research findings. Social policy related to residential and foster care is out of step with current social needs, and characterised by a lack of innovative programmes.

However, an encouraging trend observed in recent years is the dissatisfaction expressed by social workers concerning their role and task, and associated calls for improvements in their training and the services provided to children and families in need.

Future research

Future research in the fields of residential and foster care in Greece should be targeted on the following : (a) evaluation of existing services from the point of view of children as consumers of services; (b) the development of fostering, especially for pre-school children and children under 10 years; (c) the difficulties associated with children leaving care; (d) public attitudes towards young people who have been in care and who wish to be assimilated into the community; (e) the attitudes of families of children in care towards maintaining links with their children; (f) professional attitudes towards parenting failure; (g) the issue of 'burn-out' among child protection workers; and, (h) decision making in child protection work.

The development of a sound knowledge base for residential and foster care is frustrated by the low status of social research in Greece, a serious lack of economic resources, and the low political priority assigned to child protection. In a country where social policy, especially that pertaining to children in need and their families, is so closely linked to political pressure, children's inability to vote will always limit the extent to which their voice is heard. Furthermore, the parents of children in care are themselves often powerless and immature, trapped within chronic psychological and social crises, mistrustful of authority, and living on the margins of society. Such parents would be the last to form a group in order to exert pressure for their own and their children's sake. Therefore, much appears to rest with professionals, acting as child advocates, and with the state. Unfortunately, the needs of the state often appear to conflict with, and to take priority over, the needs of professionals and the children they serve. Measures are required to ensure that child-centred policies are developed, accompanied by a corresponding caring approach for staff to improve their training, status, and salaries. Unless such steps are taken, child welfare services in Greece will remain an inadequate response to the needs of vulnerable children and their families.

References

Agathonos H. (1987), 'The Crisis Unit : a new child protection scheme for abused and neglected preschool children', in H.

Agathonos (Ed.), *Child Abuse and Neglect*, Institute of Child Health, Athens.

Berridge D. (1985), *Children's Homes*, Basil Blackwell, Oxford.

Ministry of Health and Social Services 'Five Year Plan 1988-1992'.

Ministry of Health, Welfare and Social Security, Department of Family and Child (1991).

National Welfare Organisation, Department of Research and Planning (1991), 'In-service reports'.

New Family Law 1329/1983.

Panopoulou-Maratos O., Stangou L., Georgas D., Lambidi A. and Doxiadis S. (1988), 'Schemes of institutional care for children in Greece : the functioning of institutions and their effect on children's mental health', in *Growing up in an Institution*, Greek Society of Mental Hygiene and Child Neuropsychiatry, Athens.

Paritsis N., Lambidi A., Todoulou M. and Dedouli M. (1989), *Reducing behavioural problems in residential care : an experiment based on system's approach*. Paper presented at the First European Conference on Residential Care, De Haan, Belgium, December 1989.

The Government's Stationary Office (1961), Issue 158/1961 a Royal Decree 669/1961 ch. 2 1.

Triseliotis J. and Kousidou T. (1989), *Social Work in Adoption and in Fostering*, Babies' Centre 'Metera', Athens.

Vorria P. (1988), 'The effect of long-term institutionalisation on children's social behaviour', in *Growing up in an Institution*, Greek Society of Mental Hygiene and Child Neuropsychiatry, Athens.

Vorria P. and Denegri Z. (1991), *Social profile of mothers whose children have been admitted into institutional care in Greece*, Paper presented at the 3rd European Conference on Child Abuse and Neglect, Prague, June 1991.

Vorria P. (in press), *Social behaviour of preschool children living in institutions*, Psychologika Themata.

6 Ireland

R. Gilligan

Recent political history : Since late January 1993, Ireland has been governed by a coalition composed of the majority party, Fianna Fail (centre right populist, and partners of the Gaullists in the European Parliament), which holds two thirds of cabinet seats, and the Labour party (Social democrats), which has one third of cabinet seats. Economic problems such as unemployment (currently running at a national average of 20%) and the constraints of a public debt which is estimated to consume 26.7% of current expenditure tend to dominate the political agenda. Welfare state provisions which have been achieved (leading, for instance to an infant mortality rate of 8 per 1,000 in 1990, which compares very favourably with that of many wealthier nations) seem increasingly under threat for fiscal and ideological reasons.
Geographical Size : 84,421 Km².
Principal industries : Agriculture, food processing, tourism, computers, chemicals.
Date of EC membership : 1973.
Total number of inhabitants (Census of population 1991, provisional result) : 3,523,400.
Age of majority : 18 years.
Number of people under the age of majority (1986 Census) : 1,230,150.
Number of children and young people (31.12.89) :   in residential care :   734
    in foster care :   1,980

The nature of residential and foster care provision

Public care for children in need became a responsibility of the Irish state on its establishment in 1922, following the cessation of British rule in all but the north-eastern part of the island (now known as Northern Ireland). While it is beyond the scope of this chapter (or indeed the available data) to bring the reader a detailed history of alternative care provision[1] in the period since, a number of major points can be made.

118

Over this period, the numbers of children in residential care have fallen dramatically. In 1930, approximately 6,000 were in care in Industrial Schools (the previous administrative title of the forerunners of today's residential homes) for reasons of 'poverty and neglect' (Commission of Inquiry into the Reformatory and Industrial School System, 1936). A further substantial number of children in that period - 1,582 in 1925 - were in care in poor law institutions for adults (a provision thankfully then in its last throes) (Commission on the Relief of the Sick and Destitute Poor (including the Insane Poor), 1927). So in the late 1920s, something of the order of 7,500 children were in residential care, compared to roughly a thousand or less in the late 1980s.

Residential care today is a considerably more humane and intimate experience than that available in large forbidding institutions in earlier decades (Streetwise National Coalition, 1991).

The numbers of children in foster care have fluctuated over the decades : 1,907 in 1925 (Commission of the Sick and Destitute Poor (including the Insane Poor), 1927); 2,351 in 1945 (Department of Local Government and Public Health, 1946); a low of 932 in 1972 (Gilligan, 1990) and the latest available figure of 1,980 in 1989.

The character of foster care has also changed dramatically over the decades, with a much more rigorous approach to selection and support of foster parents and hopefully with considerably less stigma and risk of exploitation for the foster child.

The responsibility for the care of non-offender children historically had fallen between the health and education authorities. This anomaly has finally been resolved and responsibility has been allocated to the arm of government (health) responsible for general welfare and personal social services (see below).

As will be clear from the above, the total number of children in care for welfare reasons has fallen from approximately 9,500 in the 1920s to 2,500 in the 1980s. The easing of extreme poverty, the introduction of legal adoption in 1952, growing public scepticism about all forms of institutional care, and the development of various community services are likely to have contributed to this reduction in children in care.

Trends affecting children in the care of health boards 1970-1989

Eight regional health boards were established as a result of the Health Act 1970 and these have come to play an ever increasing role in relation to children in care and children at risk. In 1970, there were 1,665 children - or 1.64 per 1000 under 18 years (Gilligan, 1990) - in the care of health boards. By 1989, the numbers of children in health board care had risen to 2,756 (Department of Health, 1991) - or 2.24 per 1000 under 18 (derived from ibid; Central Statistics Office, 1987). In the same period, the numbers of children fostered rose from 950 to 1,980 and the numbers in residential care remained almost static - 715 in 1970 and 734 in 1989, although these figures disguise a peak in numbers of children in health board care in residential placement of 1,186 in 1983 (Department of Health 1986). The 1980s saw a dramatic increase in the proportion of children in care fostered, from 49.9 per cent in 1981 to 71.8 per cent in 1989. Conversely the percentage of children in residential care had fallen from 43.7 per cent in 1981 to 26.6 per cent in 1989. The remaining balance in each year was made up of children in various residual categories of care.

Children in the care of health boards in 1989

There were 2,756 children in the care of the eight regional health boards in Ireland on 31 December 1989 (Department of Health, 1991), the latest date for which figures are available at the time of writing. These national figures inevitably mask some important regional differences. The proportion of children fostered in 1989 ranged from 58.1 per cent in the South Eastern Health Board (responsible for 9.2 per cent of all children in care nationally) and 65.9 per cent in the Eastern Health Board (responsible for 38 per cent of all children in care) to 92.9 per cent in the North Western Health Board (which provides for 5.1 per cent of children in care nationally) (derived from Department of Health, 1991).

Historical antecedents of services

The mid-19th century saw considerable activity in the establishment of orphanages (see Robins, 1980). Legislation in 1858 provided for the establishment of 'reformatory schools' for young offenders, and this was followed in 1868 by legislation to provide for 'industrial schools' for children at risk because of their social circumstances (see Barnes, 1989).

In this century, the system of residential child care has been subject to long periods of relative neglect. A Commission reported in 1936 to the Department of Education which was then largely responsible administratively. Whatever improvements may have ensued, they did not deter an independent review committee (Tuairim, 1966) from being exceptionally critical of the state's performance in this field when it examined the situation in the 1960s. Whether by coincidence or not, a new Committee of Inquiry was appointed in 1968 (Committee on Reformatory and Industrial Schools, 1970).

By contrast with its fate in earlier decades, the 1970s saw a remarkable improvement in the fortunes of residential care. The influence of the Committee of Inquiry (ibid), extra state funds and the liberating influence of Vatican 2 encouraged the employment of lay professional staff, the improvement of living standards, and the development of modern smaller units run on more intimate and much less austere lines.

With growing numbers of professionals in field settings and residential care, their voices were often heard in the media and the corridors of power commenting on deficiencies in provision. An early, and particularly influential, example of this kind was the Campaign for the Care of Deprived Children, which put forward proposals for the future of residential care, foster care, community services, background law and policy (CARE 1972). Due, in part, to the influence of this report and its sponsors, a new government gave, in 1974, the Department of Health a 'lead role' in relation to child care services and appointed a Task Force on Child Care Services to review all aspects of provision. In its interim and final reports, this committee gave considerable coverage to matters concerning fostering and residential care (Task Force on Child Care Services 1975, 1981).

In 1984 the Department of Health (and the eight regional health boards) finally acquired overall responsibility for all residential centres accommodating youngsters with welfare rather than 'offending' problems. This transfer represented the culmination of a trend of disengagement by the Department of Education and growing involvement by the health boards and the Department of Health in provision for non-offenders.

This growing role for the health services in relation to children in care was spurred by three key factors (i) a government decision to expand the number of health board field social work posts in 1973; (ii) a government decision referred to above to give a 'lead role' for child care services to the Department of Health in 1974 (Minister for Health, 1974); and (iii) the recommendations of the Task Force on Child Care Services to assign core responsibility to health boards for the development of child care services (Task Force on Child Care Services, 1981).

Perhaps the most crucial factor was the decision that health boards should develop their own social work services. The social workers appointed quickly identified child care as a priority area for their attention. This had a number of knock on effects, all of which hastened the ultimate eclipsing of the role of the Department of

Education in relation to 'non-offender' children in care; a role it had performed since 1928 when, in what was at that time rightly seen as a progressive step, it had acquired responsibility for this area from the prison service (O'Sullivan, 1979).

Social workers quickly established a decisive role as 'gatekeepers' to the care system. They not only determined whether a child should enter care, but also the legal route into care (subject, of course, to any necessary court approval) and the type of placement. The growth of the health board's own social work child care service led to the shrinking and final cessation of the child protection role of the non-statutory Irish Society for the Prevention of Cruelty to Children (ISPCC). This came about because the emerging health boards elected (with, it seems, the encouragement of their own social work staff) to subsume rather than subsidise the former ISPCC role.

The ISPCC employed Inspectors who investigated the home circumstances of children and had been important 'suppliers' of children in care who had come under the ambit of the Department of Education. Not only did this source dry up, but the legal route for the committal of children to the administrative responsibility of the Department of Education was also closed off. This was due to the increasing reliance by health board social workers, from the early 1970s onwards, on an alternative and previously forgotten provision in the Children Act 1908 for 'fit person order' applications. Initiated by Eastern Health Board social workers, this approach was also to be adopted by the other boards as the route to compulsory care for children. In assuming this role of 'fit person' in respect of a child before the court the health boards thus supplanted the previous role of ISPCC inspectors, gardai (police) or others who might have presented a child to court for its protection.

It is suggested that the various factors listed above had the effect of rendering the role of the Department of Education redundant. It had no local field staff and therefore had no means for ongoing local monitoring of a placement, for which it would have been administratively responsible under the previously used 'committal to the care of the Minister' mechanism in the Children Act 1908. It could not compete in terms of ongoing monitoring of placements, nor could it provide non-compulsory care, or offer foster care which was increasingly pressed for by social workers themselves and by various pressure groups.

The above account illustrates a fairly typical feature of the Irish social service system. Change often occurs slowly and organically rather than by 'decree'. State organs are often reluctant to act as lead regulators and enforcers in the development of services. The possible reasons for such reticence are explored in Gilligan (1989).

Legal framework

Children may come into care on a voluntary basis, that is with the consent of their parents, under welfare provisions in the Health Act 1953. They may also enter care on a compulsory basis under child protection provisions in the Children Act 1908. When in care, there are effectively two forms of placement, residential care and foster care. The current legal framework governing residential care provision is somewhat confused. For historical reasons, some centres are certified as Industrial Schools under The Children Act 1908 (and subject to related regulations). Others, which are approved under the Health Act 1953 for their suitability for the placement of children, appear to have no regulatory controls dealing specifically with their day to day operation. The Child Care Act 1991 contains provisions to close this loophole, and also to prevent residential units from opening and operating without any official authorisation. (Although in practice there is little incentive to do so since placements or, perhaps more importantly, payments will only be made by health boards to approved or certified homes).

Health boards are the only body permitted to place children in care in foster families. Their day to day practice in foster care is governed by the Boarding Out of Children Regulations of 1983. Since 1954, there has been an obligation to give priority to foster, rather than residential, placement for the child in care. Under section 4 of the Boarding Out of Children Regulations 1954, a child was not to be placed in residential care 'unless such a child cannot be suitably and adequately assisted by being boarded out' - a clause retained in the current 1983 regulations. These regulations impose certain duties on health boards. They must arrange a medical examination of a child to be placed. They must take up medical and personal references for foster parent applicants. They must conduct an assessment as to the suitability of the applicants and of any proposed match between a child and a family. The child and foster family must be visited within one month of placement and at intervals of not more than six months thereafter. The 'health and well-being' of every child in foster care must be reviewed within two months of placement and at least every six months thereafter.

While there is no corresponding obligation on health boards to review the progress of children placed in residential care, in practice, many such reviews do occur. Regulations governing reviews for all children in care are provided for in the Child Care Act 1991.

The picture regarding the legal status of children in the care of the health boards has changed quite dramatically during the 1980s. In 1981, only 16.3 per cent of children were in care on the basis of a court order. By 1989, this proportion had soared to around 50 per cent. This sudden change may indicate that the historical tendency for high proportions of children in care to be there on a court ordered basis is reasserting itself, despite the changes in administrative, legal and professional practices in recent decades. Equally, the steep rise in court orders may reflect attempts by hard pressed social workers to cope with expanding social problems in the 1980s. Unemployment rose from a rate of 10.1 per cent in 1981 to 17.2 per cent in 1990 (Central Statistics Office, 1992). There was a dramatic tenfold increase in the annual numbers of confirmed cases of child abuse referred to health boards in 1989 compared to those for 1983, and an increase by a factor of fifteen in the sub-set of confirmed cases involving sexual abuse in the same period (Gilligan, 1992). There has also been a growth in drug misuse and AIDS - and all of this has occurred against a backcloth of public service cutbacks because of serious national debt problems. There were 298 social workers in 1981 and 309 in 1987 (O'Connor, 1987). It is possible that these embattled social workers sought to assert some control over a worsening situation by recourse to court ordered care in the (probably vain) hope that it might reduce the stress and uncertainty with which they had to deal.

Administrative framework

At the level of national policy, provision for children in the care of health boards is the responsibility of the Department of Health. In terms of operational policy and day to day practice, it is the individual health boards which are responsible. Operational policy tends to be managed by senior career administrators, who may avail themselves of the professional advice of social work teams which manage the service to children and their families.

Health boards social work teams are deployed on the basis of community care areas, of which there are thirty two nationally. Each team's role may vary with local circumstances, but most commonly they will deal with child protection investigations and assessment; family support work; adoption - related counselling and advice; and children in, or in need of, care. In relation to children in care, each team would be responsible for (i) the assessment of a child's circumstances where the question of placement might be a consideration, (ii) consultation

124

with legal advisers where court proceedings might be deemed necessary to protect the interests of the child; (iii) identification of a suitable placement in the light of the child's needs, legal considerations, parental preferences and, in practice most critically, vacancies available (iv) negotiation of the emotional and practical implications of placement with child, parents and new caretakers; (v) ongoing oversight of placement and liaison with, and support for, child, family and caretakers; (vi) conduct of reviews as necessary (vii) attention to any necessary administration arising from the placement and (viii) recruitment, assessment and support of foster parents.

The expenditure by the health services nationally in 1989 was estimated to be IR£2.92 million or UK£2.75 million on foster care and IR£ 6.94 million or UK£6.0 million on residential care (Department of Health, 1990).

Fostering   The modern system of foster care in Ireland can trace its roots to legislation in 1862, which gave authority to 'board out' children of up to five years of age outside the workhouse (the dreaded last resort of the poor under the regime of that time). Fostering was seen as protecting young children from the corrupting influences of the workhouse (Burke, 1987).

The current system of foster care is governed by the Health Act 1953 and Regulations of 1983 (Department of Health 1983). (This framework will be replaced by provisions in the Child Care Act 1991 when they become operative - on a date yet to be announced).

Analysis of 1982 data on children in care nationally revealed a tendency for children in foster care to be younger than those in residential care, to have been younger on admission and to be less likely to have come into care on a compulsory basis than their counterparts in residential care (O'Higgins and Boyle, 1988:93). More recent analysis of figures for one region in relation to age and type of placement also found this tendency for lower present age and lower age at admission to be associated with placement in foster care (O'Higgins, 1991).

While there are no published data on the numbers of foster families nationally or the numbers of children placed with each family, such information has been kindly made available to the author by the Eastern Health Board (which serves Dublin city and county and two surrounding counties and is responsible for 38 per cent of all children in care nationally). As of 30 September 1991, the Board had 799 children in foster care (including 69 in day foster care) with 504 active foster families. Of these, 311 families (61.7 per cent) had a single child placed with them. A further 128 families (25.4 per cent) had two children placed. Of the remaining families, 40 (7.9 per cent) had 3 children, 18 had 4 children, 4 had 5 children, 2 had 6 children and 1 had 8 children. (It should be noted also, as mentioned above, that 69 children (8.6 per cent) were placed on a day fostering basis, that is they were not resident with the family).

Conversely, three in five of the children (61.1 per cent) fostered with the board were placed with one or more other foster children, and one in nine (11.5 per cent) were placed with three or more other foster children (Eastern Health Board, 1991). These figures may reflect a wish to secure placements together for sibling groups in care belonging to what are, not infrequently in Ireland, large families. It is worth noting that these foster families may often have at least some birth children living with them. Berridge (1985) has observed that, in terms of the experience of the child in care, larger foster families may have many similarities with smaller children's homes. In the light of the above, Berridge's point, which is based on his British research, may also have considerable relevance in Ireland.

A successful foster care system depends on a ready supply of new foster parents. The Board had recruited and approved 45 new foster families in 1990 and 29 for the eleven months ending 30 November 1991 (Eastern Health Board, 1991).

One factor in the recruitment and retention of foster parents is the rate of allowance paid per child placed. There is a national rate of IR£38.80 or UK£36.50 per child per week, plus clothing allowances of IR£115 or UK£108 paid twice yearly in long term placements. Supplements may also be payable to meet agreed exceptional expenses or to reflect the exceptional need of a particular child. These latter payments are at the discretion of individual boards and there are considerable variations in practice and policy.

The value of the allowance has declined relative to its worth in 1982. To merely maintain that value, it should now be worth IR£42.20 or UK£39.70. To achieve this would require a IR£3.40 or UK£3.20 or 10 per cent hike in its actual value (derived from Central Statistics Office, 1991). Moreover, earlier work by the present author shows that the allowance has also been losing value against the average industrial wage (Gilligan, 1990).

Residential care Non-offender children placed in residential care are usually to be found in group homes which emerged following the recommendation of an official Committee (Committee on Reformatories and Industrial Schools, 1970). These residential settings will typically be managed by Roman Catholic religious congregations, who are responsible for 84.4 per cent of places (Gilligan, 1991a) in the purely 'non-offender' sector. In some instances, a centre may operate more than one unit - or group home - on its site, or dispersed throughout its locality. Any single constituent unit will probably accommodate no more than 8-10 children and possibly fewer.

The location of residential settings in the majority of cases is a function of history. The home is where it always has been, in the sense that the modern facilities are often built on the site of an old institution or are to be found in adapted and refurbished parts of previous centres. Thus, the location of some provision may tend to be resource driven rather than need driven, although there have been instances of a residential service transferring from a redundant to a relevant location.

One feature of recently emerging provision has been an increasing focus on serving the needs of adolescents. One aspect of this has been a tendency for some new facilities to be located on the basis of localisation, i.e. in or close to the community of origin of the youngsters requiring care. In some instances these facilities are starting from scratch. In the Dublin region four such units have opened, the first in 1979 (Yeates, 1988); three serve adolescents and one the immediately pre-adolescent age group (Gilligan, 1982). These units tend to be small, catering for six residents or so. Accommodation tends to be unexceptional, not unlike that available to families in the same neighbourhood.

The special needs of Traveller (native Irish gypsies) children within the care system have begun to be addressed with the establishment of two units dedicated exclusively to such needs. They are sponsored by voluntary organisations already engaged in the provision of a wide range of other welfare services to the general 'Traveller' community. The first, for boys, opened in 1976 and the second, for girls, in 1984. Both are in a rural setting near to each other and close to the capital.

Staffing in residential care Recent research has established that the current ratio of care staff to children varies between 1.5 and 2.5 across 26 different group homes surveyed (Streetwise National Coalition, 1991). Of 270 full time staff in these units, the majority were appropriately trained (National Diploma in Child Care, or other social work/residential/child care qualification acquired in Ireland or overseas), but 35 per cent had no child care or relevant qualification (ibid). In the case of 24 adolescent units surveyed (including a small number which act as probation hostels and strictly therefore fall outside the remit of this chapter), the care staff to adolescent ratio varied from 1:1 to 1:3. Again, the majority of the 109 full time staff employed in the units had received appropriate training, but a substantial 32 per cent had no child care or relevant qualification (ibid).

127

It seems possible to identify a number of ideas, theories or principles which have helped shape current provision. These principles it is suggested are influential within the system; inevitably, it is, of course, possible to unearth unfortunate exceptions in terms of adherence to them if one wishes!

The importance of the child as an individual with rights and a unique set of needs, experiences and preferences It has been suggested that a view of the child in care which emphasised his or her developmental needs and individuality began to emerge in the 1970s. This new thinking replaced pre-occupation with protecting society from the risk the child posed to it, or with the 'training' of the child (O'Sullivan, 1979). The Child Care Act 1991 (not yet implemented at the time of writing, as was previously indicated) requires health boards, while 'having regard to the rights and duties of parents', to 'regard the welfare of the child as the first and paramount consideration' and 'in so far as is practicable, give due consideration, having regard to his age and understanding, to the wishes of the child' (S. 3.2.b.). Also, the Irish government has signalled its intention of ratifying the United Nations Convention on the Rights of the Child (Berwick and Burns (Eds), 1991).

The importance of seeing, and working with, the child in the context of his/her own family The Child Care Act 1991 lays down the principle that 'it is generally in the best interests of the child to be brought up in his own family' (S. 3.2.c.) and requires health boards (subject to certain checks and balances) to 'facilitate reasonable access to the child by his parents' and by other persons with bona fide interests in the child (S. 37.1).

In the view of the Task Force on Child Care Services, placement in care should generally entail the minimum possible disruption of the parent-child relationship.

> 'For many children in alternative care, their own family will continue to play a very important role in terms of the children's emotional and social development... The number of children for whom a total break in their family relationships will be necessary or inevitable, and for whom adoption or long-term foster care without family contact will be required, will be small relative to the total number of children in need of alternative care.'(Task Force on Child Care Services, 1981).

The Mid Western Health Board has declared that for the child entering care

> 'the aim is to achieve rehabilitation with the birth family. Only when it is clear that rehabilitation is not feasible, or is not in the child's interests, will alternative plans be reviewed and implemented' (Mid Western Health Board, 1991).

The same health board has declared in writing the child's 'right to maintain contact with... (his or her) ... family' (ibid); it has also said that its staff will work in 'partnership' with parents in order to help them 'retain responsibilities' towards their children in care (ibid).

Attachment theory   While it is difficult to discern any one overriding theoretical school in Irish child care practice, it is probably true to say that currently the most influential set of ideas derive from attachment theory. Its core message of the importance for the child's current and future mental health of having secure bonds with key adult caretaker(s) has been very influential, especially in field social work circles. Fahlberg, an American paediatrician and psychotherapist has certainly helped to popularise, through her conferences and books (e.g. 1981), the essentials and practical application of this theoretical approach. A critical appreciation of the theoretical underpinnings of this approach (as in Bowlby, 1988) is likely to be less familiar to busy practitioners.

The principle of normalisation   This principle holds that children in need should have the usual opportunities for the normal experiences of growing up. The price of being helped should not be to miss out on the normal features of life for one's peers. Any special help required should be grafted onto the child's family, school or community to obviate as far as possible disruptions in the child's life (Task Force on Child Care Services, 1981). The child in residential care, in particular,

> 'should receive the individual, personal care and attention which a child can be expected to receive in his own family, and ... should, as far as possible, share in the normal experiences of other children living at home. He should have a foot-hold in the ordinary community either through his own family or another family, he should attend an outside school with other children in the locality, take part in the ordinary activities of the community, and establish friendships with other children and adults there, unless there are clearly defined reasons relating to his own interests or the interests of others which require that he should not do so' (ibid).

The idea of normalisation is also implicit in the following principle.

The importance of experiences of family living for the child in care Going back as far as 1862, the importance of family experience was recognised at least in terms of the under fives (see above). By 1954, services were obliged to give prior consideration to family placement before reaching a decision about placing a child in care. In the early 1980s, it was held that children requiring long-term care outside their own families 'should as a general rule, be cared for in another family ... thus preparing them for their adult roles in society' (Task Force on Child Care Services, 1981).

The principle of minimum intervention The Task Force on Child Care Services recommended that state or voluntary agency 'intervention in a child's life should be limited to what is absolutely necessary to protect his interests or the interests of others' (1981). More recently this principle of minimum intervention has been described by a Minister in a parliamentary debate on the new child care legislation as 'one of the cornerstones of our child care policy' (Minister for State at the Department of Health, 1989). There seems to be a broad consensus among professionals, politicians and administrators who, for differing reasons, appear willing to support this principle. These reasons include scepticism of therapeutic efficacy, concerns for civil liberties and family privacy, and the state's reluctance to adopt an intervenionist role in relation to many welfare issues (see Gilligan, 1989).

The importance of care which is closely aligned to the culture/community of origin The concept of care in informal local settings was considered by the Task Force on Child Services to be

> 'very suitable for ... children with serious problems who need residential care in their own areas, but who require particularly intensive, personalised care in a very informal setting and who could find a regime of another type very difficult to cope with.'(Task Force on Child Care Services, 1981).

A more recent commentary on residential child care provision has recommended that 'residential units for children and young people should be located as far as possible in the communities of origin of the client group' (Streetwise National Coalition, 1991). One health board has declared that in deciding on appropriate placement for the child admitted to care 'the implications of a child's ethnic, cultural, social and religious background will be given careful consideration' (Mid Western Health Board, 1991).

Two marked trends in the last decade have been the increasing share of all placements in care held by foster care and the increasing reliance on compulsory placements in care. It seems likely that children who present for placement will be ever more damaged by adverse experiences in their homes prior to care. Increasing rates of unemployment and child abuse referrals (see above) reflect the risks children entering care face.

Another clear trend is the increasing pressure on services to demonstrate the adequacy of their performance in terms of value for money. A Commission which reviewed health service funding refers liberally to 'contracts' and 'accountability' as key elements in a new framework to govern relations between statutory sector 'consumer/funders' and voluntary sector 'providers' of services throughout the health services (Commission on Health Funding, 1991). It is plain that providers within the statutory sector will not be immune to these pressures either.

There is also a tentative trend towards the development of new models of service provision and organisation. The locally based adolescent units referred to earlier are one example. A further example is the use of regular meetings to achieve close integration of planning and decision making between the managers of statutory field social work services and voluntary sector residential child care services in the Mid Western Health Board (Doherty, 1991). Another is the new Carers Project in the Eastern Health Board, which aims to place young people with difficult histories with specially recruited and supported carers who receive IR£100 or UK£94.3 per week (Eastern Health Board, 1991). Yet another is the transformation of a conventional and traditional group home into a pioneering and influential family centre which offers residential but mainly day care services to families experiencing difficulties. Workers use a wide range of therapeutic techniques at individual, group and family level to join with family members in seeking to prevent the risk of children being separated from their families in the future (Butler et al., 1990). The Adoption Act 1988, which opens up somewhat further the possibility of adoption for young people growing up in care, is also likely to have some impact on the care system.

Besides changes involving specific services, one leading manager in the Irish health services has argued that child care services must prepare to operate in a quite new climate, not only due to change in the law, but also in the expectations of society itself.

'The new legislation (Child Care Act 1991), and the environment of the 1990s in which it must be implemented, will force a sea-change in attitudes, practices and policies among the professional and management staffs of the health boards and the non-statutory child care organisations. What is at stake is a fundamental underlying shift in the model of service provision and delivery from a grace and favour/deserving poor/charity model to a more participative/ consumer oriented/rights/justice model.' (Doherty, 1991).

Indeed some of what Doherty anticipates is already evident in the ever more confident assertion of their views by organised foster parents (Irish Foster Care Association, 1991), in the growth of a persuasive voice for parents and relatives with children in care (Parents with Children in Care, 1989), and in the expectation of at least one health board that the child and his/her birth parents and the caretaker(s) should be among the participants in regular reviews of placements of children in care (Mid Western Health Board, 1991).

Critical issues

Facing the future, perhaps the key word must be that of 'planning' - in order to provide for a number of factors.

Implementing the Child Care Act 1991   This is a major piece of legislation, which is set to make many fresh demands on caretakers and field social workers in the care system, over and above those which will inevitably flow from changing social conditions. The 1991 Act also imposes duties on health boards to plan and provide services, which far exceeds their previous obligations, and challenges fundamentally the traditionally low key role adopted by the health services in this field (Gilligan, 1989).

Coping with the projected increase in demand for places in care   This author has estimated that on current trends alone, an additional 350 places in care will be required by 1994. In addition, the effect of the raising of the current age ceiling of care from 16 to 18 years of age, as provided for in the Child Care Act 1991, is likely to involve an increase of 200 places on the basis of present age distributions in the care population. Assuming that fostering retains its 70 per cent share of all placements, an additional 385 places in foster families will have to be found, as well as a further 165 residential places (Gilligan, 1992). These calculations do not take account of any possible shortfalls in existing provision for troubled or homeless adolescents (Keane and

Crowley, 1990; Streetwise National Coalition, 1991), which may also need to be allowed for in projecting future care place needs.

Coping with the needs and behaviour of difficult adolescents One senior manager in the health services has publically acknowledged shortcomings in care and support provision for adolescents in difficulty. He has also conceded that failure to match the appropriate care to their needs increases the risk of their adopting a 'street' lifestyle from which rehabilitation becomes ever more difficult (Donoghue, 1988). The challenges posed by troubled adolescents have also been stressed more recently by residential care service providers (Streetwise National Coalition, 1991). Both of these sources acknowledge the importance of appropriate after care provision for adolescents leaving care. Finding resources for after care work is quite a challenge. But, striking the right balance between appropriate dependency and autonomy is perhaps the even greater challenge facing caretakers and social workers in their work to support young people after they leave long-term care.

Absorbing the effects of the current large scale withdrawal of the religious from the management and provision of residential care A rapidly ageing population in religious congregations, dwindling vocations to religious life and a re-appraisal by congregations of their traditional roles and priorities are major factors in this trend (Gilligan, 1991b). This is also accompanied by no little loss of confidence in the future of residential care. In many senses, the confidence of religious residential care providers has run aground, left behind by what they perceive as a fast running tide of support in favour of fostering, and by the complexity of problems youngsters in care now present. It seems that the state is ill-equipped in terms of tradition to fill the vacuum left by the departure of the religious. Throughout this century, long-stay, non-custodial, care in Ireland has generally been undertaken by the voluntary rather than the state sector (Gilligan, Kearney and Lorenz 1987).

Eliminating some quite bizarre regional discrepancies in levels of provision, which while largely the product of historical accident cannot be allowed to shape the fate of children in need across the country in the future Nine out of thirty two community care areas do not have a residential unit as part of their provision (Gilligan, 1991). The availability of health board social workers varies widely by region from one worker per 7,000 in the North Western Health Board, through one worker per 11,500 of the population nationally, to one worker per 21,500 in the North Eastern Health Board region (O'Connor, 1987).

133

Adequate resourcing of caretakers for the daily task in residential and foster care Caretakers will have to be equipped and supported in the challenging task of meeting the needs of damaged young people. Foster parents will need more finely tuned systems of support and they will need greater access to opportunities to acquire specific knowledge and skills relevant to the management of difficult behaviour and the therapeutic care of disturbed youngsters (Gilligan, 1990). A clear need has also been identified for advanced training opportunities for care staff in the residential sector (Streetwise National Coalition, 1991).

A commitment to excellence Professionals, policy makers and politicians must jointly and regularly renew a commitment to standards of excellence in the child care system. In practice this means, inter alia, giving recognition and practical effect to the principle of empowerment of clients in decision making processes in the child care system, the importance of training and research, the need for close integration of the efforts of different elements in the system, and the necessity for constant openness to new ideas and new approaches. It also involves finally, and most crucially,

Securing the necessary additional resources to get current services to an adequate baseline, and to cope with the costs of new provisions in the Child Care Act 1991

Research on residential and foster care

While the scale and scope of research has been limited by the availability of resources, much has been achieved within existing constraints. Examples of research work completed, or in hand, include evaluations of particular services (e.g. Whelan, no date, mid 1980s); an analysis of official data on children in care (O'Higgins and Boyle, 1988); a survey of the views and experience of residential care providers (Streetwise National Coalition, 1991); a survey of the care histories of a sample of children in residential care (Richardson, 1985); an examination of the care needs of homeless young people (Keane and Crowley, 1990; Focus Point and the Eastern Health Board Homeless Social Work Team, 1989); an investigation of the circumstances of a sample of homeless women, many of whom had been in care in childhood (Kennedy, 1985); a sociological investigation of dominant models of child care practice and policy over time (O'Sullivan, 1979); and an analysis of the residential child care task (Graham, 1992). Some of this work has been funded by the health services on an ad-hoc basis (there being no child care research programme or budget as such); some has been funded by voluntary sector providers and some from the personal resources of researchers themselves.

In terms of the influence of research on policy and practice, it is difficult to cite instances where the effects have been clear cut and positive (except perhaps in the case of evaluations which reach favourable conclusions, or the work of Kennedy (1985) which led to the formation of a major voluntary agency to work with, and campaign on behalf of, the young and adult homeless). It seems more often the case that research contributes to a constant renewal of the climate within which child care thinking and decision making occurs. Thus its influence, while more indirect than direct, remains significant.

There are endless possibilities for important research work, which includes the need for longitudinal studies of different categories of children entering care; studies of consumer (children and parents) perceptions of the care experience; a regular census of caretakers (foster parents and residential care staff) and their characteristics; studies of the morale and needs of caretakers; studies of the health and educational needs of children and young people in care; follow up studies of young people who have left the care system; analysis of factors evident in placement breakdown; international comparative studies on the statistics of national child care systems (Gilligan et al., 1990); and, not least, evaluative studies of different models of practice and care settings.

Notes

1. In accordance, with the author's brief, the treatment of children in care in the chapter is confined to the non-offender category of children, i.e. children in care for reasons of their own protection and welfare.

References

Barnes, J. (1989), *Irish Industrial Schools 1868-1908 - Origins and Development*, Irish Academic Press, Blackrock.

Berridge, D. (1985), *Children's Homes*, Basil Blackwell, Oxford.

Berwick, P. and Burns, M. (Eds), *The Rights of the Child - Irish Perspectives on the UN Convention*, Council for Social Welfare, Dublin.

Bowlby, J. (1988), 'Developmental Psychiatry Comes of Age', *The American Journal of Psychiatry*, 145, 1, January, pp. 1-10.

Burke, H. (1987), *The People and the Poor Law in 19th Century Ireland*, Women's Educational Bureau, West-Sussex.

Butler, G. et al. (1990), 'Claide Mor Family Centre', *Curam*, September.

CARE (1972), *Children Deprived - The CARE Memorandum on Deprived Children and Children's Services in Ireland*, CARE-Campaign for the Care of Deprived Children, Dublin.

Central Statistics Office (1987), *Census 86 Summary Population Report*, Stationery Office, Dublin.

Central Statistics Office (1991), Personal communication 23rd December.

Central Statistics Office (1992), Personal Communication 3rd January.

Commission of Inquiry into the Reformatory and Industrial School System (1936), *Report*, Stationery Office, Dublin.

Commission on Health Funding (1989), *Report of the Commission on Health Funding*, Stationery Office, Dublin.

Commission on the Relief of the Sick and Destitute Poor (including the Insane Poor) (1927), *Report*, Stationery Office, Dublin.

Department of Health (1983), *Boarding Out of Children Regulations 1983*, Statutory Instrument No. 67 of 1983, Stationery Office, Dublin.

Department of Health (1986), *Children in Care 1983*, Department of Health, Dublin.

Department of Health (1990), *Health Statistics 1989*, Stationery Office, Dublin.

Department of Health (1991), *Survey of Children in the Care of Health Boards in 1989 (Volume 1)*, Child Care Division, Department of Health, Dublin.

Department of Local Government and Public Health (1946), *Report*, Department of Local Government and Public Health, Dublin.

Doherty, D. (1991), 'Development of Services for Children - A Health Board Perspective', Paper to Barnardo's Conference 'A Window on Irish Children', 24 October.

Donoghue, F. (1988), 'The role of the Eastern Health Board in providing services for the homeless', in J. Blackwell and S. Kennedy (Eds), *Focus on the homelessness - A new look at housing policy*, The Columba Press, Dublin.

Eastern Health Board (1991), Personal Communication with Children Section, Eastern Health Board, 23rd December.

Fahlberg, V. (1981), *Attachment and Separation*, British Agencies for Adoption and Fostering, London.

Focus Point and the Eastern Health Board Social Work Team (1989), *Forgotten Children - Research on young people who are homeless in Dublin*, Eastern Health Board and Focus Point, Dublin.

Gilligan, R. (1982), *Children in Care in their own Community*, Society of St. Vincent de Paul, Dublin.

Gilligan, R. (1989), 'Policy in the Republic of Ireland : historical and current issues in child care' in P. Carter, T. Jeffs and M. Smith (Eds), *Social Work and Social Welfare Yearbook 1*, Open University Press, Milton Keynes.

Gilligan, R. (1990), *Foster Care for Children in Ireland : Issues and Challenges for the 1990s*, Department of Social Studies, University of Dublin, Trinity College, Dublin, Occasional Paper No. 2.

Gilligan, R. (1991a), *Irish Child Care Services - Policy Practice and Provision*, Institute of Public Administration, Dublin.

Gilligan, R. (1991b), 'The Future Role of the Church in Child Care' - A discussion Paper Prepared for the Conference of Major Religious Superiors, the Catholic Social Service Conference and the Sacred Heart Home Trust (mimeo).

Gilligan, R. (1992), 'Implementing the Child Care Act - A review of the Resource Implications', *Irish Social Worker*, (forthcoming).

Gilligan, R. et al. (1990), *The Protection of youth against physical and moral danger*, Council of Europe, Strasbourg (publiée en français aussi).

Gilligan, R., Kearney, N. and Lorenz, W. (1987), 'Intermediare Hilfesysteme Personenbezogener Dienstleistungen in der Republik Irland' in R. Bauer and A.M. Thranhardt (Eds), *Verbandliche Wohlfahrtspflege im internationalen Vergleich*, Westdeutscher Verlag, Opladen.

Graham, G. (1992), Empirical research being written up for an M. Litt. thesis under the supervision of the author.

Irish Foster Care Organisation (1991), *Blueprint for Fostercare - Principle, Policy, Practice*, Dublin.

Keane, C. and Crowley, G. (1990), *Out on My Own - Report on Youth Homelessness in Limerick City*, Mid-Western Health Board and Limerick Social Service Centre, Limerick.

Kennedy, S. (1985), *But where can I go? Homeless women in Dublin*, Arlen House, Dublin.

Mid Western Health Board (1991), *Child Care Practice Policy Statement*, Social Work Department Child Care Service, Mid-Western Health Board, Limerick.

Minister for Health (1974), 'Health Estimates Speech', *Parliamentary Debates Dail Eireann*, 28.11.74.

Minister for State at the Department of Health (1989), 'Dail Eireann Special Committee on the Child Care Bill 1988', 5 December, No. 2, Column 59.

O'Connor, S. (1987), 'Community Care Services : an Overview (Part 2)' in N.E.S.C. (same title), National Economic and Social Council, Dublin.

O'Higgins, K. (1991), 'Fragile Family Relations : Families of Children in Care', Seminar paper delivered at Economic and Social Research Institute, Dublin, 14th November.

O'Higgins, K. and Boyle, M. (1988), *State Care - Some Children's Alternative : An analysis of the data from the returns to the Department of Health, Child Care Division 1982,* Economic and Social Research Institute, Dublin.

O'Sullivan, D. (1979), 'Social Definition in Child Care in the Irish Republic : Models of the Child and Child-care Intervention', *Economic and Social Review,* Vol. 10, No. 3.

Richardson, V. (1985), *Whose Children? An analysis of some aspects of child care policy in Ireland,* Dublin, Family Studies Unit, Department of Social Science, University College, Dublin.

Robins, J. (1980), *The Lost Children - A Study of Charity Children in Ireland 1700-1900,* Institute of Public Administration, Dublin.

Streetwise National Coalition (1991), *At What Cost? A Research Study on Residential Care for Children and Adolescents in Ireland,* Focus Point, Dublin.

Task Force on Child Care Services (1975), *Interim Report,* Stationery Office, Dublin.

Task Force on Child Care Services (1981), *Final Report,* Stationery Office, Dublin.

Tuairim (1966), *Some of Our Children - A Report on the Residential Care of Deprived Children,* Tuairim Pamphlet No. 13, Tuairim - London Branch, London.

Whelan, M. (no date, mid 1980s), *Community Based Child Care in Inner-City Dublin* (unpublished report, contents of which are confidential to the management committee of the Society of St. Vincent de Paul pilot project).

Yeates, P. (1988), 'Challenging the concept of putting them away', *Irish Times,* July 22, p. 5.

7 Italy

T. Vecchiato

Recent political history : After the Second World War, there was a period of industrial growth during which the Republic was established. This led to the development of state social and health services. However, the economic crisis of recent years has resulted in a restructuring of the welfare state, and stimulated the growth of voluntary services and private initiatives.
Geographical Size : 301,311.09 Km².
Date of EC membership : 1957.
Total number of inhabitants (September 1991) : 57,805,820.
Age of majority : 18 years.
Number of people under the age of majority (1986) : 14,582,99.
Number of children and young people (31.12.91) :   in residential care :   2,827
 in foster care :   1,062

The nature of residential and foster care provision

The years 1950-1970

In the years immediately following the second world war, provision for separated children was dominated by large residential institutions. The growth of these establishments was largely due to the consequences of war. Many of the children who lost their parents were left to fend for themselves. As a result, juvenile delinquency became widespread, particularly in the larger cities.

Although it was necessary to find urgent solutions to the serious social problems that existed in the aftermath of the war, a careful analysis was nevertheless made of the adverse effects of institutional care on children's development (Aubry, 1955). This was initiated by public and private authorities responsible for the provision of services to delinquent youngsters, led by the Ministry of Justice Services for Minors (AA.VV., 1955; Occulto, 1966, 1968). It should be noted that social workers also played a key role in highlighting the problems which characterised the post-war institution based system of substitute care, and in stimulating the search for community alternatives.

In order to prevent children being treated in an impersonal and institutional manner, and to provide individualised care, it was argued : first, that residential homes should serve local areas to facilitate the maintenance of relations between children and their families; second, that they should be 'open' rather than 'closed' establishments; third, that they should only accommodate small numbers of children; and, finally, that they should be organised along the lines of family groups (La Greca, 1965).

Following the example of other European countries, small family group homes were established (Bussi 1965; Spadetto, 1978). Other initiatives included the setting up of 'guest homes' and small craft communities (Senise and Giacona 1965). In attempting to combine family style care and contact with the community, these innovations lay somewhere between traditional institutions and the family, and, as such, were the forerunner to contemporary 'intermediate' forms of provision.

The element that linked community and family life experiences was the concept of the small 'primary group'. The latter involved a high degree of direct contact between children and caregivers, and the participation of children in decision making and in the activities of the surrounding community. These conditions were considered vital for the child's welfare, and the concept of the primary group provided the foundation for developments which occurred in the 1970's and 1980's (see below).

The years 1970-1980

Community-oriented residential services The 1970's was a fertile time for the development of community based residential homes owing to widespread political and public support for such services. During this period, and as was the case in other European countries, a fundamental debate took place on the nature and role of child welfare provision, which included a critique of institutional care[1].

In the wake of disquiet about the quality of institutional care, community based alternatives were sought. Whilst it was acknowledged that institutions were somewhat less depersonalising than was formerly the case, the reforms undertaken had not been sufficient to counter the widely held perception that institutions adversely effected the development of children.

Furthermore, policies geared to ameliorating the shortcomings of institutional care had not always been realised in practice. Hence, those responsible for the administration of child welfare provisions were required to produce concrete improvements in the quality of residential services. This provided the impetus for the development of community-oriented residential homes for children, particularly in regions of northern Italy such as Piemonte, Lombardia, Emilia Romagna and Veneto, and Calabria - a region in Southern Italy.

These community homes emphasised the therapeutic value of the community not only in meeting the child's immediate, day-to-day, needs, but also in seeking to compensate the child for earlier deprivations. Moreover, it was believed that life in the community would have beneficial long-terms effects on children's development.

The common characteristics of such provisions can be summarised as follows. First, the children lived in small groups. Second, the homes were part of local life[2]. Third, the children had access to services available to other youngsters in the locality, such as schools and leisure facilities. Finally, the homes maintained close links with other child welfare services.

The innovations described occurred during a decade when important changes in the health and social services were being considered. At the end of the 1970's, legislation was passed which transferred responsibility for these services from central government to the regions (Trevisan, 1968; AA.VV., 1980; Fondazione Zancan, 1980; Falcon, Trevisan, Vian, 1980).

Foster care   Foster care is used when the child does not require specialised treatment, but needs to be placed in a substitute family. This usually occurs when factors such as mental illness on the part of parents, marital conflict, immigration, and unemployment cause a crisis within the family which necessitate social work intervention.

In such cases, it may be appropriate to place the child with an alternative family in order to safeguard his or her welfare, and as a means of helping the birth family overcome temporary difficulties by relieving the parents of their responsibility for the child.

There is a special form of family placement which may be termed 'rehabilitative foster care'. This involves pre-adolescents and adolescents with behavioural problems, including delinquency, who require the intervention of social services and the juvenile court. In such cases, children are removed from situations that jeopardise their development. The aim is to offer the youngster an opportunity to experience a nuturing family environment, with adults who are adequately prepared to meet his or her particular needs.

It should be noted that residential care developed more rapidly than foster care in the 1970's. Whilst foster care was a topic of much discussion during this decade, little progress was made with regard to expanding foster care services owing to cultural factors. Birth parents often had difficulty accepting the idea of being separated from their children, even for temporary periods; they tended to fear the social stigma associated with parental failure, and generally found it hard to come to terms with the prospect of sharing responsibility for the care of their children with others; they were also inclined to be fearful that fostering would result in the break-up of their families, and that they might ultimately loose their children (Cattabeni, 1971; Andreis, 1972). Consequently, birth parents were usually more willing to give their approval for residential care rather than consent to their children being placed with alternative and, as they saw it, 'rival' families.

This problem stimulated new thinking about the nature and role of foster care, led by organisations such as The National Association of Adoptive and Foster Care Families (ANFAA) and the Auxiliary Centre for Minors (CAM); an association founded in Milan with the aim of promoting foster care and adoption[3]. In addition, numerous articles on foster care appeared during the 1970's, which described the political and cultural context of the services, documented fostering practice, and analysed the administrative and professional difficulties associated with foster care.

The local social care departments The 1970's were a time of great change in the field of social policy. Two major pieces of legislation on the social and health services were enacted : law n. 616 in 1977, and law n.833 in 1978. These laws transferred responsibilty for social and health services from central government to regional departments and local authorities. The regional departments were given overall control and administrative responsibility, legislative powers, and responsibilty for programme planning, whilst the local authorities became responsible for service delivery at the local level. This led to the creation of new social and health care departments, which in turn contributed to the development of services for children, adolescents and their families, including residential and foster care for separated children.

At the same time, many national agencies in the field of juvenile delinquency were abolished. Such organisations were criticised for adopting inappropriate methods of intervention, and for representing obstacles to inter-agency co-operation and efficiency in the provision of services to adolescents and their families.

The new local social and health care departments were obliged to operate in very difficult circumstances. Many of the children who remained in residential care required specialised forms of help. Moreover, in order to rehabilitate separated children with their birth families, and to prevent the need to receive other children into care, it was necessary to expand support services to families. The increase in marital breakdown, together with the growing problem of drug addiction, further stretched the limited resources of the fledgling departments.

The years 1980-1990

From community experience to community services In recent years the framework of services for children, adolescents and families has been strengthened. This included a diffusion of the community model of service provision. It was finally recognised that, because of its affinity with the family, the community model takes account of the individual's fundamental psycho-social needs for a sense of identity and belonging, love and privacy, and contact with people of all age groups.

The term 'community home' is the commonly used expression to denote community based residential child care provisions[4]. Community homes may be conceived as centres in which adolescents and adults share the common experiences of daily living[5], and were first established on the basis of humanistic and religious principles. Much energy was initially devoted to ensuring that their internal life was not defined or constrained by the needs of external, bureaucratic, administrative structures.

However, the expansion of the community model of services meant that common standards of care practice were required, and there was a need to ensure that support services to children and their families were properly co-ordinated. Therefore, community homes were obliged to respond to the demands of the local departments who funded the homes; comply with the prevailing labour norms in employing professional and voluntary workers; agree criteria for the admission and discharge of children with the local authorities responsible for the social services; and, finally, allow external supervision and control so as to facilitate effective monitoring and evaluation.

These requirements helped to facilitate a shift from the original concept of community homes as autonomous communities, to the idea of community homes as a vital part of a framework of community based services for children and families. This was an important achievement; and, which is more, a necessary one, given that community homes became part of the social services system with the enactment of law n.616/1977, which defined their role and thereby contributed to understanding of their distinctive contribution (Vecchiato, 1986).

A research project carried out in 1982 distinguished the following four major types of community home (Maurizio e Peirone, 1984) : (i) quasi-

143

family communities belonging to public institutions; (ii) homes run by voluntary groups and organisations; (iii) professional communities managed by public bodies; and, (iv) professional communities administered by private organisations (cooperatives) through agreements with local authorities.

The relationship between public and private bodies is mediated through agreements or contracts which establish the responsibilities of each in relation to the following : finance, inter-agency co-operation, quality of care, monitoring and evaluation, criteria for the admission and discharge of children, and the qualification requirements for social workers.

The child's right to family life In 1983 law n.184 on adoption and foster care was passed. This contained two important provisions. The first dealt with the conflict between the birth parents' right to look after their child, and the child's right to live in a family which is able to respond to his or her needs. In recognition of the fact that unrestrained parental autonomy can be inimical to the welfare of children, law n.184 made it possible to limit parental power in situations where children are at risk and need to be placed with a foster family, or in a community home or residential institution.

The second major provision introduced by the new law follows from the first. In line with the United Nations Convention on the Rights of the Child (1989), Law n.184 recognises that children, as well as adults, have human rights, and states that the family and wider community is responsible for ensuring that children's developmental needs are satisfactorily met.

In operational terms, this meant that a strong investment had to be made with regard to expanding family support services, increasing the number of foster care placements available, and improving the quality of residential and quasi-residential provision.

Foster care is provided as a short-term measure when birth families are temporarily unable to care for their children. Applications to place a child in foster care are made to the court by the local social care department in agreement with the child's parents or guardians. A ruling on the case will then be made. Where parents or guardians withold their consent, the case will be referred to the juvenile court.

In Italy, foster care includes placement with families, single people or family type communities. The anticipated duration of the foster placement should be specified in the foster care decree made by the court. The placement ends when the birth family's difficulties have been resolved, or when continuation of the placement appears to jeopardise the child's welfare. Foster placements can also be discontinued if the child is adopted, or when the child reaches the age of majority, and becomes responsible for his or her own welfare.

The responsibilities of the foster family include providing for the child's material, emotional, social, and educational needs (both at home and school). Foster parents should also help to maintain the links between foster children and their birth parents, unless otherwise directed by the juvenile court, and co-operate with the local social care department in working towards the child's rehabilitation with his or her original family. During the foster placement, the local social care department will provide help and support to the original family.

Foster care programmes are managed by local social and health care departments within the framework of the services which they offer. In addition to the normal range of social provisions, this includes psychiatric and psychological services, and family consultancy[1]. Support to children's families (original and foster) is also provided through primary services such as day nurseries, schools, health services, and educational welfare services. Financial help may also be given to foster families[2]. In addition, foster parents derive support from attending meetings with other foster parents, at which participants share their experiences. Individual foster families can also gain access to specialist help for particular problems through the foster care agencies.

During the foster care placement, periodic evaluations are undertaken concerning relationships within the foster family, relations between the foster child's birth family and foster family, and between the child and both families. The programme of help provided to the birth family is also monitored.

Foster care is promoted by a number of public services and family associations. A particularly important role is played by the National Association for Adoptive and Foster Care Families, which has offices in all regions of Italy. The activities of this organisation include publishing information about foster care, giving legal advice, providing training for social and health workers, and recruiting foster families.

Current developments

Community services The debate on alternatives to traditional institutional care highlights the transition from the idea of the community as a space for life to the notion of community based services. Much discussion has centred on issues such as the organisational needs arising from the gradual diffusion of the community model of services, and the relationship between community provisions and other social services. This has increased understanding of the characteristics of community services based on the primary group (Palmonari, 1991); it has also contributed to the fact that community services now have a clearly defined operational role, which is complementary to that of other services.

However, there may be a sense in which the community can no longer be defined as an alternative to the institution, since the former has itself become part of the services system; a system, moreover, in which the institution continues to figure prominently, in spite of efforts to eliminate it[3].

Thus, there is a move towards the idea of meeting children's needs within the context of a comprehensive range of services, including help at home, care in open community service centres (Ministry of the Interior, 1987), care in community homes, and care in residential institutions. Moreover, family care (natural, foster, adoptive) has become a sort of benchmark against which to measure the extent that residential care adequately safeguards the child's rights and meets his or her needs.

A study is currently being carried out on family-type community services in the Region of Tuscany (Regione Toscana, 1989), which recently established a National Co-ordination Centre for such services. The topics examined by the research project include (i) the development of the services; (ii) intervention plans for children and their families; (iii) administrative relationships with local authorities; (iv) relationships with the local community; and (v) 'in-house' perfomance review.

Palmonari (1991) has pointed out that family-type community care may be appropriate when it is impossible to estimate the likely duration of the presenting problem; in cases of marital conflict where the parents contest the custody of a child; when children are placed in foster care without their parents consent; and, where adolescents are in care under penal measures.

Another topic of research is the notion of community services rooted in the local reality. Indeed, it would seem that such services are more effective when they are an expression of the values of the local community and have its active support. In recent years, social cooperation has also contributed to the development of community services and residential care.

However, action-research carried out by the E. Zancan Foundation on the care of young people (including troubled youngsters) in three different regions of northern Italy, highlights the cultural and methodological problems associated with attempts to integrate community services into the local community (Vernò, 1988 and 1989; Vecchiato, 1991).

Foster care Foster care should not simply be viewed as an important part of the child welfare system and an expression of social solidarity. For the children and adults directly involved, foster care represents a major life

146

experience. Moreover, whilst the logic of service provision means that foster care must be seen as an organisational asset in order to receive the support of administrators, foster parents are motivated by a desire to offer love and care to children and not by the organisational needs of social welfare agencies.

An important distinction is emerging between 'ordinary' foster care and foster placements which entail professionals and community services. In the case of the former, the involvement of professionals is more or less confined to the preliminary mediation process associated with the child's initial placement, and the provision of ongoing support to the foster parents and the child. By contrast, the second type of fostering is characterised by a much higher degree of involvement by professional child care workers. Together, the two forms of foster care make it possible to provide family care for children and young people with a wider range of needs than was formerly the case (Busnelli, Vecchiato, 1986).

Traditionally, foster care tended to be reserved for less problematic children. However, there is a growing willingness on the part of foster parents to accept children with severe emotional and behavioural difficulties. Further, in recent years foster care (and adoption) has been extended to embrace other previously excluded groups such as disabled children (Basano, 1987), and the children of immigrants and refugees. Attempts are also being made to provide foster families for young offenders (Zancan Foundation, 1992; Busnelli, Moro, 1990; Busnelli, Vecchiato, 1991).

One of the factors which has contributed to the extension of foster care is the increasing diversity in the kinds of people willing to become foster parents. More single people are now being recruited as foster parents, and family associations and voluntary groups are becoming increasingly involved (Iafrate, 1989).

However, despite the progress made in recent years, there are important regional disparities in foster care policy and practice. Unfortunately, because many regions do not have adequate information systems, it is difficult to assess the extent of this problem. Nevertheless, it is clear that whilst some regions have made conspicuous efforts to improve the provision of foster care[9], others have tended to lag behind.

In closing, it should be stressed that child care provision is constantly developing. In the post-war period, this evolution has been marked by a transition from seeking to help children by removing them from their families and communities of origin to a perspective which emphasises support to families, the role of local communities, and children's rights (Verno, 1989; Cendon, 1991; Moro, 1991).

Notes

1. In Italy, the following major conferences represent important landmarks in this debate : 'Against the Institutionalisation, Discrimination and Exclusion of Children' (Parma, 1971); 'Adoption and Foster Care Worldwide' (Milan, 1971); 'Problems and Perspectives in Foster Care', (Rome, 1973); 'Adoption and Foster Care' (Padova, 1974); 'Children in Everything' (Assisi, 1974); 'Towards a Regional Policy of Social Services for Children' (Abano, 1975); 'Alternatives to the Care of Children in Institutions' (Mestre, 1976); and 'Prevention and Rehabilitation in Juvenile Deliquency' (Trento, 1977).

2. The term 'group apartment', used in the region of Emilia Romagna, was coined to convey that such provisions were rooted in local neighbourhoods. In Piemonte the term 'community home' was employed to convey a similar meaning.

3. CAM studied 190 foster care placements, and found that 141 were not undertaken as part of properly formulated care plans for the children, and had no pre-established time limits. The remaining 49 were temporary placements (Ichino Pellizzi, 1983).

4. Other terms used when reference is made to community-oriented residential homes include 'group apartments', 'family group homes', 'guest homes', 'reception centres' and 'therapuetic communities'.

5. During the 1980's, the National Coordination of Care Communities (CNCA) was founded to promote the idea of community based social welfare services. Moreover, the community home approach is consistent with the report of a committee which examined the roles, education and training of child welfare professionals, including field social workers and residential caregivers, and which was published in 1984.

6. In 1984, there were some 2,301 family consultancy units in Italy, 2,124 of which were administered by the public sector. By 1986, this figure had risen risen to 2,398 (of which 2,217 were in the public sector).

7. The average monthly fostering allowance is approximately 700.000 Italian Lira or approximately £300.

8. For example, in the Piemonte region of north-west Italy, which is committed to a policy of de-instutionalisation, on 31 December, 1990, there were some 81 institutions, accommodating some 1,016 youngsters, compared with 88 community homes looking after 406 children. The following table gives a breakdown of the populations of the Piemonte institutions and community homes by age of children accommodated.

Table 7.1
Age of children in institutions and community homes in the Piemonte Region on 31 December, 1990

N Children

Age	Institutions	Community homes
0-2	38	37
3-5	43	21
5-10	226	75
11-13	306	85
14-17	403	188

9. One such region is Venetto, which carried out a three year pilot project (1987-1989) in collaboration with the E. Zancan Foundation on the education and training of social workers in adoption and foster care.

References

AA.VV. (1955), *Il trattamento in istituto dei minori traviati*, Esperienze di rieducazione, n. 11.

AA.VV. (1979), *Gruppi appartamento e interventi alternativi alla istituzionalizzazione*, Autonomie locali e servizi sociali, n. 1.

AA.VV. (1980), *Unità locale e poteri locali*, Fondazione 'E. Zancan', Padova.

AA.VV. (1983), *Le istituzioni e la comunità di fronte all'abuso del minore*, Fondazione 'E. Zancan', Padova.

AA.VV. (1984), *Quattro mura di umanità*, Regione Piemonte, Torino.

AA.VV. (1985), *Dal ricovero all'affidamento : cambia una legge o una mentalità*, Fondazione 'E. Zancan', Padova.

AA.VV. (1986), *Reti familiari e bambini a rischio*, Vita e Pensiero, Milano.

AA.VV. (1987), *L'adozione e l'affidamento : problemi e prospettive*, AAI, Roma.

AA.VV. (1987), *L'affidamento familiare temporaneo*, Mandese, Taranto.

AA.VV. (1988), *I problemi dell'intervento nell'affido familiare*, Fondazione Fontanari, Venezia.

Andreis, G., Santanera, F., Tonizzo, F. (1972), *L'affidamento familiare*, Promozione sociale n. 3-4 and 5-6.

Andreis, G., Santanera, F., Tonizzo, F. (1973), *L'affidamento familiare*, AAI, Roma.

Ass. Naz. Focolari (1976), *Sviluppo, inserimento e qualificazione dei focolari nella politica dei servizi a livello locale*, Esperienze di rieducazione, n. 2, 1976.

Aubry, J. (1955), *La carence de soins maternels*, Centre Internationale de l'Enfance, Paris.

Alloero, L., Pavone, M., Rosati, A. (1991), *Siamo tutti figli adottivi*, Rosenberg & Sellier, Torino.

Basano, G. (1987), *Storia di Nicola*, Rosenberg & Sellier, Torino.

Battistacci, G. (1981), *L'abbandono dei minori e la risposta della comunità locale*, Maggioli, Rimini.

Busnelli, E., Moro, A.C., a cura di (1990), *Minori e giustizia*, Fondazione 'E. Zancan', Padova.

Busnelli, E. and Vecchiato, T. (1991), *La promozione del benessere psico-fisico nell'età evolutiva*, Ministerio della sanità, Roma.

Busnelli, E. and Vecchiato, T. (1986), *Bisogne e Risposte per l'età evolutiva*, Servizi Sociali n° 4, Fond. Zancan, Padova.

Bussi, G. (1965), *Il 'Focolare': struttura e metodo di trattamento*, Infanzia anormale, n. 61.

Carugati, F., Emiliani, F., Palmonari, A. (1975), *Il possibile esperimento*, AAI, Roma.

Cattabeni, G. (1971), *Aspetti psicosociali dell'affidamento familiare*, Prospettive assistenziali, n. 16.

Cattabeni, G. (1983), *L'affido educativo*, Bambino incompiuto, n. 3, Unicopli, Milano.

Cirillo, S. (1983), *L'affidamento familiare*, Vita e Pensiero, Milano.

Cirillo, S. (1986), *Famiglie in crisi e affido familiare*, La Nuova Italia, Roma.

CNCA (1984), *Tra utopia e quotidiano*, EGA, Torino.

Consiglio nazionale dei minori (1989), *I minori in Italia*, Angeli, Milano.

Cendon, P. a cura di (1991), *I bambini e i loro diritti*, il Mulino, Bologna.

Dell'Antonio, A.M. (1984), *Il bambino di fronte al suo affidamento familiare*, Bambino incompiuto, n. 3, Unicopli, Milano.

Dell'Antonio, A. (1989), *Il genitore 'acquisito'*, Bambino incompiuto, n. 2, Unicopli, Milano.

Demetrio, D. (1990), *Educatori di professione*, Nuova Italia, Firenze.

De Rienzo, E., Saccoccio, C, Tortello, M. (1989), *Le due famiglie*, Rosenberg & Sellier, Torino.

Donati, P.P. a cura di (1989), *Primo rapporto sulla famiglia in Italia*, Paoline, Milano.

Donati, P.P. a cura di (1991), *Secondo rapporto sulla famiglia in Italia*, Paoline, Milano.

Falcon, G., Trevisan, C., Vian, F. (1980), *Unita locale : verifica di un modello*, Fondazione 'E. Zancan', Padova.

Fondazione Zancan (1979), *Riforma delle leggi sull'adozione e sull'affido*, Documentazioni di Servizio sociale n. 20, Padova.

Fondazione Zancan (1980), *Dopo il 616 e la 833 : l'unità locale dei servizi*, Servizi sociali, n. 4.

Iafrate, R. (1989), *L'affido familiare come intreccio di rappresentazioni*, in Bambino incompiuto n° 3, Milano.

Ichino Pellizzi, F. a cura di (1983), *L'affido familiare*, Angeli, Milano.

La Greca, G. (1965), *Il gruppo-famiglia negli istituti di rieducazione*, Infanzia anormale, n. 61.

Maurizio, R., Peirone, M. (1984), *Minori, comunità e dintorni*, EGA, Torino.

Ministero dell'Interno (1980), *Adozione, affidamento familiare*, Comunità alloggio, DGSC, Roma.

Ministero dell'Interno (1984), *Gli operatori sociali : urgenza di una normativa*, DGSC, Roma.

Ministero dell'Interno (1987), *I centri di servizi 'aperti'*, DGSC, Roma.

Moro, A.C. (1983), *I diritti inattuati dei minori*, La Scuola, Brescia.

Moro, A. C. (1991), *Il bambino è un cittadino*, Mursia, Milano.

Occulto, R. (1966), *Le istituzioni e i servizi operativi a favore dei minori disadattati*, Maternità e infanzia, n. 1.

Occulto, R. (1968), *Note in margine all'apertura degli istituti rieducativi*, Esperienze di rieducazione n. 11-12.

Palmonari, A. (1982), *Il lavoro dell'educatore-operatore nei servizi territoriali*, Scuola e professione, n. 6.

Palmonari, A. a cura di (1991), *Comunità di convivenza e crescita della persona*, Patron, Bologna.

Perico, G. (1983), *Il lungo 'iter' della nuova legge su adozione e affidamento familiare*, Aggiornamenti sociali, n. 6.

Regione Toscana (1989), *Le comunità di tipo familiare per l'accoglimento dei minori*, Giunta Regionale Toscana, Firenze.

Senise, T., Giaconia, G. (1965), *Pensionati di rieducazione e officine o aziende artigiane per adolescenti e giovani disadattati*, Infanzia anormale, n. 61.

Spadetto, G. (1978), *Un'esperienza di servizio per minori disadattati*, Rivista di Servizio sociale, n. 3.

Trevisan, C. a cura di (1968), *L'unità locale dei servizi*, Fondazione 'E. Zancan', Padova.

Vecchiato, T. a cura di (1985), *Educazione, devianza giovanile e comunità alloggio*, Scuola sup. Servizio sociale, Trento.

Vecchiato, T. (1986), *La comunità alloggio : un modello polivalente di intervento sociale*, Il bambino incompiuto, n. 3, Unicopli, Milano.

Vecchiato, T. (1988), *Dalla comunità alloggio alla dimensione comunitaria*, Animazione sociale, n. 12, EGA, Torino.

Vecchiato, T. (1991), *Minori, devianza e nuovo processo penale minorile : ruolo dei servizi e della comunità locale*, Il Bambino incompiuto, n. 3, Unicopli, Milano.

Vernò, F. (1988), *Come la comunità locale si fa carico dei problemi dei minori*, Animazione sociale, n. 2, EGA, Torino.

Vernò, F. a cura di (1989), *Minori : un impegno per la comunità locale*, Fondazione 'E. Zancan', Padova.

Volpicelli, L. (1974), *Documentazione sul ruolo dell'educatore di comunità*, Maternità e infanzia, n. 9.

8 The Netherlands

J.D. van der Ploeg

Recent political history : The Netherlands is a monarchy, and the reigning monarch, Queen Beatrix, is the third queen in succession. For the past three years, the government has been formed by a coalition between the Christian Democratic party and the Socialist party. The Christian Democrats have been the largest party for the last decade. The Netherlands is characterised by very extensive welfare provisions.
Geographical Size : 41,547 Km².
Principal industries : food and allied products, electronics and chemicals.
Date of EC membership : 1958.
Total number of inhabitants (01.01.1992) : 15,010,455.
Age of majority : 18 years.
Number of people under the age of majority (01.01.1992) : 3,786,164.
Number of children and young people (01.01.1993) :   in residential care :   9,000
                 in foster care :   10,000

Introduction

As in many other western European countries, residential care for deprived children in the Netherlands dates back to the last century. The first institutions were established by private, charitable, organisations and the church as a response to the material and social deprivation of poor children in the large cities. As time went by, government support for these initiatives constantly increased. Nowadays, all residential child care institutions are subsidised by the government, with some institutions deriving all their funding from government.

The nature of the residential task has also shifted over time. Residential institutions are presently oriented towards addressing emotional, rather than material, deprivation. Table 8.1 shows the types of residential care currently provided for children with psycho-social problems. It should be noted that provisions for children with disabilities are outside the scope of this chapter.

Table 8.1   Types of residential care

Type	Capacity
Residential treatment centres	4,200
Homes for children without behavioural problems	3,300
Treatment centres for youngsters with psychiatric problems	1,400
Centres for supervised lodging	1,000
Closed residential centres	600
Family style homes	300
Reception Centres for crisis-intervention	250
Total capacity	11,050

The age of the children accommodated in residential care homes ranges from birth to 18 years. In addition to residential care, some 3,500 places are provided in day-care centres. Further, an estimated 10,000 children are placed with foster families. Of these, approximately 2,800 children are placed in long-term foster homes, 3,400 in short-term foster care, and 3,800 children stay with foster families on a regular basis during school holidays, etc.

Residential care

Decreasing capacity

Whoever surveys the development of residential children's homes will be struck by the fact that the capacity of these homes has shrunk in recent years. This is all the more striking because in the 1960's the residential sector had continued to expand. At that time, it was believed that such growth would be maintained in line with the growth in population. However, the reverse happened. Just how sharp the fall in residential numbers has been can be judged by the following figures. In 1970, residential child care capacity totalled some 18,000 places, since which time it has plummeted to about 10,000 places.

Various reasons have contributed to this decline, not least the increase in day help; a development based on the view that assistance at an early stage can prevent more serious difficulties later on. Concern about the possible adverse effects of residential care has also played a part, along with the increasing tolerence shown by the community toward deviant behaviour.

Moreover, a policy has been pursued based on the principles that, where possible, help should be provided on a short-term basis, be close to the child's home, and be 'light' in nature. The latter point, in particular, has led to lighter forms of help, such as community help and day help, being sharply increased and heavier forms, such as day and night provision, being reduced. The guiding idea in this is that the more intensively the lighter interventions are applied, the more the heavier interventions can be prevented. Whilst this is not an illogical proposition, it is one that ignores the stubborn fact that many problems cannot be effectively solved by light intervention. Strengthening prevention and day help should not, therefore, mean a weakening of residential help.

More coherence

There has been long-running discussion on whether help for young people should be concentrated within a single ministry. Some have even advocated a separate ministry for youth. Until fairly recently, responsiblity for helping young people was fragmented between different departments, with the Ministry of Justice taking the lion's share. This situation partly reflected the lack of interest other departments had traditionally shown in problematic young people, and partly the convenience of having such youngsters dealt with by a single department. The latter, however, encountered increasing opposition, with calls for a division between welfare and justice.

Finally, in 1986, a decision was taken to siphon off a large number of children's homes operating in the field of child-protection to the Ministry of Welfare, Public Health and Culture. This step was not only aimed at rationalising the organisation of services, but also had the objective of creating internal and financial harmony between the variety of children's homes which were often funded and supervised by different agencies.

Spreading help

The policy of decentralising assistance to the young involves an attempt to achieve a good infrastructure of services at a regional level.

Working from the principle that help must be provided as close to home as possible, it should no longer be the case, for example, that a youngster should have to travel from the north of the country to the south in order to receive help. It is planned to extend the policy of decentralisation throughout the provinces and the four large cities from 1992 onwards.

How well is this attempt to achieve a more even spread of services across regions progressing? Formerly, the regions had absolutely no significance in the organisation of child care services. It was not until the 1960's that the notion developed that young people should be placed in their own region and as near as possible to their own homes. Whilst the number of young people placed outside their own region has since fallen, the ideal of treating every young person in his or her own or neighbouring province has not been fully realised. On average, as many as a quarter of young people admitted to children's homes are placed outside their own province.

Although policy makers originally thought in terms of five regions, they later opted for the thirteen Dutch provinces and have now arrived at 44 regional areas. For such a small country as the Netherlands, which has a limited capacity with regard to children's homes, forty or so regional areas seems far too many.

Running parallel to the issue of regionalisation is the question of which children's homes should have a national function. Currently, 40 residential institutions, which have a combined capacity of 1,900 places, are recognised as national facilities. This represents about one-fifth of the total children's home capacity for young people with behavioural problems, and seems far too high since it means that 2 out of every 10 young people are placed outside their region of origin; it also suggests that the goal of an even distribution of children's home capacity has yet to be attained.

When we leave national capacity out of the equation and examine regional children's home capacity, set against the number of young people resident in each region, the conclusion is inescapable : certain regions of the Netherlands still possess too much, and others too little, children's home capacity.

Doing things on a small scale

During the last ten years, attempts have been made to facilitate the provision of help in small-scale surroundings. That is, surroundings which are, in all respects, on a human scale. This not only entails striving toward smaller living-units and groups, but also locating these within populated areas. Seeing things on a small scale also creates situations in which young people know that the individuals helping them are close at hand, literally as well as figuratively.

The idea behind this is that the process of making help available is most effective if the context is familiar to the young people concerned and they feel at home there. This has not always been the prevailing view. Until recently, education in children's homes was dominated by the idea that concentration and centralisation provided the best conditions for optimal help. It was thought that concentrating residential help in one place would improve the quality of the services provided for young people, both in terms of materials and personal supervision.

It cannot be denied that a private swimming pool can be constructed in a children's home for 300 young people but not in one for 20 young people. Similarly, it is easier for a large children's home to appoint a full-time educational psychologist than it is for a small children's home. Financially and economically too, the large children's home enjoys undoubted advantages. Nevertheless, the fact remains that residential help must primarily be educative in nature.

Hence, it is important to note that small-scale facilities can certainly constitute a sound part of a larger organisation, provided that they respect the characteristics of being small-scale. Such characteristics include : location in a residential area, a limited number of residents and groupleaders, a large measure of autonomy for the group leaders, and access to the same social facilities that are available to other citizen's (e.g., schools, youth clubs, health centres etc.).

Here we are clearly a long way from the idea that residential help can be most effective in isolated, rural, settings. There is a growing belief that children's homes should be integrated within the neighbourhoods that they serve.

In addition, young people are better able to develop as individuals in small-scale provisions, and do not suffer from the anonymity of a large, bureaucratic, institution, where the application of rigid routines and rules creates an artificial living environment.

However, operating on a small scale accomplishes no miracles in itself. This point is underlined by the research of Klüppel and Slijkerman (1983). It appears from this study that young people's degree of satisfaction with living in a children's home is strongly determined by their opinion of their group leaders. Moreover it seems that the seriousness of young people's problems influence the amount of contentment they experience during their stay in a children's home.

Research by Brandjes et al. (1992) also shows that small children's homes do not automatically make for contented group leaders. Dissatisfaction expressed by such personnel was associated with receiving insufficient support from fellow group leaders, and with considerable tensions within the team of group leaders.

Naturally these findings do not imply that small children's homes are undesirable. They do, however, indicate that small children's homes do not provide the best possible help as a matter of course, and that they even have some areas of weakness, stemming from their narrow supporting structures and limited organisational framework.

Increasing problems

With a strengthening of preventive and day help for young people, one might assume that residential care would be reserved for the more problematic youngsters. In some cases, youngsters would be admitted where day help is not having the desired effect. In others, intervention would proceed directly to a residential placement because day help appears unlikely to prove successful.

To further consider the proposition that children's homes are required to cope with increasingly problematic youngsters, we may refer to two investigations carried out almost 10 years apart (Van der Ploeg, 1979 and Van der Ploeg and Scholte, 1988). Because both studies used the same methodology and involved representative random samples, it is possible to make an accurate comparison involving a number of key variables.

Manifest problem behaviour Table 8.2 provides information about changes with regard to problem behaviours which contribute to the admission of young people to residential care.

Table 8.2 Behavioural problems on admission*

	1979	1988
Running away from home	32.9%	37.4%
Theft	30.7%	26.2%
Truancy	33.0%	23.6%
Wandering	24.3%	23.7%
Burglary	5.5%	10.6%
Sexual problems	8.3%	12.7%
Extreme aggression	21.5%	14.9%

* The same boy or girl may display several behavioural problems.

It appears that truancy and aggression fall significantly, while burglary, running away from home and sexual problems increase. However, these results do not tell us whether the behaviour for which young people are admitted has generally become more or less serious over the years.

Relational problems Table 8.3 presents findings from the 1988 study on relations between the youngsters and other important people in their lives.

Table 8.3   Relations (in round percentages) with

	father (figure)	mother (figure)	siblings	children of the same age	teaching staff
good	12%	13%	22%	27%	29%
moderate	33%	43%	59%	52%	59%
bad	55%	44%	19%	21%	21%
	100%	100%	100%	100%	100%

A comparison of these results with the 1979 investigation suggests that relations between young people in residential care and all five other important persons referred to in table 8.3 have deteriorated significantly over the period concerned.

The worst relationships exist within the family. Relations between the youngsters and their fathers (or father figures) were found to be particularly poor. Moreover, relations with teaching staff and children of the same age could be described as bad for about one-fifth of the youngsters. No more than 30 per cent of the young people concerned could be said to enjoy very good relationships with significant others. Overall, one may conclude that the relationships of young people in residential care have become more unfavourable over recent years.

Family problems The family circumstances under which young people have grown up seem, in general, to be no cause for rejoicing. The question is whether changes in such circumstances have occurred during the last few years. In order to address this issue, we may refer to several indicators.

To begin with, it appears that in 1979, the original families of 42.4 per cent of young people fell apart through divorce. By 1988, that percentage had significantly increased to 57.8 per cent.

Table 8.4 provides further information on the deterioration in relations between the children's current parents (or parent figures).

Table 8.4 Parental relationships

	1979 Investigation	1988 Investigation
bad	35%	55%
moderate	38%	30%
good	27%	14%
	100%	100%

We also examined the nature of parental problems. Table 8.5 shows that, overall, the problems of both father's and mother's have increased. The increase in levels of emotional disturbance appear significant.

Table 8.5 Parental problems

Nature of problems	1979		1988	
	father	mother	father	mother
emotional disturbance	44%	57%	54%	69%
incestuous relations	6%	2%	13%	3%
problems of addiction	25%	11%	19%	13%
delinquent behavior	12%	2%	13%	2%

Further analysis revealed that emotional problems are often accompanied by other problems. It was also established that if the mother has problems, so too does the father. In other words, when dysfunction occurs it usually applies to both parents.

Finally, it may be noted that family problems increased in seriousness during the interval between the two studies.

Children's case histories What experiences did the young people in the two studies referred to bring with them when they were admitted to a children's home? We may attempt to answer this question on the basis of the following : the number of previous placements in children's homes experienced by the youngsters concerned, where they stayed immediately prior to admission, and the duration of the problem.

In 1979, some 48 per cent of the young people studied had previously stayed in a children's home. By 1988, the figure had risen to 54.3 per cent. This increase is cause for concern, given that several investigations have demonstrated an association between the number of previous children's homes placements and the seriousness of young people's problems. Further, it may be noted that almost all those resident in the children's homes containing the most problematic youngsters had one or more previous placements in residential care.

The place of stay immediately prior to admission can also give an indication of the seriousness of a youngster's problem. In general, the longer young people have remained with their family, the less adverse will be their case-history. The following table shows that in recent years the number of young people who have been admitted to a children's home directly from their family has fallen sharply.

Table 8.6 Place of stay before admission

	1979 Investigation	1988 Investigation
family	63%	45%
foster-family	9%	17%
children's home	20%	14%
centre for crisis intervention	5%	7%
wandering	0%	5%
living alone	1%	1%
various	2%	11%
total	100%	100%

The message conveyed by table 8.6 is clear : far fewer young people now live with their families before admission to children's homes than was the case a decade or so ago. Prior to resorting to residential care, the social services will have unsuccessfully tried alternative measures (e.g. foster care), or will have lost contact with youngsters.

Finally, we looked for changes in the duration of the problems of young people in children's homes. We found that the longer the duration of a problem, the less likely it became that social services would come up with a solution. This, in turn, led to a more serious problem. In the 1979 study, the average length of problems was estimated to be 3.31 years. By 1988, this had increased to 4.42 years, which represents a significant rise of just over one year.

On the strength of the above findings, it appears that over the past 10 years or so young people in children's homes have become more problematic. Their family situations are now more troubled, their relations with significant others have deteriorated, and they have longer and more traumatic case-histories.

Reduced length of stay

The average length of stay in children's homes has clearly become shorter over the years. When one considers the average length of stay as the ratio between the number of young people leaving residential care each year and the annual average number of resident youngsters expressed in months, one finds that over the last twenty years the average length of stay has dropped from 18 to 13 months.

However, these averages are misleading, for they include data on runaways whose length of stay varies from short to ultra-short. This means that the average length of stay for youngsters who complete their course of therapy is much longer than the period of just over one year reported above. Moreover, it is now recognised that length of stay is not only determined by internal treatment considerations, but also by external factors. Vissers (1988) established that young people whose family situations are unfavourable automatically stay in the children's home longer.

From further investigations it appears that a lessening of young people's problems is not always consequent upon length of stay (Edward and Kelly, 1980). Moreover, Klüppel and Slijkerman (1983) found a curvilinear relationship between length of stay and problems. In other words, a reduction in problems can be expected for a period following admission, after which the youngster's problems are likely to recur. Thus, it seems that the effect of the treatment received in the children's home reaches a peak, but then ceases to be effective. This suggests that young people often stay too long in children's homes.

Increasing professionalism

Over the years, growing importance has been attached to the position of group leaders. Indeed, the idea that they are the key figures in the helping process is now widely accepted. The consequences of this are clearly visible.

The number of leaders per living group has constantly increased in past years. The extent of this development can be judged from the fact that, whilst in 1959 an average of 2 people worked with each group the figure has since more than doubled to 4.5 group leaders per group. It is not only educational considerations that have driven this trend; other factors have played a part, not least the reduction in working hours, which looks set to continue.

In addition, the size of living groups has been reduced since the second world war, thus providing conditions more favourable to a professional approach. Whereas in the 1940's and early 1950's one could still observe groups comprising 30 children, a rapid change took place halfway through the 1950's. Thus by 1959, the average group size was down to 14, since which time it has been further reduced to 10.

The increased importance attached to the role of group leaders is also reflected by improvements in their training. The first large scale investigation into child care practice in children's homes in the Netherlands, conducted by Clemens Schröder and Koekebakker (1955), established that 67 per cent (N = 843) of those comprising a representative sample of group leaders had not completed a professional training course. Some thirty years on, much has changed in this respect. A recent study by Van der Ploeg and Scholte (1988) on the functioning of group leaders revealed that only 17 per cent still had no professional training.

Furthermore, there has been a remarkable rise in the numbers of allied professionals (e.g. psychologists, psychiatrists) working in children's homes over the years. In 1951, no such professionals were employed on a full-time basis in children's homes, and only 36 were available for a few days a week. However, by 1985 some 200 were employed part-time, whilst the number of full-time staff had risen to 177 (Van der Ploeg, 1986).

Performance of group leaders

Has increasing professionalism improved the functioning of group leaders? This question is difficult to answer because the context in which group leaders operate has changed a good deal since the 1950's. Nevertheless, we are able to comment on variations in the functioning of contemporary group leaders on the basis of the research carried out by Brandjes et al. (1982). A number of important conclusions may be drawn from this study.

First, it appears that the chances of dysfunction are increased by certain personal characteristics. Those who have low self-esteem, who suffer from anxiety and vague physical complaints and respond to everyday problems with a passive, pessimistic approach would be better advised not to opt for the profession of group leader. Such persons run a higher than average risk of failing as a group-leader. Although one might expect a solid professional training to lead to a successful career, this does not seem to be the case. At present, one is obliged to

163

conclude that certain personal traits have a greater impact on the functioning of group leaders than professional training or other biographical characteristics.

Second, individuals who have failed to come to terms with recent traumatic experiences are extremely vulnerable as group leaders. The more such unresolved, stressful experiences, the group leader has undergone, the greater his or her susceptibility to dysfunction. This finding supports a hypothesis which has been confirmed more than once by research; namely, that vulnerability to stress increases as further, unresolved, traumatic experiences are acquired. Nevertheless, it is clear that vulnerable individuals continue to opt for the profession of group leader in the hope that working with underprivileged youngsters will compensate them for, or help them come to terms with, the adversity they themselves have experienced. Unfortunately, unresolved personal problems often result in group leaders handling relationships and conflicts with young people inappropriately. This may suggest that the notion that group leaders who have personally suffered traumatic experiences are ideally placed to help troubled young people should be treated with caution.

Third, it appears that group leaders who receive insufficient social-emotional support from their immediate colleagues are more likely to be ineffective. By contrast, role performance is much enhanced when one is surrounded by people on whom one can count. This is especially important at times of increased tension, given that social support increases our capacity to cope with stressful situations. In this respect, it is also worth pointing out that support which group leaders receive from their own teams, consisting of others who are directly involved, has a greater impact on performance than the support provided by supervisory staff; although the latter is by no means unimportant.

Fourth, in spite of good personal traits and the support of colleagues in the children's home and even the group itself, the group leader can still fall victim to dysfunction if the children's home possesses the following two negative characteristics : an authoritarian organisational structure and a high turnover of group leaders. Whilst the latter problem has greatly decreased, it nevertheless appears that the repeated departure of colleagues demoralises those remaining behind.

Finally, only one group characteristic appears to be significantly related to dysfunction among group leaders : group atmosphere. This concerns how youngsters perceive one another. The more negatively young people view their peers, the worse the group leadership seems to function.

An oppressive environment is particularly likely to be created when the young people involved are unhappy about factors such as the low level of involvement by group leaders, and feel unable to express their emotions. Group leaders can be so deeply affected by this that their performance suffers as a consequence. Moreover, the interaction between a bad group atmosphere and a badly functioning group leader creates an even worse situation for all concerned.

Increasing attention to the family

Until quite recently, when a young person was admitted to a children's home, very little attention was given to his or her family. Somewhat illogically, the focus was almost exclusively on the young person's problems, while the family was more or less ignored. Consequently, by the time the young person returned home, little had usually changed. Since by far the greater part of problems experienced by young people originate within the family, a return to the latter, even after years in a children's home, often spelled little good for the youngster. Typically, the problems flared up again, and this resulted in a new residential placement.

However, in the 1950's it was recognised that admitting a young person to a children's home was pointless if the family was not also included in the treatment programme. Thus, residential staff began to work with families outside the walls of the institution.

Social welfare services are relieved of a great deal of pressure when troubled young people enter children's homes. Resources can then be devoted to households where young people continue to live. In particular, children's homes alleviate the strain on social welfare services with large caseloads. Given that the majority of children's homes do not have the resources to offer counselling to families, many families remain excluded from treatment.

In a recently completed investigation (Van der Ploeg and Scholte, 1988), it appeared that 75 per cent of the children's homes studied maintained contact with the young person's family. But such contact could be termed intensive in only 39 per cent of cases. In other words, over 60 per cent of the homes surveyed did not engage in the sort of contact which indicates that families were included in the treatment process.

Nevertheless, the idea that the families of young people in care ought also to receive help is growing. Further, measures geared to preventing the need for an institutional placement are increasingly being deployed. A diverse range of home-training projects have been introduced which, by means of intensive help to families, aim at preventing residential placements. Optimists believe that the need for residential care can be averted altogether if sufficient help is offered to families. Some have even advocated the abolition of children's homes on the grounds that residential care adversely affects children's development and competencies.

Two questions arise at this juncture. First, whether the need for residential placement can be prevented by further optimisation and intensification of help. Second, whether children's homes can make a positive contribution to modifying problem behaviours in young people.

The answer to the first question depends not only on the quality of the family therapy provided, but also on the nature of the problems confronted. It is unrealistic to suppose that the positive forces existing within families are always conducive to effective treatment through which youngsters can remain at home. Therefore, care orders will remain inevitable. The question as to whether it is better for a youngster to be admitted to a foster family than a children's home is, generally speaking, not difficult to answer. A foster family is a more ideal choice than a children's home because a family situation offers the child a better chance of developing into an autonomous person in natural surroundings.

Unfortunately, however, not every young person is able to fit into a foster family. Equally, foster families cannot always be made to fit the child. These points particularly apply to older children with behavioural difficulties of long-standing.

Consequently there will continue to be young people who require a residential placement. This bring us to the issue of whether children's homes can make a significant contribution. The opponents of children's homes sometimes cite the misleading slogan that the worst family is always better than the best children's home. They also often refer to the percentage of criminals who spent part of their early lives in a children's home. However, anyone who has experienced at close hand the psychological damage inflicted on children by a dysfunctional family knows better. It is also clear that the high percentage of criminals with a children's home background is easily exceeded by the percentage of law-abiding people who spent time in residential care in childhood. Follow-up studies show that between 60 and 70 per cent of such persons turn out well.

However, this does not alter the fact that a children's home upbringing takes place in an artificially created environment. Thus, great care must be taken to ensure that children's homes are nurturing environments in which young people are helped to further their own development, and where they learn how to maintain themselves and to participate fully in society.

Foster care

Varieties of foster care

It is possible to distinguish six major types of foster family care in the Netherlands. First, common foster homes, where the majority of children are looked after on a temporary basis for an indefinite period. Second, therapeutic foster families, which care for severely disturbed children. Third, crisis-reception families, which provide short-term and emergency care. Fourth, so-called weekend or holiday foster families, where children spend a specific period of time during weekends or holidays. Fifth, common boarding foster families that accommodate older children who require less intensive care and guidance. Finally, there are a number of new initiatives, which include foster homes where foster parents receive extensive guidance in providing for groups of four foster children while maintaining a close relationship with local residential institutions. In what follows attention will be concentrated on the common types of foster families that provide temporary placements for children.

In 1991, some 8,971 foster children were placed under guardianship either through voluntary arrangements with their birth parents or as a result of compulsory child care and protection measures.

Some statistics

On average, around 10,000 children are placed under guardianship each year. However, statistics show that some striking fluctuations have occurred over time. In the past, the majority of guardianships resulted from compulsory child care and protection measures. However, table 8.7 shows that the number of compulsory placements has fallen dramatically since 1970.

Table 8.7 Number of foster children placed as a result of child care and protection measures

Year	Number
1970	9387
1977	6803
1984	6501
1991	5183

Whilst the number of children under child care and protection measures receded sharply between 1970 and 1991, voluntary receptions increased from less than 1,000 to over 4,000 in the same priod. The reduction in the number of judicial foster families correlates with the decline in the total number of children under child care and protection measures, which fell from 36,146 in 1970 to 18,930 in 1986. This reflects the large decrease in the number of parents deprived of parental rights, which automatically places children under guardianship of an institution. Usually, such children will then either be placed in another institution or with a foster family.

A second important point to note from the available statistics concerns gender differences. Over the years boys have constituted a slight majority among judicially placed children (around 53 per cent). Conversely, girls now form a majority (approximately 65 per cent) of those placed in foster families by voluntary arrangement.

A further point that can be deduced from the available statistics is that it is mainly younger children who, by way of child care and protection measures, experience mandatory placements in foster families. By contrast, older children constitute a majority of those in voluntary placements. About two-thirds of all children in voluntary placements are over 12 years of age.

The characteristics of foster children

In the Netherlands, there is a dearth of representative research on the characteristics of foster children. Still, several investigations have been conducted that tell us something about such children.

Research by Van Ooyen-Houben (1991) looked at children under 12, whilst that of Reeuwijk and Berben (1987) studied children aged from birth to 21 years (N=207) in voluntary placements. With regard to the latter, it must be borne in mind that children placed as result of child care and protection measures generally come from more problematic family backgrounds. Table 8.8 shows the percentages of foster children in Reeuwijk and Bergen's (1987) study manifesting or experiencing six types of problems.

Table 8.8   Problems of foster children

	%
recalcitrancy	29
absconding	19
relationship problems	14
dependency on others	12
depression	11
loneliness	10

It should be noted that the problems listed in table 8.8 were far more prevalent among older children.   Problems such as absconding, depression, and so on, hardly occur among younger children.   For a better insight into the problems experienced by children under the age of 12, we may refer to the work of Van Ooyen-Houben (1991), who observed the development of 52 children placed in foster families. The following problems were the most frequently observed : quickly irritated, lack of feeling, childish, tense, withdrawn and stubborn. Although at first glance this seemed to suggest that the problems necessitating placement often stemmed from the children themselves, the latter was found to be true for no more than 3 per cent of the children.   In 47 per cent of cases, the reason for placement was attributed entirely to adverse family circumstances, whilst in 50 per cent of cases placement was due in roughly equal measure to both children's behavioural problems and adverse family circumstances.

Many of the foster children studied by Reeuwijk and Berben (1987) were from broken homes.   In 55 per cent of cases this was due to divorce. Some 16 per cent of the foster children had experienced the death of a birth parent, and 8 per cent were born to single mothers. In addition, the original families of 2 per cent of the foster children had broken up as a result of the imprisonment of one of their birth parents, and 19 per cent of the children had experienced family breakdown for other reasons.

Research further reveals that almost two-thirds of all breadwinners in single-parent families are unemployed. Of those in work, 57 per cent hold jobs which require little, if any, schooling.

Table 8.9 shows the proportion of foster children in Reeuwijk and Berben's (1987) study who had experienced various types of family problem prior to placement.

Table 8.9 Problems within foster children's families of origin

Problems	%
relationship problems between child and parents	64
pedagogic incapacity of parents	31
relationship problems between parents	29
emotional problems of parents	28
child abuse	17
addiction	15
affectional neglect	12
incest	8
delinquency	5
prostitution	3

Prior to placement with their foster families, many of the youngsters studied by Reeuwijk and Berben (1987) had already received a good deal of professional help. Some 58 per cent had previously been placed with foster parents. Further, two-thirds of the children and their birth families had received help from social welfare agencies. Thus, the idea that all foster children move straight from their birth families to foster families is erroneous, and held for only 54 per cent of the youngsters in Reeuwijk and Berben's (1987) study. Of the remaining 46 per cent, 24 per cent came from other foster families, 10 per cent from an institution and the remainder from other places of residence.

A comparison with children in institutions

It is generally assumed that children in institutions are more problematic than foster children, and that institutions are better able than foster families to deal with difficult youngsters. In commenting on the Dutch situation, we are able to refer to an investigation by Van Ooyen-Houben (1991) in which she observed 140 children aged from birth to 11 years who no longer lived with their own families. Of these children, 66 per cent were initially placed in institutions and 34 per cent went to foster families. Van Ooyen-Houben (1991) carried out a systematic comparison of the two groups, and found significant differences in age, sex and family problems. There were also significant differences in the physical, social-emotional and cognitive functioning of the two groups. According to their caregivers, the foster children tended to show more socially desirable behaviour than the children in institutions. Among the latter, children in treatment settings manifested the most undesirable behaviour. For the most part, these differences could be attributed to differences in age. However, there were some differences in the functioning of the two groups which could be accounted for in terms of differences in their backgrounds. Even when these differences were controlled for, the foster children were still seen as significantly less withdrawn and more intelligent than the children in institutions.

Characteristics of foster families

In considering the characteristics of families, we may return to the work of Reeuwijk and Berben (1987). Two-thirds of the foster families in their study consisted of a foster father and foster mother. Single-parent foster mothers were more prevalent than foster families headed by single fathers.

The average age of the foster fathers was 39, compared with 40 for the foster mothers. The age of foster mothers ranged from 19 to 72 years, which was wider than that of the foster fathers whose ages varied between 22 and 65 years.

Sixty-six percent of the foster parents had children of their own living with them, whose ages ranged from 0 to 27 years. In one-third of the cases, the foster parents shared accommodation with the foster children's natural parents. A further 22 per cent of foster families lived in the same district as the foster children's birth parents. A comparison of the occupations of foster and natural parents revealed that the socio-economic status of foster families was generally higher than that of natural families.

The effects of placement in foster families

It has been known for some time that foster families experience difficulties in coping with troubled youngsters. Indeed, a high proportion of foster placements breakdown. In the Netherlands, the breakdown rate ranges from 25 per cent to over 50 per cent, depending on the population of foster children concerned.

These figures are taken from research carried out by Kaas-Fontaine (1981) and De Groot (1981). The former study, which involved over 300 foster children aged from birth to 21 years, found an average breakdown rate of around 26 per cent. For children under the age of 10 a breakdown rate of 14 per cent was obtained, while some 41 per cent of placements for youngters aged 10 years and over brokedown. De Groot's (1981) study, which also entailed over 300 children of all ages, found a breakdown rate of 48 per cent. A third investigation by van Thiel (1987) indicates that up to two-thirds of foster placements may fail.

Some 44 per cent of the foster placements studied by Reeuwijk and Berben (1987) brokedown. The majority of these involved youngsters aged between 13 and 18 years. Moreover, significant correlations were found between fostering breakdown, the severity of foster children's behavioural problems, and their family backgrounds.

However, table 9.10 shows that it is incorrect to regard every placement that ends sooner than was originally planned negatively. Further, it should also be emphasised that the breakdown rates reported above include cases where the decision to end the placement cannot be equated with failure.

Table 8.10   Reasons for termination of foster placements

	%
conflict between foster children and foster family	25
absconding by foster children	16
foster parents unable to cope	9
foster child rehabilitated with natural family	11
objective of placement reached earlier than planned	6
child wanted to leave foster family	4
foster placement no longer seen as appropriate	4
other reasons	25

The question of whether a foster family is more beneficial to the child than placement in an institution has long been debated, and remains difficult to answer given the wide range of reasons as to why children are placed in foster families. The problems of foster children vary, as do their family backgrounds.

Nevertheless, conventional wisdom assumes that placements in foster families are more beneficial for children than institutions. However, Van Ooyen-Houben's research (1991) casts doubt on this view.

She reports significant differences in development between groups of children living in foster homes and institutions. The children in institutions stood out as being the most problematic group, whereas the foster-family children emerged as relatively non-problematic. However, there were significant differences between the composition of the two groups, their scores at the outset of placement, and in the frequency of visits they received from their birth parents. After controlling for these differences, there remained only one significant difference between the development of the two groups; namely, that the children in institutions were generally less easily distracted than the foster children after two years in placement. The most important factors associated with desirable or undesirable courses of development were age and level of functioning at the outset of placement. Van Ooyen-Houben (1991) also found that younger children developed in a more desirable direction than older children, and that a higher initial level of functioning was associated with a higher level after two years, and vice versa.

It is clear from this research that groups of children in foster families and institutions differ significantly in composition and in initial level of functioning. When these differences are not controlled for, the subsequent development of foster children compares favourably with that of institutional children. However, when background variables are taken into account, the results do not support the view that children in family settings function better than those in institutions.

Some significant bottlenecks

Despite the improvement of foster care in the Netherlands in recent years, two issues represent bottlenecks to further progress.

Recruitment and selection of foster parents Attempts are increasingly being made to find families that are genuinely able to look after foster children for an indefinite period of time. Academic commentators have identified a number of factors pertaining to foster parents which may impede the development of foster children. These include authoritarian attitudes and possessiveness toward foster children (Van Oever et al. 1979). Research also suggests that a child's progress is likely to suffer if the foster parents view development as wholly dependent on hereditary factors (Wit et al., 1971). Conversely, it appears that foster parents who are prepared to seek help and guidance tend to perform their roles more successfully than those who are not (Hart de Ruyter, 1968).

Unfortunately, the recruitment of appropriate foster parents is hampered by the fact that this task is handled by too many authorities. Moreover, there is no central register of foster families, and the selection criteria used by the different agencies involved vary considerably.

Supervison of foster placements Effective supervision of foster placements is undermined by a shortage of expertise and specialist skills among social workers.

In this respect, it has been argued that social workers too often refrain from explicitly supporting foster children in conflicts with foster parents (Weterings, 1977). It also appears that the prospects for a successful placement are reduced when insufficient time is devoted to preparing the foster child and parents for the placement, and when the foster parents receive insufficient background information about the foster child.

Finally, there is considerable debate about the extent to which birth parents should share in the care of foster children. Opinions vary strongly. Some take the view that the involvement of birth parents should be kept to a minimum, or even that birth parents should be excluded altogether. Others believe in an 'inclusive' model of fostering, which is premised on the notion that children benefit when foster care involves partnership between birth and foster parents.

Conclusions

In retrospect, the 1950's can be seen as a period of quantitative expansion for the residential child care sector. By contrast, the 1960's were marked by calls for improvements in the quality of such provision (a tendency which is on going). In the 1970's, emphasis was placed on reorganisation. This not only produced a sharp reduction in capacity, but also a move towards greater differentiation and a more even geographical spread of children's homes. The 1980's was a period of important policy development on a macro-level. Improved co-ordination and cooperation has been brought about in the care of young people, while a clear impetus has also been given towards further continuity and quality.

Over the next ten years, a more effective system of quality evaluation should be the order of the day. Individual residential centres will be required to systematically map out their own role and identity with regard to population served, methods and outcomes. This will make it clear to all concerned just what care capabilities a given children's home possesses and what its strengths and weaknesses are.

With regard to fostering, it is evident that the number of children placed in foster families under compulsory child care and protection measures is falling, while the proportion of children voluntarily placed in foster care by their birth parents is increasing. Girls are more likely to be accommodated with foster families than boys. Children placed in foster families generally turn out to be less troubled and troublesome than those placed in institutions. However, the likelihood of placement in a foster family increases when a child is young, less troubled, and comes from a less problematic family. The selection and supervision of foster parents is generally unsatisfactory. Further research is required on this area, together with efforts to promote the development of specialist skills and knowledge.

References

Brandjes, M., Nass, C., Defares, P.B. and van der Ploeg, J.D. (1982), *Arbeidsbevrediging en verloop onder groepsleiding*, IOPS, Wageningen.

Clemens Schröder, B.F. and Koekebakker, J. (1955), *Verzorging en opvoeding in kindertehuizen*, Den Haag.

Edwards, D.W. and Kelly, J.G. (1980), 'Coping and adaptation : a longitudinal study', *American Journal of Community Psychology*, VI, n. 2.

Groot, de M.E. (1981), *Hoe gaat het ermee? Achtergronden van kind/jongere en pleegadres en het verloop van de plaatsing. Een follow-up onderzoek*, Jeugd Onder Dak, Deventer.

Hart de Ruyter, Th. (1968), *Het moeilijk opvoedbare kind in het pleeggezin*, Van Gorcum, Assen.

Kaas-Fontaine, P. (1984), *Een enquête onder pleegouders : follow-up III*, Centrale voor Pleeggezinnen, Amsterdam.

Klüppel, J.E.J. and Slijkerman, A.J.M. (1983), *Gebruik en beleving van kindertehuizen*, IOPS, Wageningen.

Oever, van den A.C.C., Hoogheid, B.J. and Hirschfeldt, L.J.A. (1979), *Plaatsing in pleeggezinnen*, Rijksuniversiteit Leiden.

Ooyen-Houben, M. van (1991), *De ontwikkeling van jonge kinderen na een uithuisplaatsing*, dissertatie Rijksuniversiteit, Leiden.

Ploeg, J.D. van der (1976), *Isolement, angst en agressie*, Samson, Alphen aan den Rijn.

Ploeg, J.D. van der (1979), *Elfhonderd jeugdigen in tehuizen*, Wijn, Utrecht.

Ploeg, J.D. van der (1985), *Jeugd (z)onder dak II*, Samson, Alphen aan den Rijn.

Ploeg, J.D. van der and Scholte, E.M. (1988), *Tehuizen in beeld*, Rijksuniversiteit Leiden, COJ, Leiden.

Reeuwijk, P.M.C. and Berben, E.G.M.J. (1988), *Vrijwillige pleegzorg, een kwantitatieve analyse*, C.W.O.K, Den Haag.

Thiel, M. van (1982), *Vrijwillige pleeggezinplaatsingen : een dossieronderzoek*, Centrale voor pleeggezinnen, Rotterdam.

Vissers, J. (1988), *De residentiële carrière van jongeren in de kinderbescherming*, CWOK, Den Haag.

Weterings, A.M. (1977b), *Het pleeggezin als opvoedingssituatie : een empirisch onderzoek naar de opvoedingsrelatie van voogdijpupillen in een pleeggezin*, Brouwer, Groningen.

Wit, O.C. and Adriani, P.J.A. (Eds) (1971), *Pleeggezinonderzoek*, Rijksuniversiteit, Utrecht.

9 Portugal

M. Calheiros, M. Fornelos and J.S. Dinis

Recent political history : For some 48 years, Portugal was a totalitarian state. This was put to an end by the revolution of 25 April 1974. Since then, Portugal has been a democratic republic; it has a President, who was re-elected in 1990, and a Prime Minister belonging to the PSD (Social Democratic Party), which was elected in 1991.

Geographical Size : 92,131 Km.²

Principal industries : Manufacture of food, textiles, chemicals and paper products.

Date of EC membership : 1986.

Total number of inhabitants (31.12.1991) : 9,846,000.

Age of majority : 18 years.

Number of people under the age of majority (31.12.1991) : 2,620,600.

Number of children and young people (01.11.1990) :   in residential care :   12,010
in foster care : no figures available

The nature of residential and foster care provision

All children who are separated from their birth families should have the opportunity of being placed in one of the possible provisions available, i.e. residential or foster care, so as to ensure the necessary continuity and stability of their relationships with the environment.

As such placements are temporary, at least in principle, no effort should be spared to maintain the links between the child and his or her family of origin. The psychological processes inherent in development elicit a great need for stability and continuity in the child's environment. Therefore, substitute care practice must be geared to the individual needs and circumstances of each child.

In Portugal, children deprived of their normal family environment as a result of intervention from social welfare services, health centres, child mental health teams or the courts, are sent to the Social Security Regional Centres, IPSS (Private Social Solidarity Institutions), the *Misericórdias* and the *Serviço de Tutela de Menores* (Juvenile Guardianship Service). In Lisbon, children under 6 years of age are placed with the *Santa Casa da Misericórdia de Lisboa*. Those aged 6 years and over are looked after by the *Casa Pia de Lisboa*. Children with physical or mental disabilities are placed under the care of the Social Security Regional Centres.

For the most part, when negligence, abandonment or ill-treatment has occurred, and where there is a need for intervention in order to safeguard the physical and psychological development of the child, placement away from home is preceded by a legal and juridical decision.

Whenever possible, the rights of parents should be protected, and contact between parents and their children should be maintained. Above all, however, intervention should ensure that the basic needs of the child are met.

Types of provision

Foster care Foster families and residential homes for children and young people are appropriate forms of placement when the child's separation from his or her parents is likely to be transitory. By contrast with adoption, the rights of parents of children placed in foster and residential care can be limited but never completely annulled.

In Portugal, the legal status of foster families is similar to that in other European countries, particularly France. Foster families are families who have one or more children placed in their care by the Social Services (in Lisbon, the Misericórdia or the Regional Centres). Placement in a foster home involves 24 hour care, seven days a week. Foster parents receive fees for the services they provide, and are directly responsible for the care and education of foster children throughout the placement. However, foster children do not legally belong to their foster parents.

The length of foster care placements vary. But many are long-term, and foster children often remain with their foster families until they reach the age of majority. In general, foster children maintain contact with their natural families through short visits, weekend stays and holidays. Typically, the birth parents of foster children do not wish to abandon their children, but rather lack the means to look after them.

Because the reasons underlying the inability of birth parents to adequately care for their children are often complex and multi-faceted, the task of rehabilitating children with their families of origin can be exceedingly difficult.

The Social Services reserve the right to remove the child from the foster placement at any time. Foster families and the children placed with them are supported by interdisciplinary teams of social workers, psychologists and public health nurses.

Residential homes In many residential homes an interdisciplinary team, co-ordinated by a Director, and consisting of social workers, psychologists and teachers, is responsible for meeting the needs of the children and young people looked after.

The present trend is for units accommodating not more than 15 children and young people, aged between 3 and 18 years. Contact with the community is encouraged, and youngsters attend school in the local area and participate in neighbourhood recreational activities.

Numbers of children

In December, 1991, the Misericórdia of Lisbon had a total of 158 children and young people in its care. Some 86 of these were accommodated in 5 residential homes, known as 'residences'. The numbers in each 'residence' were as follows : 26, 23, 14, 7, and 16. The remaining 72 youngsters were accommodated in 'care centres'. At the same time, the Misericórdia of Lisbon had 78 children placed in foster care.

Historical antecedents

We may begin this historical overview of the development of services for children deprived of a normal family with the evolution of the 'House of Mercy' of Lisbon (Santa Casa da Misericórdia de Lisboa). This was founded in 1498 by Queen Leonor, wife of King João II, to 'aid and succour' the destitute and needy. In 1543, the Santa Casa da Misericórdia de Lisboa was called upon by Royal Charter to care for 'foundlings in the charge of All Saints Hospital', Lisbon, and in 1775, by letters-patent, to assume 'total and definitive responsibility for the Exposed'.

At about that time, the 'Turn' of the Misericórdia of Lisbon was introduced. This device was similar to those used by convents. The unwanted newborn child was placed in a revolving cylinder, spun around and taken in by the Hospice on the other side of the wall.

179

An order dated 26 March 1912 extended the care of children by the Misericorida of Lisbon to orphans and abandoned children. From a study of contemporary documents it is clear that by the 1860's the Misericórdia had large, and rapidly increasing, numbers of needy children in its care. For example, in 1869, the Misericórdia provided accommodation for some 14,134 children, of which 2,980 were received through the Turn.

In 1870 a decision was taken to abolish the Turn, following the introduction of a number of alternative measures, such as the concession of subsidies to destitute mothers to enable them to maintain their children.

By 1902 there were only 40 to 50 children in the residence, with a further 2,600 'put out to nurse'. However, the number of children in residential care was to increase considerably during the next 50 years, despite the fact that Portugal did not suffer the consequences of two world wars to the extent of the majority of other countries in Europe.

Residential homes - The beginning of great changes In 1956 the restructuring of the residential sector was begun. This included the recruitment of qualified residential care workers and teaching staff; the reorganisation and modernisation of existing residential homes, thereafter open to all children of both sexes; the incorporation of kindergardens; and the opening of two more infant homes for a total of 80 children. Further measures included a feasibility study for the building of new infant homes in 1958 and the subsequent closure in 1960 of the main residential home for young children. Two additional homes were opened in 1961. In accordance with new thinking, one of these units was a flat located in the centre of town, which accommodated a small number of children who participated fully in the daily life of the surrounding community. During the remainder of the 1960s, investment was concentrated on the training of residential staff.

New ideas In the 1970s two more residential flats were opened. Moreover, a decision was taken by the Misericórdia to continue to care for children beyond the prescribed age of 7 years. This was accompanied by other measures that, unfortunately, were only partially realised in practice. These included: the introduction of family style residential homes in 1975, which were closed down after only one year; the addition of psychologists to the interdisciplinary teams; a fresh emphasis on training for residential staff; and reductions in the numbers of youngsters accommodated in the homes. In 1985 the infants home (0 to 3 years) was closed, following the creation of short-term care centres.

The structure of the services Along with the changes introduced in relation to residential care, the Misericórdia also recognised the need to review the care of the children which it placed 'out to nurse'. In 1961 there were some 83 such children. At that time, there was no organised family placement service to take responsibility for facilitating the initial placement of children and the subsequent supervision of placements.

The first step towards making good this shortfall in provision was taken in 1962 with the establishment of rules concerning the recruitment of nursemaids, and the definition of the role of foster care provision and conditions of service for foster parents. In 1966 the term 'foster family' was introduced in place of 'ama' or nursemaid. This reflected a growing awareness that the alternative to the birth family should be another family rather than one person only - the nursemaid.

Children placed in foster care include those with a strong need for individualised care and the warmth and affection of an adult, and those whose links with their birth families have been completely severed. Such children were traditionally referred to as 'abandoned'.

The first attempt to establish foster care as a legal entity came in November 1967. However, the relevant legislation was not enacted until August 1979.

Children placed with foster families usually come from households headed by single mothers. The birth parents of foster children often have problems such as drug addiction, and serious personality disorders. Typically, foster children are from families beset with multiple problems. Since the 1980s, most of the children placed in foster care have birth parents who, while not wishing to have their children adopted, are for various reasons unable themselves to provide adequate care for their children. As previously noted, some children remain in foster care until reaching the age of majority. Following this, the young adult may continue to be helped until he or she is able to live independently.

Legal framework of the services

Residential homes In October 1980 Ministerial Dispatch no. 57/80 was published which made provision for the reorganisation of existing residential homes. This included the introduction of smaller homes integrated into the community. The Dispatch also established the conditions for the admission of children and young people to residential care.

In January 1986, Decree-Law no. 2/86 was published, which stipulated the basic principles for the structure of residential homes, and proposed that existing facilities be re-appraised with a view to improving the quality of residential services.

Foster care In 1979 the publication of Decree-Law no. 288/79 of 13 August established the legal position of foster care, the regulation of which was provided for by Decree-Regulation no. 60/80 of 10 October. Further, on 2 December 1980, Dispatch no. 366/80 of 29 October was published fixing the rates of monthly subsidies for the maintenance of foster children and the remuneration of foster parents.

Administrative framework of services

In Portugal, voluntary work has no particular administrative framework, and most of the voluntary work undertaken is provided by the Private Social Solidarity Institutions (IPSS), which are largely supported and technically assisted by the State.

Expenditure on residential and foster care

In 1991 expenditure on residential care, including Care Centres, totalled Escudos 53,100,000$00 or approximately £265,500 (excluding staffing and installation expenses), while spending on the Foster Care Service amounted to Escudos 47,950,000$00 or approximately £239,750.

Major theories and ideas

The conceptualisation of children's placement services entails the recognition that the child's needs are not met simply through transfer from a disorganised social environment to a more organised one.

Within the framework of early prevention, an interdisciplinary approach is necessary to safeguard the welfare of children deprived of a normal family environment.

The quality of care the child receives in the first years of life is of vital importance for his or her future mental health. Infants and young children have a fundamental need to establish a warm, intimate and continuous relationship with their mother, or permanent substitute mother; that is to say, a person who regularly and constantly acts as the child's mother. The first basic need of any child is to be able to establish a secure link with the caregiver, normally but not necessarily the mother.

The separation of the infant from the mother will lead to emotional deprivation if the child is placed in a situation where the quality of care provided by the substitute mother is inadequate. In cases where family crisis is followed by frequent interventions, with the child experiencing multiple placements in institutions or with nursemaids, the adverse consequences may be irreversible. There are numerous cases of seriously retarded development and impoverishment of psychological life which could lead to permanent depressive states or future anti-social behaviour.

The Children's Care Service, whether alerted by the social services or by the courts, provides help to families which, despite their individual differences, have common characteristics. As a rule, such families belong to disadvantaged groups whose conditions of life have been unsatisfactory for several generations. This is often associated with psychiatric problems.

When the problem goes beyond a temporary crisis situation, the causes generally involve an interplay between serious internal family problems, the personalities of the parents and the external social environment.

As the children are dependent and incapable of safeguarding their own interests, and need to receive intimate and continuous care from an adult, it is incumbent on the State to assume responsibility for their welfare. The laws on the placement of vulnerable children are part of the contribution which society makes towards their protection when the parents of such children are unable to perform their roles satisfactorily.

Innovations and trends

'Placement' and 'follow-up treatment', which entail the intervention of interdisciplinary teams, are inseparable. The child placed in foster or residential care remains dependent on the placement service which is directly responsible for his or her care and education.

In the case of foster care, the foster family has to respond to the needs of the child and at the same time cope with the changes in its own family dynamics engendered by the child's placement. In addition, the foster family is required to co-operate with the foster child's birth family, and accept the supervision of the fostering service.

Whatever the form of placement, we consider the link between care and treatment of fundamental importance. The successful integration of the child into a foster or residential setting requires a care environment which is therapeutically-oriented in order to allow an understanding of the child's reactions to the experience of separation from his or her birth family. The psychological effects of separation play an important part in the child's reaction and also that of the birth parents, not only at the moment of separation and placement but also in later periods of stress. The child's great vulnerability to loss and change, as well as to disruptive experiences, requires stability and continuity in his or her primary relationships. The responsible service, through the interdisciplinary team, should ensure this stability and continuity as far as possible, thus avoiding the fragmentation of care and treatment created by the various parties involved in the process - parents, social work services, and the courts.

Critical issues

The need to place a child in care presupposes the existence of a crisis in the birth family. An understanding of that crisis should be the first consideration. For example, what are the reasons for the crisis? How serious is it? What are the prospects with regard to rehabilitating the child with the birth family? And, within what time-scale? Which members of the family of origin will be able to maintain contact with the child during the critical period? Will such contact be regularly maintained? And will it be conducive to a positive outcome?

If the answers to these questions tend to be negative, a careful assessment should be made on the basis of the known facts - social, psychological, juridical - as to whether adoption should be considered. As earlier stated, adoption entails the severance of ties between the child and the birth family. Decisions about whether or not the child should be adopted will be strongly conditioned by the child's age, and by the presence or absence of serious pathological factors at both the psychological and somatic level.

Foster care presupposes that contact with the family of origin, or at least with some of its members, can be maintained on a regular basis. This contact should be facilitated within the framework of a care plan for the child, in which the child's return to the birth family is a genuine, and not too distant, possibility. The foster family should be informed that the child's rehabilitation with the birth family is one of the goals of intervention. Naturally, the foster parents will require help in coping with a difficult situation in which they are asked to devote themselves to the child's needs and participate fully in the work undertaken with the birth family in order that contact should not be lost. The motivation of prospective foster parents should be carefully appraised, given that the foster parent role demands a nuturing relationship with the child whilst at the same time forming part of a response to a situation of family crisis. For the child placed in foster care, the foster family must be seen as a 'friend' of the birth family and never perceived to be in opposition to them or as a possible source of rivalry. It should be recognised that in certain cases it may be particularly difficult for the foster family to achieve these aims. It is important not to overlook such issues when defining criteria for the selection of foster families and in the supervision of foster placements.

Placement in a residential home does not entail the possibility of conflict or rivalry between two families. Birth parents tend to perceive residential staff as 'professionals' rather than 'rivals'. Thus, relations between residential caregivers and birth parents are, in principle at least, less likely to involve conflict than those between foster parents and birth parents. Nontheless, a residential placement lacks some of the advantages which a family environment provides, particularly with regard to younger, and emotionally fragile, children.

It is not always easy to distinguish between children who should be placed with a foster family, and those who are more likely to benefit from residential care. Age is one of the key considerations in selecting the type of placement for separated children, since older children may experience greater difficulty settling into a strange family than younger children. The characteristics of the birth family is another factor that must be taken into account. Some birth families may not be predisposed to co-operate with a foster family. In such cases, the prospects of a successful foster placement are severely circumscribed.

In view of the above, it is considered desirable to attempt to recruit foster families from an entirely different socio-cultural and economic level than has hitherto been the case. It is essential that foster parents should be predominantly motivated by a strong sense of social responsibility. Such foster parents are more likely than others to establish a good relationship with the family of origin, and to be more effective in raising the parenting standards of birth parents and in helping them to overcome their difficulties. It is necessary, however, to ensure that the socio-economic difference between the two families does not create new forms of rivalry or a sense of paternalism.

It would also be useful to create a group of foster families who would be specifically selected and prepared for the task of undertaking therapeutic work with abused children.

With regard to residential homes, it is necessary to define their roles clearly, according to whether they receive children or adolescents. However, the style of care offered should not be based on rigid age criteria, but should be geared to the needs of the individual child.

Research on residential and foster care

Little research has been carried out on the separation of children from their biological parents, despite the fact that a study undertaken by the Centre for Judicial Studies (Amaro, 1988) indicates that each year around 30,000 children are subject to abuse and neglect in Portugal. Moreover, studies carried out during the last 15 years (Bichão, 1989; Conçalves, 1991; Proença, 1979; Vala; 1986), show a rise in the number of requests for admission to institutions with regard to children under 7 years of age, and an increasing use of residential homes or correctional homes as a measure for dealing with young offenders who are subject to the jurisdiction of Minors Courts (8.6 per cent of the cases tried in 1983). This is an important fact given that, although delinquency figures are lower in Portugal than in most other European countries (Vala, 1986), there has been a sharp increase in the number of young offenders brought before the courts.

It should also be borne in mind that not all children separated from their biological families in Portugal are accommodated in residential institutions or formally placed in foster homes. Many children are abandoned and left by their parents with someone who will look after them (generally known as 'ama') or with other relatives. Such children are not included in the official statistics, and the authorities lack any real knowledge of their living conditions.

Residential care

Because research on foster care is particularly scarce, this review of research will necessarily concentrate on residential care.

Research of a more academic and theoretical nature which informs residential and foster care services is predominantly drawn from other European countries. Studies carried out in Portugese universities relate mainly to associated areas, such as juvenile delinquency, domestic violence, and children's rights. Research on residential and foster care in Portugal is usually undertaken by the agencies responsible for providing the services. The focus of such studies is on evaluating provision with a view to promoting programmes for adapting services to social developments and changing needs.

For example, in 1979 a project was initiated to study residential homes administered by the 'Santa Casa da Misericórdia de Lisboa', in response to the fact that children over the age of 7 had been living in the homes since 1974. Awareness of the negative effects of moving children who had reached 7 years of age (the prescribed age limit) from residential homes run by the 'Santa Casa da Misericórdia' and placing them in residential homes belonging to other organisations, prompted a study of the Misericórdia's residential services with the objective of adapting them to the needs children over 7 years of age.

Historical background With regard to the historical development of residential and foster care, several studies are of interest. Among these is the work of Pessoa Jorge (1985) on developments in residential homes between 1956 and 1985. The author analyses the circumstances of children cared for in residential homes from the theoretical perspective adopted by Goffman (1970, cit. in Jorge, 1985) in his analysis of total institutions. Jorge's (1985) study was also informed by the work of Carugati et al. (1981, cit. in Jorge, 1985) on de-institutionalisation. By way of analysing all the documents and laws enacted on residential care, Jorge (1985) evaluates the reforms, changes and improvements made during the period referred to. Using the method of semi-structured interviews with 44 staff members who worked in the residential homes and 20 individuals who grew up in the homes, the author also examined the problems that interview subjects considered most important within the residential homes.

Despite positive and significant developments, Jorge (1985) concludes that by 1985 all the residential homes studied continued to manifest elements associated with total institutions. Furthermore, de-institutionalisation was restricted to attempts to prevent the reception of children into residential care, and did not extend to measures geared to making care practice within the residential homes less institutionally-oriented.

Organisation and functional framework Several studies, using methods such as questionnaires (Calheiros, 1991), direct observation (Guimarães and Iria, 1991; Jorge, 1985; Proença, 1979) and interviews (Jorge, 1985), have sought to identify the major problems and needs of residential homes in terms of their organisational and functional framework.

The major problems distinguished with regard to the structures for social welfare intervention include a lack of resources, the inadequacy of co-ordination between services, and poor facilities (Jorge, 1985; Proença, 1979). Further, insufficient numbers of qualified staff are employed in the services, and the training provided for the latter is inadequate (Calheiros, 1991; Guimarães and Iria, 1991; Jorge, 1985; Proença, 1979). Difficulties have also been encountered in relation to implementing common work programmes among residential staff (Jorge, 1985). Other serious problems which undermine the quality of residential and foster services include the long waiting periods for admission, together with the complexity and seeming intractability of some of the problems presented by the children and families served. These difficulties appear to be related to the large numbers of children cared for, the protracted length of many placements, the lack of community alternatives to residential and foster care, and the low level of involvement by birth families.

From a study carried out by Calheiros (1991), in which a questionnaire was given to social workers and psychologists, it is also possible to draw conclusions about the deficiencies related to care practices in residential homes. Those interviewed highlighted the need to evaluate and improve methods of intervention, and the need for greater knowledge of the social reality of children separated from their biological families (Calheiros, 1991). A number of studies also indicate the need for intervention programmes designed to prevent the reception of children into residential care (Jorge, 1985), and for greater interaction between residential homes, families and the community (Guimarães and Iria, 1991).

However, the problems associated with residential care must be seen within the wider context of the macro-structure of social welfare provision. The success of any attempt to resolve the problems identified depends on the implementation of preventive social welfare policies aimed at increasing the capacity of vulnerable parents to provide adequate care for their children. At the same time, however, there is a need for reforms to ensure a higher degree of professional expertise on the part of the staff employed in residential and foster care and other measures aimed at improving the daily lives of the children looked after.

Characteristics of children in care The lack of adequate research on this topic means that the available data do not cover the whole of the subject group. This means that caution must be exercised in drawing conclusions from the limited number of studies undertaken. Most of the studies on the characteristics of children in residential and foster homes, refer to data obtained at the time of admission and during the period of placement. The methods used involve the analysis of children's case files (Bichão, 1989; Gersão, 1988; Proença, 1979; Vala, 1986), the Justice statistics published by the National Institute of Statistics and the Directorate of the Minors Tutelage Services (Gonçales, 1991), and the application of questionnaires (Gersão, 1988).

It appears that the majority of children under the age of 7 admitted to the residential and foster homes of the Social Action Service in Lisbon were abandoned. However, in recent years there has been a slight decrease in the number of children admitted for this reason

(Bichão, 1989; Gersão, 1988), which seems to be related to the increase in the number of children given up for adoption. Other factors associated with admission to care are imprisonment and illness (physical and mental) on the part of parents (Bichao, 1989; Vala, 1986), along with abuse and neglect (Bichão, 1989; Gersão, 1988; Vala, 1986).

Findings on the placement of youngsters aged between 9 and 16 years in homes administered by the Minors Tutelage Services, which are scattered around the country, reveal that three-quarters of such children were placed in residential care for· criminal offences (Gersão, 1988; Vala, 1986).

Requests for the admission of younger children to residential care are usually made by social workers employed in the community or by agencies such as general hospitals, maternity hospitals and the police (Bichão, 1989; Gersão, 1988). Hardly any such requests are made by parents (Bichão, 1989).

Requests which lead to placement by court order of youngsters who commit criminal offences, or who manifest serious behavioural problems, are usually made by the police (Gersão, 1988; Vala, 1986). Parents are responsible for making just under one-third of such requests (Vala, 1986).

Socio-demographic data show that a slightly higher percentage of male than female children are separated from their families (Bichão, 1989). Further, over three-quarters of the youngsters placed by order of the courts are boys (Gersão, 1988; Vala, 1986), who tend to come from the major urban centres.

With respect to age on separation, half of children admitted up to the age of 7 are under 2 years old (Bichão, 1989). Furthermore, in 1988 a little over half of the children who were admitted to care having been abandoned, or because they were in danger, were under 6 years of age (Bichão, 1989; Gersão, 1988). Some 60 per cent of youngsters committed to care by the courts in 1986 were aged over 13 years (Vala, 1986).

The problems characteristically associated with children in residential homes seem to be related to difficulties in behaviour, socio-cognitive and affective development, psycho-social integration (Jorge, 1985), lack of progress at school (Gersão, 1988; Gonçalves, 1981; Guimarães and Iria, 1991), and difficulties in moving toward an adult identity. However, there is a need for more longitudinal research and comparative studies of the psychological and social variables involved. Such studies should monitor the development of youngsters into adulthood and evaluate the contribution made by residential and foster care.

Although there is no objective data on the school performance of children and young people in residential care, most of them complete the compulsory period of schooling (which in Portugal is 9 years) and some go on to obtain college and university degrees. The data on young people placed in correctional homes are not very encouraging. A considerable percentage can read and write, but few progress beyond the compulsory period of schooling (Gonçalves, 1991; Guimarães and Iria, 1991).

The family characteristics associated with the separation of children from their biological parents include : material deprivation (Gersão, 1988); marital break-down and prolonged absence on the part of parents (Vala, 1986); single-parenthood (Gersão, 1988); serious conflict between children and their parents, other adults or institutions (Vala, 1986; Gersão, 1988); maltreatment (Bichão, 1985); parent-related problems; large families (Vala, 1986); and problems concerning the family's socio-professional and cultural integration.

Current trends

Over the last decade there has been ongoing and lively discussion about how best to safeguard the welfare of children in vulnerable families. This debate has centred on the question of whether the possible negative effects of growing up in families where there is a lack of adequate basic care, outweigh the adverse effects of separation from the primary attachment figure. Studies have highlighted the negative short- and long-term effects of separation on the development and behaviour of children.

In response to such findings, various forms of preventive intervention have been developed at the individual, family and community levels with a view to tackling the problems which lead to separation. In addition, attempts have been made to improve the quality of support services for children and families in need.

Research has an important role to play in providing information about the scope of the problems confronting social welfare practitioners, analysing their causes, and studying the effects of social welfare interventions on children and families. This kind of research can inform the development of more effective and efficient social welfare interventions. In closing we will outline our own contribution towards this goal.

The socio-psychological factors associated with maltreatment, neglect and the separation of children from their birth families Within a community prevention perspective, we intend to study all the factors associated with the process of separation. In so doing, we hope to clarify the relationship between the global and specific variables, external and internal, within the different systems (children, families, and the community) and evaluate the complex interaction between the internal capacities of individuals, types of personal coping skills, life events and social networks. The variables that will studied include: social experience; social mobility; stressful life events; lifestyles; type, adequacy and level of use of formal and informal social support; and the characteristics and abilities of parents and children. It will also be important to examine the nature of parent-child relationships, parenting styles, and the beliefs and values of the parents.

The study is being carried out in a Lisbon community which has the highest recorded levels of separation and maltreatment in Portugal. The subject group comprises some 200 families of children up to the age of 15 years.

The first phase of the research project will involve an attempt to study the characteristics of the subject group in order to obtain an experimental and a control group. This will be followed by an intensive study of sub-samples with a view to formulating hypotheses and identifying the specific variables that will be examined.

During the third phase, different methods of evaluation will be used (e.g. semi-structured interviews and paper and pencil instruments) to study the whole of the sample group.

The project should contribute towards a better understanding of the social action resources of the community that can be utilised to minimise the problems associated with the separation of children from their birth parents. The study will also help in creating alternative programmes that will benefit vulnerable families within the context of prevention and community intervention.

Life history and psycho-social integration of individuals following discharge from residential and foster care There has been considerable doubt as to whether placement in long-term residential or foster care is an appropriate answer to the needs of separated children, even though a substantial number of children and young people are accommodated in such settings.

In some quarters, long-term residential or foster care has been rejected in favour of other options, such as the reunification of children with their birth parents or adoption. According to this view, residential and foster care should be used only as a time-limited tool in permanency planning.

Others have argued in favour of long-term residential or foster care as a desirable option in some situations, especially when the crisis within the family which resulted in separation remains unresolved, therefore prolonging the child's stay in care. Although the duration of placements continues to be a controversial issue, the problem also has much to do with the variable quality of substitute care. High standards of care are essential to facilitate recovery from the accumulated negative effects not only of separation, but also of the long and successive periods of substitute care which often form part of the life histories of the children concerned.

Research on the effects of growing up in foster and residential care is inconclusive, but findings do raise questions regarding the variety of untested assumptions currently guiding service delivery.

More intensive examination is required of the different types of placement and their short- and long-term impact on children, as they vary with socio-demographic factors, reasons for placement, developmental level, life history before, during and after the placement, contact with the biological family, preparation for leaving care, and the use of services and social networks in the post-discharge period.

To this end, we are carrying out research on children in residential and foster homes run by the 'Santa Casa da Misericórdia de Lisboa'. The young people involved in the study are aged between 15 and 25 years, and may be separated into the following three groups : (i) those who still use the services; (ii) those who have been rehabilitated with their birth families; and, (iii) those who have gained full independence.

During the first phase of the research project, evaluation methods will include the analysis of data from the children's case files (e.g. information about socio-demographic factors, family and development history, behaviour, etc.) and interviews with professional staff who work, or worked, with the youngsters. During a second phase, we intend to collect information about socio-psychological and academic and/or professional variables.

Our findings should enable us to identify needs, and develop new policies and practice guidelines with the aim of improving services for separated children.

References

Amaro, F. (1988), *Crianças maltratadas, negligenciadas ou praticando a mendicidade, I, Cadernos do CEJ, Gabinete de Estudos Jurídico-Sociais*, Ministério da Justiça, Lisboa.

Anuário Estatístico de 1984 a 1989, INE, Lisboa.

Bichão, S. (1989), *Análise das admissões de crianças na Divisão de Acolhimento Socio-Educativo do Serviço de Acção Social*, Santa Casa da Misericórdia de Lisboa.

Calheiros, M. (1991), *Avaliação dos problemas, expectativas, necessidades e intervenção dos técnicos do Serviço de Acção Social*, Divisão de Estudos e Planeamento, Santa Casa da Misericórdia de Lisboa.

Castro, M. and Calado, R. (1990), 'Anenoria Fiarice - Peritagem Psicológica - Tribunal de Menores de Lisboa, ano de 1989', *Infância e Juventude*, Outurbro - Dezembro, n° 4, DGSTM, Lisboa.

David, M. (1989), *Le placement familial - de la pratique a la théorie*, Les Editions ESF, Paris.

Gersão, E. (1988), 'Estudos de casos de menores carecidos de apoio urgente detectados em Lisboa e Porto' in *Crianças maltratadas, negligenciadas ou praticando a mendicidade*, II, Cadernos do CEJ, Gabinete de Estudos Jurídico-Sociais, Ministério da Justiça, Lisboa.

Goldstein, J., Freud, A. and Solnit, A. (1980), *Dans l'intéret de l'enfant? Vers un nouveau statut de l'enfance*, Les Editions ESF, Paris.

Gonçalves, I. (1991), *Delinquência juvenil : Caracterização do caso Português e reflexões para a implementação de programas de prevenção*, F.P.C.E. de Lisboa.

Guimarães e Iria (1991), *Estabelecimentos Tutelares de Menores em Portugal - que futuro par a este presente?*, Provedoria da Justiça, Lisboa.

Jason, L.A., Thompson, D., and Rose, T. (1986), 'Methodological Issues in Prevention', in A. Barry, E. Edelstein and L. Michelson (Eds), *Handbook in Prevention*, Plenum Press, New York.

Jorge, P. (1975), *Reflexão sobre a situação actual dos Internatos Infantis da Misericórdia*, Santa Casa da Misericórdia de Lisboa.

Jorge, P. (1985), *O possível e o necessário - Algumas reflexões sobre a Educação em Internato*, Santa Casa da Misericórdia de Lisboa.

Kline, D. and Overstreet, M. (1972), *Foster Care of Children*, Columbia University Press, New York.

Maior, R. (1869), *As finanças e a mortalidade dos expostos em Portugal*, Santa Casa da Misericórdia de Lisboa.

Oliveira, C. (1956), *Nota breve sobre a Santa Casa da Misericórdia de Lisboa*, Santa Casa da Misericórdia de Lisboa.

Pinto, G. (1828), *Exame crítico e histórico sobre os direitos estabelecidos pela legislação antiga e moderna, tanto pátria como subsídiária, e das nações mais vizinhas e cultas relativamente aos Expostos ou Engeitados*, Typographia da Academia Real das Sciências.

Proença e colaboradores (1979), *Estudo dos Internatos*, Santa Casa da Misericórdia de Lisboa.

193

Proença e Rodrigues (1984), *Caracterização dos utentes do sector de acolhimento socio-educativo*, Santa Casa da Misericórdia da Lisboa.

Ribeiro, V. (1902), *A Santa Casa da Misericórdia de Lisboa*, Typographia da Academia Real das Sciencias.

Vala, J. (1986), *Caracterização dos menores internados nos estabelecimentos dos Serviços Tutelares de Menores*, Presidência da República, Instituto de Pesquisa Social Damião de Gois, Programa de Investigação sobre Marginalidade e Violência em Portugal, Núcleo de Estudos Sociais, Lisboa.

Veloso, E., Lopes, M., Matias, M., and Santos, M. (1986), *Marvila : Contribuição para um diagnóstico social*, Santa Casa da Misericórdia de Lisboa.

10 Spain

F. Casas

Recent political history : Spain has had a democratic Constitution since 1978. This created what has become known as the 'State of Autonomies' - a decentralised political system with a Parliament for every region, as distinct from a Federal State. Most 'Autonomous Communities' have child protection laws based on Spanish law, and are responsible for the administration of child protection services in their region.
Geographical Size : 504,750 Km²
Principal industries : Tourism, construction and agriculture
Date of EC membership : 1986
Total number of inhabitants in 1991 : 39,433,942
Age of majority : Civil : 18; Penal : 16 years
Number of people under the age of civil majority : 9,278,487
Number of children and young people (31.12.89) :   in residential care :   18,626 (protection)
          847 (reform)
         in foster care :   3,203

The nature of residential and foster care provision

Any discussion of residential and foster care in Spain must be set within the context of the recently created democratic state. This transformation means that current child welfare provision has been influenced by many recent political, legal, and social changes.

In legal terms, two crucial changes occurred: first, the establishment, and subsequent development, of the Spanish Constitution in 1978; second, the introduction of Law 21/87, which reformed procedures concerning the custody of children, particulary those relating to adoption and fostering.

From a political standpoint, the crucial event was the transfer of responsibility for children to the Autonomous Communities. The Spanish Constitution created what has become known as the 'State of Autonomies', a form of political organisation which goes further than a purely decentralised State in that each of the 17 Autonomous Communities has its own Parliament. In practice, however, the degree of power devolved to the Autonomous Communities varies considerably, and their actual development has been markedly unequal.

Beyond the particular situation of each Autonomous Community, and in spite of the fact that the new Law on 'Bases de Régimen Local' 1985 gives control of social services to the local authorities (town and provincial councils), it is necessary to highlight the considerable geographical disparity in the actual development of services for children in each area of Spain. This reflects differences in the political priority given to child welfare, and major inequalities in the availability of human and material resources.

Sociologically speaking, it is not possible to speak of a precise 'historic moment' when the current pattern of services took shape. Recent years have witnessed many changes in the child care system. Although improving the quality of provision has been an exasperatingly slow process, there is no doubt that progress has occurred. Positive change began in the early 1970s - that is, before the important political and legal changes referred to took place - and was driven by a wide range of ideas, influenced by varying outside trends, and originated in different parts of Spain. Practitioners or teams of professionals were the real pioneers of the major changes. Such teams organised themselves at local level in order to secure better conditions and treatment for children in residential care. Sometimes there was a high level of communication between the main participants, and sometimes mutual ignorance and even serious disagreements between them.

The contrasting nature of the approach to change adopted in different geographical areas led to regional differences in professional child care cultures which, in turn, have considerably affected the nature of current service provision. It may also be noted that the lack of defined regulations for the education and training of some of those who work with children with social difficulties in Spain (for example, social educators) has handicapped the development of services. This leads us to the conclusion that we are still in the difficult process of establishing an extensively agreed professional culture that would help to facilitate the changes in child care provision that are required. At present, therefore, it must be said that the pattern of child care provision in Spain, despite increasingly convergent trends, is still very uneven.

A similar point can be made about our knowledge base in this field. We still lack sufficient data for the whole of Spain. The reasons for this shortcoming include: first, the tradition (understandable, given the historical context) of data collection focused on one territory; second, the fact that not all the Autonomous Communities have made the same effort to obtain and publish data on the circumstances of children in need; third, the lack of a standardised system of data collection; and, finally, the low priority given to research on child welfare within the context of the low budget for social science research in Spain.

It seems that the small amount of national data so far produced is mainly due to the persistence of a limited number of organisations and individual researchers who have worked against the tide. One such organisation that deserves special mention is the 'Centro de Estudios del Menor' (C.E.M.) of the Directorate-General for the Legal Protection of Minors.

In view of all that has been said, it is not possible in this account to offer a detailed description of residential and foster care in Spain. To merely cover the regional and local differences which exist would require considerably more space than a single chapter. Therefore, it is proposed to present only a broad outline of the points that the author considers most important in order to put recent developments into context, and to establish a foundation for future research on child welfare, with particular reference to foster and residential care.

Historical antecedents

During Franco's dictatorship, there were only two possible ways of responding to the needs of children with social and family problems in Spain. Such children could either simply be left at home, with aid from charities in a very limited number of cases, or be placed in residential care. This was despite the fact, as numerous commentators have pointed out (e.g. Giménez-Salinas, 1981), that the law on the Custody of Minors 1948 made other alternatives possible.

The 1948 law served to reinforce a major dichotomy in the care of separated children in that it introduced different procedures for those in need of protection, on the one hand, and young offenders, on the other. The current age of majority in criminal law is 16. However, child protection orders could, in certain cases, remain in force until the young person's 18th birthday, which coincides with the age of majority in civil law.

Placing a child in foster care involved a lengthy and complex legal process, which meant that it was only feasible in a very small number of cases. This situation did not change until 1987, when a new law was passed. Further, residential homes tended to be large, impersonal, institutions, characterised by authoritarian regimes based on religious dogma, well into the 1970's.

However, influenced by ideas from other western countries, those who had contact with children in residential institutions began to criticise this state of affairs. Two groups of professionals led the way. The first comprised those working in the field of residential child care or social education (which at that time was called 'special education' in Spain); the second consisted of social workers in the primary health care system.

The first group or movement was informed by ideas that entered Spain through Catalonia, and which were brought by people educated in the training colleges for workers in special education in the south of France. In 1969, the first such Spanish college was founded in Barcelona (Centre de Formació d'Educadors Especialitzats, 1978). The ideological core of this movement was the principle of 'normalisation', which originated in the Scandinavian countries at the end of the 1950's (Monereo, 1985). Parenthetically, it is interesting to note that 'normalisation' had, in effect, been practiced under a different name in Catalonia at the beginning of the century by Pedragosa (Santolaria, 1984).

However, the new ideas adopted by social workers in the field of primary health care came from diverse sources. The notion of community based social welfare services was one of the ideas which attracted the greatest following, and was borrowed from Latin American writers. Among the most important of these authors was Ander-Egg (Casas, 1990).

Gradually, the two movements referred to, along with others which originated in psychology and the health sciences, began to coalesce. The work of Paulo Freire (see, for example, Ortega, 1978) represents a prototype for the confluence of ideas drawn from education and social work. By the beginning of the 1980's, the new ideas resulted in calls for legislative change, led by those who were critical of traditional approaches to child welfare (Gonzalez Zorrilla, 1985).

The first attempt to reform the system of child care for children with family and social problems occurred in the Catalonian city of Barcelona in 1977. This entailed a programme to improve the quality of life for the 700 children in the city's three residential institutions (Centre de Formació d'Educadors Especialitzats, 1978; Ajuntament de Barcelona, 1980 and 1983). Shortly after this, reform programmes were introduced in Valencia, Navarre, the Basque Country, and in other parts of Catalonia (Casas, 1981; Generalitat Valenciana, 1981;

Diputació de Barcelona, 1982; Gobierno Vasco, 1985; Diputació de Valencia, 1986).

These early reform programmes addressed the urgent need to improve the quality of day-to-day care in residential homes for abused and neglected children and young offenders, and the necessity of revising the process of admission to residential care, beginning with the network of community based or field social work services. However, it took longer to establish the case for non-residential alternatives for young offenders, such as probation (Funes, 1984; Fransoy, Bellido, Funes and Gonzalez, 1986), and the equally pressing need to expand foster care services (Generalitat de Catalunya, 1985; Caritas Española, 1985; Gobierno Vasco, 1987).

The present legal framework

With the implementation of Act 21/87, the removal of abused and neglected children from their families and into foster or residential care must proceed through the appropriate administrative body in each Autonomous Community. Moreover, the Court must be immediately informed of the measures adopted. The appropriate administrative body, usually a Directorate General for child welfare services, is also responsible for coordinating the resources, both public and private, available in its territory.

Thus, for each Autonomous Community there is a single route by which children may enter care. Further, the new law introduced the concept of 'automatic guardian' (Ministerio de Asuntos Sociales, 1991a), which allows administrative measures to be taken without recourse to the courts, thus speeding up the process of admitting children to care. However, the parents of the child have a right of appeal against the decision of the administrative body. Such cases are presided over either by the Judge of the Court of First Instance or the Family Judge. The latter are not found outside the large cities. The new Law also makes the fostering of children less complex and easier to arrange than was previously the case, and provides for pre-adoption fostering.

It should also be mentioned that the law stipulates that the assessment of child care cases requiring administrative or legal action should be carried out by expert inter-disciplinary teams. Some Autonomous Communities have created a special network of such teams, which include, for example, the E.A.I.A. (Teams for the Care of Children and Adolescents) in Catalonia (Generalitat de Catalunya, 1988) and the C.A.I. (Centres for Child Care) teams in Madrid.

Several Autonomous Communities have developed their own legislation based on Law 21/87, with the aim of formulating detailed procedures for protecting abused and neglected children in their territories (Ministerio de Asuntos Sociales, 1989).

By contrast with children in need of protection, youngsters who have committed offences are sent directly before a judge. This procedure is still based on the law for the Custody of Minors of 1948. The only important recent change in the juvenile justice system was the creation of special Juvenile Judges who specialise exclusively in hearings for young offenders. In addition, special police teams who deal with young offenders have been created within the national police force (the G.R.U.M.E.), and in some of the Autonomous Communities.

A current development which seems to presage fundamental change in the treatment of young offenders, is the proposal for the reform of several chapters of the 1948 Law that was put before the Spanish Parliament at the beginning of 1992. In 1991, one of the chapters in question was even declared illegal by the Constitutional Courts. Many hope to see a new law passed that will render the present juvenile justice system less dependant on legal procedures, and will enlarge the range of non-custodial alternatives available to judges.

Some overall data

According to official statistics, from 1976 to 1989 between 16,000 and 18,000 proceedings were taken annually against young offenders throughout Spain. Table 10.1 shows that the numbers of children in corrective custody rose steadily between 1985 and 1987. However, the total number of children detained in remand homes has decreased over recent years. On 31 December, 1989, some 847 young people were held in detention centres, of which only about 5 per cent were girls (see the report of the Spanish Ombudsman : Defensor del Pueblo, 1991).

Table 10.1

Children in corrective custody in Spain 1985-1987

Year	Cases opened and reopened	Sentences pronounced	Accumulated at end of year
1985	16,869	16,070	8,957
1986	17,614	16,395	10,311
1987	16,696	14,887	12,125

Source: I.N.E., (National Statistics Institute). Estadisticas de los Tribunales de Menores, 1985-1987

It is more difficult to specify the number of children in care under protective measures. This is because of the variety of means which existed for taking children into care prior to 1987. Hence, statistics from the Courts for the Custody of Minors represent only part of the total figure. Table 10.2 shows that during 1984, 1985 and 1986 these Courts heard 4,522, 5,240 and 6,487 cases respectively, of which about 40 per cent resulted in children being placed in residential care (Ministerios de Asuntos Sociales, 1991b). Table 10.2 also gives the overall or accumulated numbers of children accommodated in residential homes between 1984 and 1986 by virtue of orders made by the Courts. However, we do not have reliable figures for the number of children taken into care through the 'Committees for the Protection of Minors' (Juntas de Proteción de Menores), the social services, and charitable organisations, which together deal with a much higher number of cases than the Courts.

Table 10.2

Minors under 16 in protective custody 1984-1986

Year	Cases opend and reopened	Sentences pronounced	Accumulated at end of year
1984	4,522	3,783	12,330
1985	5,240	4,078	12,003
1986	6,487	5,339	13,651

Source: I.N.E., (National Statistics Institute). Estadisticas de los Tribunales Tutelares de Menores, 1984-1986.

The statistics for Spain as a whole based on Act 21/87 must be calculated from data on each of the 17 constituent Autonomous Communities. This means that the system for producing statistics is complex, and it has so far proved unreliable. For a majority of cases, the administrative procedure of 'automatic custody' is the prior step to placement in foster or residential care. Table 10.3 shows the number of automatic custodies taken in 1988 and 1989.

Table 10.3
Automatic custody of children in Spain (1988-1989)

Year	Automatic custodies*
1988	2,574
1989	2,853

* The concept of automatic custody is defined in Article 172 of the Civil Code using the wording of Act 21/1987 of November 11.

Source: Dirección General de Protección Juridica del Menor.

Provisional data show a gradual increase in the numbers of children fostered and adopted, and a corresponding gradual decline in the number of children placed in residential care. Table 10.4 shows that in 1989, some 1,090 children were placed in foster care through administrative decisions, and that there were 553 proposed legal fosterings (Ministerios de Asuntas Sociales, 1991b). Table 10.5 shows that the number of adoption orders made in 1989 more than doubled the figure for the previous year. On 31 December, 1989 a total of 3,203 children in Spain were in foster care, and 24,406 children were accommodated in residential homes because they were considered to be in need of protection. Just under two-thirds of the latter (62.55 per cent) were placed in publically administered homes, whilst the remainder were in privately run establishments (Defensor del Pueblo, 1991).

Table 10.4
Fosterings in Spain 1988-1989

Year	Fosterings*		
	Administrative	Legal	
		Proposed	Orders
1988	725	385	119
1989	1,090	553	280

* The concept of fostering is defined in Article 173 of the Civil code, based on Act 21/1987.

Source: Dirección General de Protección Juridica del Menor.

Table 10.5
Adoptions in Spain 1988-1989

Year	Adoptions of Spanish Children		Adoptions of non-Spanish Children
	Proposed	Order	
1988	596	317	93
1989	1,085	812	94

Source: Dirección General de Protección Juridica del Menor.

Over the last 10 years the average size of residential homes has been considerably reduced with the introduction of much smaller living units. However, the process of such change has been very uneven across Autonomous Communities. In some regions (e.g. Catalonia, the Basque Country and Valencia), there are hardly any large institutions left, and there has been a normalisation of daily life for children in residential care in these areas. A number of Autonomous Communities have introduced legislation on the quality of residential child care provision. However, in other parts of Spain (e.g. the Canary Islands, Castile and Leon, Extremadura and Galicia), the process of reform has only just begun.

As previously indicated, a large proportion of children in residential care are accommodated in privately run establishments. Most of these institutions receive a public subsidy of a fixed sum per day and per place occupied. No official figures are available on the nature of these payments, although we do know that they vary greatly across Autonomous Communities.

With regard to foster care, there is currently a debate about whether payments should be made to short-term foster parents. Those in favour of financial allowances argue that they are necessary to cover the expenses involved in temporary foster placements, so as to ensure that the foster families do not suffer additional strain due to financial hardship (Gobierno Vasco, 1987 and 1989).

An important new development in child protection is the increasing deployment by the Autonomous Communities of inter-disciplinary teams. Some of these teams specialise in the assessment of cases prior to decisions being taken as to the form of help required. Once such decisions have been made, the teams then play a supportive role in the programme of intervention undertaken (Generalitat de Catalunya, 1988). In some areas, there are also special support teams for professionals working with children in residential care. Several parts of Spain also have teams which specialise in the selection and supervision of foster families.

It appears that the inter-disciplinary teams referred to suffer from the fact that this approach is in its infancy in Spain. Consequently, the workers involved have no established body of knowledge to which they may refer. Naturally, this hinders the development of expertise. At the same time, some teams are simply overwhelmed by the sheer scale of their workload. Concern has also been expressed by public authorities about the difficulties associated with the establishment of new teams. This owes a good deal to the lack of adequate training for child welfare professionals.

Future prospects

During the last 15 years the expansion and improvement of the substitute child care system has been accompanied by attempts to develop a comprehensive framework of community based social services aimed at preventing, recognising and responding to child abuse and neglect. Whilst this goal has not been fully realised, the *Plan Concertado* (Adopted Plan) sponsored by the Ministry of Social Affairs, has allowed considerable progress to be made in the past 3 years. As a consequence, some of the gaps in provision have been reduced.

Steps have also been taken to ensure that child welfare professionals are equipped with the knowledge and skills to identify and respond to situations in which children are at risk, and to monitor and evaluate their interventions. The 'Centro de Estudios del Menor' has initiated professional training courses, and has been active in promoting the dissemination of knowledge to child welfare practitioners (Ministerio de Asuntos Sociales, 1992b). The Autonomous Communities of Catalonia and Castile and Leon also have their own training centres. These play an important role in facilitating the exchange of knowledge and skills among residential and field social workers.

Although the resources devoted to research in Spain continue to be very limited, the evidence pointing to the lack of information about the circumstances of vulnerable children has prompted a number of organisations to work towards improving the routine collection of such data (Casas, 1989; Ministerio de Asuntos Sociales, 1991b).

A further encouraging recent development is the proposed Children's Rights Act which, if introduced, would provide a general framework for improving the quality of life for children in Spain.

Finally, attempts have been made to increase public awareness of child abuse and the social needs of children at risk. In early 1991, the Ministry of Social Affairs launched a media campaign using the slogan 'Listen to them'. Several non-governmental organisations, most notably parents' associations, have followed this up to ensure that the objectives of the original campaign are achieved.

Research on residential and foster care

As previously indicated, research on foster and residential care is still very limited in Spain. However, growing concern about child abuse is proving to be an indirect stimulus for research on substitute care. A large number of conferences have already been organised with a view to promoting the exchange of knowledge and experience between practitioners and researchers, and a number of articles on child abuse have been published (e.g. Montané, 1990).

Financial support for research on foster and residential care has come from central government in the form of the Directorate-General for the Legal Protection of Minors of the Ministry of Social Affairs, a number of Autonomous Governments, and a few regional and town councils. Research has also been sponsored by private bodies such as savings banks.

205

Despite the limited amount of research carried out in Spain as a whole, measures designed to improve the quality of residential care and to restructure the community based framework of services for children in certain territories have often been informed by fairly comprehensive research studies (see, for example: Casas, 1981; Diputació de Barcelona, 1982; E.D.I.S, 1982; Grandal, 1984; Pareja, 1984; Miranda, 1985; Lopez et al., 1985; Gobierno de La Rioja, 1986).

However, the research that has been carried out has tended to be descriptive rather than explanatory (see, for example, Agelet et al., 1981; Generalitat de Catalunya, 1985; Gobierno Vasco, 1989; Ministerio de Asuntos Sociales, 1991c). Hence, measures are required to encourage academic research on foster and residential care. So far, research carried out in the universities has mainly involved individual initiatives, including dissertations undertaken for degrees (Casas, 1984) and doctoral theses (Amorós, 1987; Trigo, 1989; Ripol-Millet, 1990). The university sector has been responsible for pioneering research on the social climates of residential homes, which provided the subject matter of the first doctoral thesis on residential care (Fernández, 1991).

Although the 'Centro de Estudios del Menor' (C.E.M.) does not employ a research team of its own, it has sponsored several extensive research programmes on child cruelty, six of which were begun in 1991. Three of these programmes were carried out through agreements with universities (Madrid, Salamanca and the Basque Country), while the other three were carried out by researchers employed by private institutions. The C.E.M. has also sponsored research on adult perceptions of children and their problems (see, for example, Aguinaga and Comas, 1991), whilst the 'Centro d'Estudis Juridics i Formació Especialitzada' de Catalonia has funded research and published several papers, mainly on young offenders (see for example, Egea, 1989; Del Rincón and Santolaria, 1989).

Moreover, the C.E.M. has started to publish a 'Directory of Studies and Research on Children' (Ministerio de Asuntos Sociales, 1992), which provides an overview of recent research. Only 8 research projects on fostering are included in the Directory, whereas there are 18 on residential care. Apart from research sponsored by the C.E.M., the majority of research projects on foster and residential care are carried out in individual Autonomous Communities, particularly Catalonia, the region of Valencia, the Basque Country, La Rioja, Andalusia and Madrid.

References

Agelet, F., Calvo, R., Carretero, A., Casas, F., Flotats, J., Majado, F., Paès, M., Pi, R., Serranos, C. and Diez, A. (1980), 'El treball de l'educador especialitzat a un barri perifèric de Barcelona: Equip d'Educadors del Collectiu Infantil Canyelles', *III. Jornades sobre la prevenció i el tractament de la delinqüència juvenil a Catalunya*, Barcelona, 29 November.

Aguinaga, J., and Comas, D. (1991), *Infancia y adolescencia: La mirada de los adultos*, Centro de Publicaciones. Ministerio Asuntos Sociales, Madrid.

Ajuntament de Barcelona (1980), *Una nova alternativa de serveis per a la infància*, Area de Serveis Socials. Col. lecció 'Serveis Socials' 2, Barcelona.

Ajuntament de Barcelona (1983), *Els Centres municipals d'infància*, Area de Servicios Sociales, Barcelona.

Alvira, F. and Canteras, A. (1985), *Delincuencia y marginación juvenil*. Public. de Juventud y Sociedad, Barcelona, 1986.

Amorós, P. (1987), *La adopción y el acogimiento familiar*, Narcea, Madrid.

Amorós, P. (1988), *Situación actual de los servicios de adopción y acogimiento familiar, 1988*, Centro de Estudios del Menor. M.A.S., Madrid, 1990.

Arana, J. and Carrasco, J.L. (1980), *Niños desasistidos del ambiente familiar*, Karpos, Madrid.

Berjano, E. (1986), *Drogas y delincuencia: Población de alto riesgo*, Dir. Gral. Serveis Socials, Generalitat Valenciana, Valencia.

Bonal, R., and Costa, J. (1979), *La delinqüència juvenil avui: el cas de Mataró*, Publicacions de la Fundació Jaume Bofill, Barcelona.

Bueno, A., Cantó, N, Cascales, C., Galindo, D., Moullor, F., Olmos, J., Rives, A. and Segura, M.A. (APISMA-GESE) (1981), *Marginación social del menor*, Publicaciones Caja Ahorros Alicante y Murcia, Alicante.

Canales, R. and Navarro, F.J. (1981), *La marginación social del menor*, Dir. Gral. de Juventud y Promoción Socio-cultural, Madrid.

Caritas Española (1978), 'Inadaptación y delincuencia juvenil', *Documentación Social, 33-34*, (Monográfico), dic-marzo.

Caritas Española (1985), 'Menores marginados', *Documentación Social, 59*, (Monográfico).

Casas, F. (1981), 'Política de infancia y adolescencia planteada a partir de la Direcció General de Serveis Socials de la Generalitat de Catalunya. El nacimiento de las Comunidades Infantiles', *Cuadernos INAS*, 5, enero-marzo, pp. 61-65.

Casas, F. (1982), 'Informe de l'actual normativa, estructura i recomanacions sobre l'àmbit de la infància i l'adolescencia, orientat a la confecció del Mapa de Serveis Socials de Catalunya', Dir. Gral Serveis Socials, Generalitat de Catalunya, Barcelona.

Casas, F. (1983), 'Les noies acollides a equipaments residencials a Catalunya', *Quaderns de Serveis Socials*, 3, pp. 40-45.

Casas, F. (1984), *Els internaments d'infants a Catalunya*, Obra Social de la Caixa de Barcelona, Barcelona, 1985.

Casas, F. (1987), 'Informe sobre la incidència dels fets delictius relacionats amb menors a la ciutat de Barcelona', Comissió Tècnica de Seguretat Ciutadana de l'Ajuntament de Barcelona, Barcelona.

Casas, F. (1988), 'Las instituciones residenciales para la atención de chicos y chicas en dificultades socio-familiares: apuntes para una discusión', *Menores*, 10, pp. 37-50.

Casas, F. (Coord.) (1989). *Infància i risc: Dades Bàsiques*, ICASS, Generalitat de Catalunya, Barcelona.

Casas, F. (1990). 'La psicología social comunitaria en Cataluña', in G. Musitu, E. Berjano, and J.R. Bueno, *Psicología Comunitaria*, Nau Llibres, Valencia.

Casas, F. and Biosca, L. (Coord.) (1985), *Els centres diürns a les comarques barcelonines*, Diputació de Barcelona, Barcelona.

Casas, F., Flotats, J.M. and Pi, R. (1984), 'Una experiència pedagògica: La Comunitat Infantil de Gavà', Memoria de convalidación del título de Educador Especializado, Barcelona, Unpublished.

Casas, F., Fransoy, P. and Rueda, J.M. (1983), *Proposta de treball en els serveis d'atenció al menor*, Federació de Municipis de Catalunya, Barcelona. Policopiat.

Centre de Formació d'Educadors Especialitzats (1978), *Els Col. lectius Infantils: Memòria curs 77-78*, Centre d'Educadors, Barcelona.

Colectivo I.O.E. (De Prada, M.A., Actis, W. and Pereda, C.) (1989), 'Infancia moderna y desigualdad social', *Documentación Social, 74* (Monográfico), Enero-marzo 1989.

De Paul, J. (Ed.) (1987), *Los malos tratos y el abandono infantil*, Servicio Ed., Univ País Vasco, S. Sebastián.

Del Rincón, D. and Santolaria, F. (1989), *Análisis de la vivencia y evolución de un grupo de menores que han sido objeto de medidas de internamiento*, Departament de Justicia, Generalitat de Catalunya, Barcelona.

Defensor del Pueblo (1991), *Menores*, Publicaciones del Defensor del Pueblo, Madrid.

Diputació de Barcelona (1982), *Informe i proposta de reestructuració de les Llars A.G. de Mundet*, Barcelona.

Diputación de Valencia (1986), *Una alternativa: Centros para menores marginados*, Institut d'Assistència i Serveis Socials, Valencia.

Diputación Foral de Alava (1988), *Menores marginados en Alava*, Departamento de Bienestar Social, Vitoria.

E.D.I.S. (1982), *Estudio sobre la situación y problemática de los niños de La Rioja*, Logroño, Ciclostil.

Egea, J. (1989), *La protecció de menors a Catalunya. Els diferents règims de protecció*, Departament de Justicia, Generalitat de Catalunya, Barcelona.

Escartí, A. and Musitu, G. (1987), *El niño abandonado en la Comunidad Valenciana*, Dir. Gral. Serveis Socials, Generalitat Valenciana, Valencia.

Fernandez del Valle, Jorge (1991), 'Evaluación de contextos en centros de protección de menores', Universidad Complutense, Departamento de Psicologia Biologica y de la Salud, Madrid, Unpublished doctoral these.

Fransoy, P., Bellido, J., Funes, J. and Gonzalez, C. (1986), *Els nens de carrer*, I.C.E.S.B, Barcelona.

Funes, J. (1984), *La nova delinqüència infantil i juvenil*, Edicions 62, Barcelona.

Gimenez-Salinas, E.(1981), *Delincuencia juvenil y control social*, Circulo Editor Universo, Barcelona.

Generalitat de Catalunya (1985), *Jornades d'Estudi i formulació de propostes d'actuació a Catalunya. Families acollidores*, 1984, Girona. Collecció Arnau d'Escala, Generalitat de Catalunya i Diputació de Girona, Girona.

Generalitat de Catalunya (1988), *Què són els E.A.I.A.?* Direcció General d'Atenció a la Infància, Barcelona.

Generalitat Valenciana (1981), *II Jornades sobre Menors Marginats*, Conselleria de Sanitat y S.S. D. Gral. Serveis Socials, Valencia.

Gobierno de La Rioja (1986), *Informe para la Comisión de relaciones con el Defensor del Pueblo y los Derechos Humanos sobre los Centros de protección de menores de La Rioja*, Gobierno de la Rioja, Logroño.

Gobierno Vasco (1985), *Hogares funcionales familiares*, Departamento de Trabajo, Vitoria.

Gobierno Vasco (1987), *Adopción, acogimiento familiar*, Servicio Central de Publicaciones, Vitoria.

Gobierno Vasco (1987b), *Principios básicos de actuación en el ámbito de los servicios sociales para la infancia y la juventud*, Servicio Central de Publicaciones, Vitoria.

Gobierno Vasco (1989), *Primeras Jornadas sobre adopción y acogimiento familiar*, Servicio Central de Publicaciones, Vitoria.

González Zorrilla, C. (1985), 'La justicia de menores en España, Epílogo a de Leo', *La justicia de menores*, Teide, Barcelona.

Grandal, M.I. (1984), *Centros provinciales de menores en Galicia: Cambio y evolución*, Diputación Provincial, La Coruña.

Guanter, P., Masó, J., and Parramón, E. (1990), *Les necessitats socials de la infància i l'adolescència a les comarques de Girona*, ICASS, Generalitat de Catalunya i Diputació de Girona, Girona.

Guerau de Arellano, F. and Trescents, A. (1987), *El educador de calle*, Rosselló Impr, Barcelona.

Inglès, A. (1991), *Els maltractaments infantils a Catalunya*, Dir. Gral. d'Atenció a la Infància. Generalitat de Catalunya, Barcelona.

López, J., et al. (1985), *Hogares funcionales: Una alternativa al internamiento para la integración social de menores marginados*, Diputación Provincial, Sevilla.

López Cabello, P. and Bergaretxe, G. (Coord.) (1987), *Menores institucionalizados en la Comunidad Autónoma del País Vasco*, Dep. Trabajo y Seg. Soc. Gobierno Vasco, Bilbao.

Marqués, J. (1986), *Acogimiento familiar y servicios sociales,* Diputació de Valencia, Valencia.

Ministerio de Asuntos Sociales (1989a), *Servicios Sociales, Leyes Autonómicas*, Centro de Publicaciones, Madrid.

Ministerio de Asuntos Sociales (1989b), *Adopción, Ley 21/87, Guía de aplicación y normativa de las Comunidades Autonomas*, Centro de Publicaciones.

Ministerio de Asuntos Sociales (1991a), *Adopción y acogimiento familiar, Ley 21/87, Guía de aplicacion,* Centro de Publicaciones, M.A.S., Madrid.

Ministerio de Asuntos Sociales (1991b), *Población menor de dieciocho años en España, Datos estadisticos generales 1991,* Centro de Publicaciones, M.A.S, Madrid.

Ministerio de Asuntos Sociales (1991c), *I Congreso Internacional Infancia y Sociedad. Bienestar y derechos sociales de la infancia,* Noviembre 1989, Direccion Gral. Protección Jurídica del Menor, Madrid.

Ministerio de Asuntos Sociales (1992), *Anuario de estudios e investigaciones de infancia en España*, Centro de Estudios del Menor, Dir. Gral. Protección Jurídica del Menor, Madrid.

Ministerio de Asuntos Sociales (1992b), *El Centro de Estudios del Menor,* Centro de Publicaciones, Ministerio de Asuntos Sociales, Madrid.

Ministerio de Justicia (1987), 'Adopción y acogimiento familiar', *Menores, 2*, (Monografico), marzo-abril 1987.

Miranda, M. J. (1985), *Factores de marginación social de niños y jovenes*, Instituto Regional de Estudios, Comunidad Autonoma, Madrid.

Monereo, C. (1985), 'Un análisis crítico de los conceptos vinculados a la integración escolar', *Siglo Cero, 101*, set-oct., 1985.

Martínez Shaw, C. (1986), 'L'assistència pública a la Barcelona Moderna', *L'Avenç*, març 1986.

Montané, M. J. (Coord.) (1990), 'Acogimiento Familiar', *Infancia y Sociedad, 6* (Monográfico).

Musitu, G., Escartí, A., Ruiperez, M.A. and Clemente, A. (1985), 'El niño institucionalizado: agresión y autoestima', Departament de Psicologia Social, Universitat de Valencia, Valencia, Policopiado.

Ortega, J. (1978), *Delincuencia, reformatorio y educación liberadora*, Zero, Madrid.

Pareja, M. C. (1984), *Investigación sobre las causas psicosociológicas del abandono infantil*, Diputación Provincial, Granada.

Ripol-Millet, A. and Rubiol, G. (1990), *El acogimiento familiar,* Centro de Publicaciones, Min. Asuntos Sociales, Madrid.

Sánchez Moro, C. and Pérez Peñasco, A. (1979), *El menor marginado (I) (II)*, Ministerio de Cultura y EDIS, Madrid.

Santolaria, F. (1984), *Reeducació social: L'obra pedagògica de Josep Pedragosa*, Departament de Justicia, Generalitat de Catalunya, Barcelona.

Trigo, J. (1989), *Deprivación socio-familiar e institucionalización de menores: Hacia una intervención psicosocial*, Universidad de Sevilla, Unpublished doctoral these.

Valverde, J.M. (1988), *El proceso de inadaptación social,* Popular, Madrid.

Vega, A. (1984), *Pedagogía terapéutica e inadaptados en Cataluña*, EU-Publicaciones y Edic. Univ. Barcelona, Barcelona.

Vega, A. and Casas, F. (1983), *Informe sobre servicios y centros de Cataluña dedicados a la atención de la infancia y la adolescencia con problemáticas socio-familiares*, Dir. Gral. Serveis Socials, Generalitat de Catalunya, Barcelona.

Ventosa, L. and Recolons, L. (1982), *La delinqüència juvenil a l'Hospitalet de Ll., 1976-1981*, Ajuntament de L'Hospitalet de Ll. y Obra Social de la Caixa de Barcelona, Barcelona.

Zabalza, A. (1989), 'Estrategias de intervención socioeducativa ante los inadaptados sociales: una reflexión desde la práctica de trabajo en pisos', *Menores*, 15, mayo - junio 1989, pp. 17-39.

11 The United Kingdom

R. Bullock

Recent political history : The United Kingdom comprises, England, Wales, Scotland and Northern Ireland. Each has its own legislation and administration within a framework agreed by the national government in London. Wales was unified with England in 1535, Northern Ireland was annexed in 1541 and Scotland joined in 1707. Policies in the 1980s encouraged devolution of power to each area and the establishment of separate assemblies, but in Northern Ireland, as a result of civil unrest, direct rule from London has replaced the provincial government since 1974.
Geographical Size : 244,100 Km².
Principal industries : 40 per cent of the gross national product comes from manufacturing and financial products, 30 per cent from tourism and public services and 18 per cent from energy, construction and transport. Forestery and agriculture account for only 1 per cent.
Date of EC membership : 1973.
Total number of inhabitants : 55.5 million.
Age of majority : 18 years.
Number of people under the age of majority : 13 million.
Number of children and young people : in residential care :

residential child care establishments :	15,000
boarding schools for children with special needs :	13,000
penal establishments :	1,000
in foster care :	40,000

The nature of residential and foster care provision

Like most things in the United Kingdom, services for children and families have long historical antecedents and reflect a preference for piece-meal reforms rather than radical policy shifts. This means that much of what exists today can only be understood in its wider context.

212

For example, present child-care services developed from the Poor Law which itself expanded to meet the lacuna left by the dissolution of the monasteries in 1539. Some features of the Poor Law system are still apparent today, such as in regional variations in policy and provision, in the separation of education from child welfare services and in discussions about the principle of less eligibility, namely that recipients of services should be no better off as a result of our intervention. Moreover, different parts of the United Kingdom have their own welfare histories, legislation and administrative systems, so structures for decision making in England and Wales are not the same as in Scotland or Northern Ireland. Hence, any overview of services in the United Kingdom has to be general.

The administrative and legal system

A feature of the British system is its high degree of centralisation; laws and procedures are laid down by the London government and most funding comes from the public exchequer. This centralisation has increased over time, partly as a result of the urbanisation following the industrial revolution in the last century and the two world wars which increased the need for a nationwide service. It is local agencies, however, which actually deliver most services in the United Kingdom and they have considerable freedom to define policy and fix budgets. Because of its high population, 55 million, many parts of the United Kingdom are densely populated and some of the 133 local authorities can be responsible for the welfare of as many as a million individuals.

There is also a small but active voluntary sector, some of which has its roots in the last century and predates state intervention; but this tends now to provide services purchased by local authorities. For example, voluntary associations may provide a special facility, such as a family centre or residential unit, or may undertake a particular area of welfare work for a social services department. However, their contribution nationally is relatively small compared with state agencies. For example, although they have been contracted to co-ordinate child abuse referrals in some local authorities, only a fraction of all child abuse work in Britain is undertaken by voluntary bodies. Indeed, the total expenditure of the largest such organisation is only equal to that of the child-care budget in one large local authority. Private enterprise, whereby services are provided for profit, is uncommon in child-care, although it is more extensive in the provision of special education boarding schools and other areas of social work, such as residential care of the elderly.

Three state agencies provide services for children and families. These are health, education and social services. However, for older teenagers who commit offences, the probation service can also be involved and it is possible for serious older adolescent delinquents to be sentenced to detention in prison department institutions. All these agencies are required by law to offer a free service. Nevertheless, apart from obvious areas of departmental responsibility, there is much overlap, particularly with the provision of services for children who present a variety of difficult problems, as is often the case with offenders or abuse victims. For example, as well as treating the physically and mentally ill, health authorities provide community and hospital facilities for disturbed, abused and neglected children. Similarly, schools are expected to help pupils with learning and behaviour problems and are complemented by a psychological service, a set of parallel day and residential establishments and peripatetic teachers able to give home tuition. Social services, too, offer a wide range of provision ranging from family support and community projects to specialist care in foster homes or even secure units should they be necessary.

It is possible, therefore, for a deprived or delinquent child and his or her family to receive a wide range of assistance from a single administrative agency, be it health, education or social services. However, when a family faces multiple problems, such as alcoholism, housing difficulties, criminality and child neglect, it is equally feasible for one agency to assume overall responsibility for the case but to employ the services of others. For some groups of children, such as the physically and mentally handicapped, the abused and delinquent, several agencies may be involved even though the child remains the responsibility of social services. The local authority is required by law to promote the child's best interests by providing whatever help, therapy and protection is deemed necessary.

Naturally, this overlap of responsibility and variety in the agencies providing services raises the question of why some children enter one administrative system while young people with similar problems go elsewhere. In some cases it may be a matter of chance, such as what facilities are available locally or who initially refers and defines the problem, but a range of other factors, such as referral routes, social class and differences between agencies in the tolerance of children's difficult behaviour have been suggested by research studies. For example, a government study of admissions to child-care secure units (Cawson and Martell, 1979) found that the factors associated with successful applications had less to do with the seriousness of the child's behaviour than with the number of letters written to support the request and the proximity of the referring authorities to the units.

In short, it was the determination of the applicants and the availability of the services that mattered most.

We have stressed that services in Britain have evolved over a long period and that change has been somewhat piece-meal. However, in recent years, there has been a conscious attempt at both national and local level to rationalise services and avoid duplication. Yet, despite these good intentions, change has not been easy because of the increasing awareness that the needs of many children can only be met by a multi-disciplinary approach. Several recent reports and legislative changes, such as the Cleveland Child-Abuse Inquiry (Department of Health, 1988) and the 1989 Children Act, are examples where clear definitions of agency responsibility accompany a requirement for inter-agency co-operation. Whilst professional ideologies and roles will always conflict and communication between agencies seems universally problematic, at least the agent responsible for managing and co-ordinating the work and the procedures for making important decisions is specified.

Responsibility for child welfare, as opposed to education and health, rests largely with the social services department in each local authority. They deal with families at risk, children in need of substitute care, young people who present serious control problems and children with physical and mental handicaps. They are free to work in any way possible to promote the welfare of children apart from giving income support, which is administered by the central government on a national basis, and housing which is the responsibility of another local authority department. Social Services help can be very varied. It may mean providing a family aide, educating parents or offering child-minding facilities to allow a family to function. On the other hand, it may require placing the child in another living situation. This can be achieved by voluntary agreement between parents and social workers or by order of a court. Courts are only involved when children are at serious risk of abuse, when their difficult behaviour is persistent or when some parental responsibilities need to be taken over by the state.

The power of the court to specify where children committed to care should live varies in different parts of the United Kingdom. In Scotland, those ordering care can specify what happens to a child in care, including their place of residence, but elsewhere the court order, called a care order, only serves to transfer parental powers to the local authority. Social workers are generally free to make whatever professional decisions they choose about the placement of the child and are only directed by the courts in cases of criminal remands or if they wish to place a child in secure accommodation. Thus, the interpretation of the child's best interests is open to considerable professional discretion.

Provision for children in need

In the United Kingdom, there are some 75,000 children looked after away from home at any one time (Department of Health and Social Security, 1990), although the numbers legally in care have fallen since 1991 as voluntary separations no longer require an official entry to care. Voluntary situations usually result from temporary family breakdowns due to parental illness, confinement or marital discord whereas committals by a court usually follow serious abuse or persistent anti-social behaviour. Each year, some 35,000 children separate from home. Thus, alongside a core of long-stay cases, there are numerous short-term situations. This combination of acute and chronic cases means that statistics on each group contrast; the snap shot view of the population looked after at any one time shows a large proportion of long stay cases, mostly adolescents living in foster homes, residential units or with relatives or friends whereas a scrutiny of children separated within a specified time period reveals many more voluntary arrangements and younger children placed in foster homes with siblings. The single year band in which children are most likely to experience separation has always been the first twelve months of life but, as many of these infants stay away for only a short time, they are under-represented in the snapshot statistics.

This variety in the types of children looked after by social services is confirmed by the very considerable differences in children's length of stay away from home. Out of every 100 separated children, 10 will have returned home within a week, half by three months, three-fifths by two years and five-sixths by five years (Bullock, Little and Millham, 1993). The short-stay cases will tend to be those where a family problem is quickly resolved, for example when a mother returns from hospital or new family accommodation is found. The long-stay group consists of three groups : severely neglected and abused children who cannot return home and who are likely to be adopted, troublesome adolescents usually placed in residential settings and older children who have no home to go back to and who need help in moving to their own accommodation. Separated children in Britain are, therefore, extremely heterogeneous. Nevertheless, there are clear subgroups with common situations and each has its own reasons for separation, patterns of placement while away and mode of return to the family or home community. It is important to stress that no one of these groups dominates the total population of children in need. Indeed, separated

216

children and their families are sometimes stigmatised by the imputation of abuse or delinquency when the majority of such children display neither of these problems.

The provision for children who require substitute care is varied but the most important categories are foster families and residential units. Traditionally, foster care was preferred for younger children, those without physical and mental handicaps and those who presented few behaviour difficulties. Residential care, in contrast, was used for older children, for those needing control and as a reception or emergency facility. However, in recent years there have been successful moves to reduce the amount of residential provision and to use fostering for children previously considered unsuitable for family placements. Thus, numbers in residential care have fallen by two-thirds since 1980. This policy has been implemented differentially across the country and some local authorities, such as Warwickshire, have ceased to provide residential services for child welfare cases, although they do purchase a few places when necessary from other local authorities and the voluntary and private sectors (Cliffe and Berridge, 1992).

In addition, community services to prevent children, especially young offenders and truants, entering foster or residential care and to support those that do on return home have been widely developed. Indeed, we have estimated that for every child placed away from home, social workers are helping another five in the community. Thus, it is possible for children to be legally in care and for some parental responsibilities to rest with the state, yet for them to live at home with parents or relatives. Many seriously delinquent and abused children both in and out of care are supported in this way. For example, adolescents remanded for very serious crimes may be allowed to live at home but be visited five times each day by a social worker as an alternative to custody. The success of community care for difficult teenagers has encouraged the government to extend this approach to young people between the ages of 18 and 21.

All of these changes have had the effect of reducing the number of children living in residential child care. There are fewer units, they are of smaller sizes and stays are shorter. However, the numbers of children who experience residential care at some point in their separation has fallen less than these changes imply. For many children, residential care is still part of the care process, along with fostering and placements at home (Rowe et al., 1988). In addition, the numbers of children in need living in residential care provided by other agencies, such as special boarding schools run by education, have fallen less. It has been argued that the decline in child-care places has increased referrals to other types of institutions, but this process has proved difficult to confirm. There is certainly no simple relationship which suggests that one sector having curtailed its provision simply off-loads its cases to another, even though in the case of offenders an attraction for local authorities is that central government pays for prison places. The most recent survey estimates that about 6 per 1,000 young people aged 0-18 in Britain live in some kind of residential facility, a fall in the rate of a quarter since 1970 (Parker and Dartington Social Research Unit, 1988). However, because of a drop in the child population in Britain, the actual numbers in residential settings have declined even more and, as we explained, in social services child-care the fall in numbers is considerable.

This change in child-welfare policy has particularly affected establishments such as reform schools and remand homes. For example, Greater London, with a population of 10 million, now has only 400 such beds compared with 4,000 in 1970. The residential provision that has survived tends to fall into two types : small, local, short-stay units on the one hand and highly specialised facilities, such as therapeutic communities and secure units, on the other. It is now unlikely in the United Kingdom that a child under the age of eleven would be considered for a long-term residential care placement although residence may be used for reception, assessment or to meet a crisis. In addition, the regimes of any such units would be open and flexible, with co-education and accessibility to children's families the norm. Recent changes have, therefore, affected both the amount and style of residential services while at the same time they have probably led to their being used for the most problematic child-care cases, thus posing considerable problems for staff and institutions.

Changes in the perception and use of residence can also be seen in the private boarding schools used by the middle classes in Britain. These shelter some 150,000 children at any one time, a number some ten times greater than that for poorer children in welfare provision (Millham, Bullock and Little, 1987). Revised perceptions on the shortcomings of residence have also affected provision for mentally handicapped children and influenced the growth of community care, trends which reflect new solutions to enduring problems. Indeed, the retreat from residential life is affecting many other settings from monasteries and kibbutzim to universities and mental hospitals. Thus, it is important to stress that the move away from residential care is not just a reflection of the changing needs of clients, such as the decline in the number of the orphans who dominated Victorian child welfare, but of much wider social processes and values in post-industrial societies.

These changes in child-care services have affected staffing patterns and recruitment in child welfare. In 1971, child-care was incorporated into the government department responsible for all social work activity. At the same time, local authority social services departments were established to care not only for children and families but also for other groups in need, such as the elderly, the mentally ill in the community, the physically and mentally handicapped, the deaf and the blind. A social worker in the United Kingdom is trained and expected to work with all such problems. They also have full responsibility for each case even when the client is placed in residential care. These changes have reduced the power of residential staff in that key decisions about cases are made by others elsewhere. Obviously, good professional practice requires consultation but the best social work career opportunities are now in field work rather than residential care. The staffing of residential units is, therefore, increasingly difficult and staff turnover is high. Young, inexperienced and untrained staff are often left to tend and work with the most problematic clients.

Special training courses, including a qualification undertaken while working *in situ*, have sought to raise the status and skills of residential staff but the adults looking after children are still more likely than not to be untrained and isolated from fellow professionals. While there is much goodwill to change this situation, including the Government commissioned Wagner Report (NISW, 1988) entitled *Residential Care : A Positive Choice*, the run down of services and declining belief in residential interventions seems to overwhelm attempts to improve services.

To compensate for these changes in the residential sector, foster care and community services have had to provide for an increasing number of difficult and disturbed young people. The type of fostering pioneered in the early 1970s by Nancy Hazel in Kent, where adolescents were fostered instead of placed in residential care, is now common practice and every local authority will seek to recruit foster parents willing to undertake such work (Hazel, 1989). However, despite some remarkable achievements, only a small proportion, about 6 per cent, of all adolescent fosterings are specialist in that the clients present serious problems and the foster families receive enhanced payments, usually some £150 per week in addition to normal allowances. Children who in former years would have been candidates for residential care are, more often than not, kept at home or supported in the community. In this, schemes such as intermediate treatment, backed by arrangements which facilitate close co-ordination between social workers, schools and police, obviate the need for removing the child to an institution.

Child-care services in the United Kingdom, therefore, continuously change and in 1991 a new Children Act came into force. This was a radical piece of legislation as it combined private and public law, improved protection for children at risk, tightened the criteria for removing children, especially troublesome adolescents, from home and introduced new concepts, such as parental responsibility.

The new Act seeks a balance between several seemingly conflicting child-care perspectives; the rights of parents versus the rights of children, the need to protect some children but rehabilitate others, the promotion of social work initiative but under central control and the benefits of reconciling the views of clients and professionals. All these are tackled within a fundamental welfare principle, namely that the child's best interests must be paramount. Historically, these changes reflect an amalgamation of the severance policies which dominated child-care philosophies before World War II, the emphasis on rehabilitation that followed and more recent concerns with effective child protection.

Future developments in child welfare services

Given these recent developments, what future changes are likely in British child-care services? Initially, there is the cynical view that economics and politics will prevail whatever social workers want. However, this seems unduly pessimistic as child welfare has been less affected by restraints on Government expenditure than many other services, such as housing or income maintenance, and policies seem to be influenced as much by research as by dogma. So, there seems to be considerable scope for further professional development. Indeed, two important constraints on future child-care services are likely to be external in that they arise from demographic and employment factors. The number of children and adolescents in British society is set to rise in the 1990s putting additional demands on agencies which have run down residential options. At the same time, an expected shortage of labour at the end of the decade seems likely to affect the recruitment of foster parents.

Child-care services in the future will be based around a balance between residential, community and foster care. Each will be part of a child-care process in which the strengths of one approach will be used to offset the weaknesses of others. Each will expand to include a wide variety of approaches to children and families, such as preventative work, rehabilitation, substitute care and therapy. There seems little probability of a resurrection of residential provision on a large scale although the number of specialist facilities may increase, mainly as a result of initiatives by voluntary associations. The additional pressures on services resulting from the growth in the number of adolescents in the general population will, therefore, have to be met without recourse to residential options. What residential provision exists will have to adopt a more specific and specialist role but one that is much reduced within the gamut of available services.

Secondly, social work is likely to become more professional as training standards improve. At the same time, it will have to be more accountable, both in response to media attention and the more rigorous legal testing required by the 1989 Children Act. The simple provision of substitute care for children and an uncritical belief in welfare will not be enough as concerns with outcomes and standards increase.

Thirdly, along with increasing professionalisation of child-care services, the clients will demand more information and rights. This is part of a general social trend to increase customer choice and to limit the power of professionals. Welfare services will have to respond to this and the 1989 Children Act requires that agencies produce clear written information on their services for parents and children and that clients' views are ascertained and considered when decisions are made.

Fourthly, the growing awareness of the complexity of children's problems, coupled with an ecological perspective that views them as part of an extended family and local community with its own history and culture, mean that no single person or agency will be able to provide all the necessary services. Thus, responsibility for a case will become increasingly separate from the provision of care and support. Co-operation between local authorities, private and charity services will need to increase.

Finally, research evidence, particularly longitudinal studies which relate present situations to future outcomes, will increasingly influence practice. We live in an age of audit and the anecdotal evidence and zeal which sustained practitioners in the past will no longer be acceptable. While some research findings, such as the intractability of persistent delinquency or the continual dangers posed to children by abusers, may depress practitioners, their ability to interpret and apply research will be a hallmark of the new professionalism.

Research on residential and foster care

The recently implemented Children Act is unusual by European standards in that it is based on a considerable body of case law and of Government commissioned research rather than on fundamental legal or social principles. As the United Kingdom has no written constitution or Bill of Rights, key judgements, some from the European

Court of Human Rights, and findings from research can be very significant. Adjudications on parental access and the placement of juveniles in security have been particularly influential as have recently published studies on the fate of children removed from home in emergencies, the effects of interventions with delinquents, the problems faced by parents in maintaining access to separated children, the instability of substitute placements, the length and complexity of legal procedures and the difficulties of leaving care. Almost every section of the legislation seems guided by research findings and the Act can be seen as a model of a successful relationship between research, policy and practice.

The structure for commissioning research

We noted previously that the administration of child-care in the United Kingdom is highly centralised. The national government in London provides regulations and inspection of services and has considerable control over policies and expenditure at a local level. This centralisation also extends to the commissioning and use of research and largely affects the amount and type of child welfare research undertaken. It will be seen that while this approach has considerable strengths compared with many other countries, there are also some weaknesses.

Separate departmental responsibility for child welfare at national and local level was only established in 1948. Before then, several government and local authority departments shared responsibility for different aspects of child-care. Initially, the government department responsible, the Home Office, instigated a research structure capable of producing annual statistics but showed little interest in more fundamental investigation of such areas as the needs of deprived children or the nature of child-care services and their effects. The most relevant theoretical and empirical work was seen to be done in academic institutions, for example in psychological analyses of child development and studies of the separation of children from families. Child-care policy makers seemed content to draw on the findings from the research of authors such as Winnicott and Bowlby rather than commission work of their own.

As the child welfare service grew, however, several important child-care studies were undertaken and in the 1960s several classic studies which were to have a major influence on policy were published. For example, Parker (1966) scrutinised foster care breakdown, King, Raynes and Tizard (1971) measured the effects of residential care on children with physical and mental handicaps and Packman (1968) explored differences in child-care needs and numbers in different parts of the country. These studies tended to be one-off projects undertaken by interested academics receiving small grants from charitable foundations and, although the government department then responsible (Home Office) had its own in-house research unit, child-care other than for delinquents was given relatively little priority.

In 1971, responsibility for child-care services passed to a newly formed government Department of Health and Social Security. Social Security has since become the responsibility of a separate government department and child-care remains in the Department of Health. At the same time, a report prepared by Lord Rothschild (Department of Health and Social Security, 1971) on government commissioned research recommended that such work should be organised on a customer-contractual basis. The civil servants and government ministers who make policy were the customers and their priorities were to determine the nature and scope of any funded research.

At the Department of Health, an early decision was made that more research was needed in the child-care field but that it should be contracted to outside agencies. Only statistical monitoring was retained within government. As a result, several external child-care units, each with their own area of specialisation, were established. Among these were the Thomas Coram Unit in London which focuses on the under-fives, the Dartington Research Unit which concentrates on children looked after by the state, the National Children's Bureau which specialises in inter-disciplinary research and the Hester Adrian Unit in Manchester which studies physical and mental handicap. Each was funded on the basis of a research programme rather than an individual project as this offered greater job security to staff, allowed them to develop an area of expertise and facilitated cumulative knowledge which builds on earlier work. Grants were also made available for specific projects nominated by individuals and for programmes of work associated with particular issues, such as child abuse. The total expenditure by the Department on child-care research is over £3 million.

An example of effective research planning was the Department's commissioning of three complementary projects concerning children in care. Each focused on a specific problem but overlapped with others in the sense that there were areas of mutual interest, such as the initial separation, the stability of alternative placements and processes of decision making. The first of these projects looked at differences between vulnerable children who were separated and those who were not (Packman, Randall and Jacques, 1986), the second explored the factors affecting a child's length of stay away from home (Vernon and

Fruin, 1986) and the third analysed the problems of maintaining links between the children and their families while they were away (Millham, Bullock, Hosie and Haak, 1986). Many of the findings in each study were confirmed in the other two, so enhancing the authority and reliability of the research programme.

Although most child-care research is supported by the Department of Health, the government funded Economic and Social Research Council can award grants to academics seeking to undertake research. Naturally, the scope of this body is wide as it has to cover all the social sciences. In 1980, however, funds were specifically set aside for a programme of work in child welfare and a number of grants were made to universities and research institutes. In this package, the studies focused particularly on clients' views on the care experience. It is also possible for the Research Foundations, such as Rowntree, Nuffield and Leverhulme, to provide funds and they have contributed considerably to work on child care law as well as to action research and developmental projects.

Child-care research in the United Kingdom, therefore, is more established than in most other European countries and in terms of theoretical and exploratory empirical work is probably equal in amount to North America. However, there is a sharp contrast between the countries in that in the United States there is also far more routine evaluation and monitoring of programmes. Moreover, private foundations as well as central government control the funding with the result that there are more independent research institutes capable of conducting continuous research and development on a national basis.

Strengths and weaknesses of the British research structure

At first sight, the research arrangement in Britain seems generous and satisfactory in the opportunities and freedoms it affords academics. Indeed, colleagues from other countries often express envy of this structure. It may seem churlish, therefore, to criticise the situation just described but it does have weaknesses which need airing.

The term research is often used globally whereas, of course, it involves several distinct activities. Research can be theoretical in that it develops concepts and typologies; it can be empirical in that it produces and analyses new data or it can consist of a scrutiny of particular situations, such as an evaluation of a situation or service. These three types of research are not exclusive; theory needs to be tested by evidence, empiricism bereft of a theoretical structure becomes mindless and small-scale evaluations need to be placed in the context of wider knowledge if they are to be useful. The research structure we have described with its high level of central control leads to an abundance of studies which are policy relevant, a situation that is hardly surprising given that decisions are the business of government. Hence, theoretical research rarely gets financial support and the empirical studies undertaken tend to reflect government policy priorities rather than academic relevance. Thus, delinquency studies were generously funded in the 1970s but interest dwindled thereafter as reform schools closed and community options developed. Very little work in this area has been undertaken since and in the 1980s the pressing issues have been more concerned with value for money, the effectiveness of interventions, clients' views, community care, child abuse and AIDS.

It is also difficult under the British system for researchers to persuade the government of the value of radical as opposed to reformist research. Hence, studies that explore questions about the structure of society or which seek to challenge existing thought and practice are increasingly uncommon; unless of course the government of the day is seeking to stir up controversy. Similarly, as child care problems overlap, the distinct areas of responsibility allotted to specific government departments make it hard to get funding for studies adopting a wider brief, such as linking health, housing, education and so on. It would be hard at the present time to get funding to scrutinise the relationship, if any, between changes in income maintenance and the problems faced by older teenagers leaving care. The research problems under scrutiny also tend to reflect problems as perceived by government, placing the local authorities and social work profession in a relatively weak position. This can be self defeating as critical results can do much to undermine the confidence of staff, so alienating them from research relevant to improving their work.

There are also scientific weaknesses in this research structure. Investigators hired to undertake applied studies cannot afford to take too many risks in developing new methodologies or in pursuing interesting side issues. Macro surveys which provide reliable material of national situations are thus preferred to insightful micro studies. In addition, there is the limitation that experimental designs and random allocation are ruled out on ethical grounds. Thus, the research is usually presented in the form of written reports which tend to be thorough but dull and somewhat over-reliant on well tested approaches. These are, perhaps, some of the reasons why research can be unattractive to practitioners, a problem we shall discuss later.

Nevertheless, despite these deficiencies, the range of child-care studies produced in the United Kingdom in the last twenty years is impressive. New information of high quality has been produced about almost every aspect of the child welfare process and a clear body of specialist knowledge has been built up. This is largely an outcome of adventurous government policy with regard to the management and use of research.

The dissemination of research findings

Government activity on such a broad scale inevitably raises questions about the function of applied social research. Is it a genuine attempt to expedite social progress or is it a cover designed to delay change, divert criticism or neutralise threat? The use made of social policy research has long been of interest to academics, although some commentators clearly argue from a political as well as a research position (Bulmer, 1986, 1987). Nevertheless, a general conclusion has been that in social services the value of much good academic work is lost because of the poor relationship between research, policy and practice. This certainly seemed to be the case for a long period in child welfare with social workers seemingly unaware of research results that could be useful to them. This ignorance reflected the fact that most research was undertaken by academics. They, by nature of their interest, tend to think from the particular to the general, thus giving practitioners, whose thought processes need to be in the opposite direction, the opportunity to avoid accountability for their lack of knowledge. There were further tensions in that policy makers tended to be suspicious of researchers, accusing them of producing lists of further problems for investigation rather than providing applicable results. Similarly, government civil servants were seen by academics as having unrealistic perceptions of research and posing questions which were impossible to test scientifically. Thus, frustration was widespread.

These problems partly arise from the difficulties of setting up models to link social work research and practice. In medicine, the teaching hospital provides an arena for combining practice, training and research. In contrast, in the natural sciences, fundamental exploration in the laboratory is taken up by private agencies seeking to improve profitability and efficiency. Social work falls between these two models; practitioners rarely feel that they own the research and so resist its implications and professional problems which could benefit from research remain poorly articulated.

It was this situation of general mistrust that led the Department of Health in the early 1980s to focus on ways of improving the dissemination of research findings in social work (Department of Health, 1990). Having commissioned a large programme of work, the need was to get its results fed into practice. This was achieved by a carefully staged programme. First, the government department prepared summary reports based on completed projects (Department of Health and Social Security, 1985; Department of Health, 1991). The research summary is accompanied by practical exercises enabling social workers to ask, how can we find out if this situation is true for us? In conclusion, clear messages are given to social workers about what they could do immediately to improve their practice. As these recommendations are based on such unequivocal evidence, no social services department can afford to ignore this advice.

The dissemination exercises then proceeded by publishing the summary reports attractively and cheaply and by sending copies to every local authority and voluntary agency. In addition, they were launched at national and regional conferences attended by professionals and political representatives from all social services departments. Furthermore, there then followed a set of three-day regional seminars attended by local social workers and trainers. It was hoped that this would lead to closer relationships between academic institutes and practitioners. There is no doubt of the success of the dissemination exercise, indeed every social worker in Britain knows the summary reports, which have come to be affectionately known as the 'pink' and the 'red' book. However, the relationships between agencies has proved more difficult to engineer and has varied in success in different parts of the country.

This review of recent child care research activity in the United Kingdom may seem somewhat glowing but the fact is that the programme of child-care research in the early 1980s and its subsequent dissemination were the largest exercises of their kind ever undertaken in Britain and for that alone the government department deserves some credit. But that is not to say that all is well.

The limitations of British child-care research dissemination

One of the weaknesses of the programme of research dissemination has been the lack of certain types of development work. As with research, this term is used globally whereas it has many aspects. For example, it can seek to disseminate research findings and incorporate them into practice and legislation, on the other hand it can set up action or demonstration projects while a third possibility is to fashion indicators and predictive criteria to aid professional practice. All three types of development have to be viewed in the light of the three types of theory previously described. For example, theoretical concepts may need to be demonstrated in practice while empirical data is needed to derive indicators of success.

While the government initiatives we have described were clearly effective in the dissemination of research findings and incorporating them into government policy and the framing of legislation, there has been less emphasis on ensuring that the necessary changes in ethos, structure and practice are made in the agencies expected to apply them. It is still too easy for welfare organisations in the United Kingdom to ignore research findings or to neutralise the threat of change arising from new knowledge (Bullock, Hosie, Little and Millham, 1990). There are many techniques for doing this, such as denying the existence of the problem or incorporating new perspectives into existing role structures, so reducing their impact. Many care workers have altered their titles to abuse specialist oblivious to the changes that this suggests.

A further limitation of the government's recent research and development initiative is that because it was very much a one-off exercise, replication is not possible. The single broad sweep obtained from the set of complementary studies cannot offer much more than a sophisticated natural history. It can lay out processes, typologies and outcomes but can only offer tentative causal explanations. If the findings are to become eternal truths, several replications would be necessary. These would need to involve testing hypotheses using predictive criteria applied to longitudinal, prospective study cohorts. This is inevitably expensive and unlikely to take place for all aspects of child care. Thus, the tools derived from research to help social workers make assessments and to select appropriate strategies are not yet validated sufficiently for them to gain uncritical acceptance.

The focus of child-care research in Britain also needs to be widened. In order to develop child-care services, all sorts of bureaucracies and professions have developed. While such structures may be necessary, they can develop a *modus vivendi* of their own, displacing the needs of clients, being reluctant to change and seeking continuity. Welfare interventions themselves can also generate problems for participants and there is a case for encouraging social workers to sensitise the public to a more radical stance. There is a need, therefore, to expose bureaucracies more to external scrutiny, which is a major role of research. There is a need to redress the emphasis on issues proposed by policy makers with studies that begin with the problems as perceived and approached by other groups, such as clients and practitioners.

Future research needs in Britain

So, what research needs to be undertaken in Britain to expand and build on the government programme of the 1980s and to fill the gaps we have highlighted? We have already stressed the need for research which is broad in focus and which looks at the inter-relationship between agencies concerned with children. There is also a need for more cross-disciplinary inquiry, particularly in the light of publications such as Giller and Rutter's (1983) review of delinquency research which emphasised the inter-relationships between medical, genetic, psychological and social factors. Comparisons of alternative child-care approaches would also do much to evaluate interventions with troubled and troublesome children. In some areas, such as the effects of different residential regimes in homes for the mentally handicapped and in reform schools, comparative instruments have been developed. Moreover, there have been successful comparisons between residential and fostering approaches (Colton, 1988). But, in most other areas, there is not yet an established methodology let alone a body of comparative research knowledge.

Comparative research could also be beneficially extended across countries and across sub-cultures within a society. Social research tends to be hide-bound by the difficulties of making international comparisons and the need to view events in their historical and social context. Important as these problems are, cross cultural studies are useful even if they only serve to increase awareness of one's own situation. The conclusions of Bronfenbrenner (1971) on the status of childhood in the United States and Soviet Union and of Harragan and Bullock (1992), for example, could help us better fashion hypotheses on the pressing problems that face all countries, such as the over-representation of certain ethnic groups among child welfare populations.

In closing, it can be concluded that in light of the very considerable research knowledge in child care that has been built up in the last decade, two research perspectives would best take knowledge forward in the United Kingdom. These are research that is broad in focus, looking at the inter-relationships between agencies, and, secondly, studies that highlight conflict and tensions in policy rather than seeking to achieve a false consensus. It is too easy to imply that everybody is going to benefit from proposed change; we need to acknowledge more readily that some participants are likely to lose out.

References

Bronfenbrenner U. (1971), *Two Worlds of Childhood*, Allen and Unwin, London.

Bullock R., Hosie K., Little M. and Millham S. (1990), *Access to Children in Care : Practitioners' Views*, Bristol University Papers N° 17.

Bullock, R., Little, M. and Millham, S. (1993), *Return Home as Experienced by Children in Care*, Aldershot, Dartmouth.

Bulmer M. (1986), *Social Science and Social Policy*, Allen and Unwin, London.

Bulmer M. (ed.) (1987), *Social Science Research and Government*, University Press, Cambridge.

Cawson P. and Martell M. (1979), *Children Referred to Closed Units*, HMSO, London.

Cliffe, D. and Berridge, D. (1992), *Closing Children's Homes*, National Children's Bureau, London.

Colton M. (1988), *Dimensions of Substitute Care*, Avebury, Aldershot.

Department of Health (1990), *Taking Research Seriously*, HMSO, London.

Department of Health (1991), *Patterns and Outcomes in Child Placement*, HMSO, London.

Department of Health and Social Security (1971), *the Organisation and Management of Government Research and Development*, HMSO, London.

Department of Health and Social Security (1985), *Social Work Decisions in Child Care : Recent Research Findings and their Implications*, HMSO, London.

Department of Health and Social Security (1988), *Report of the Inquiry into Child Abuse in Cleveland 1987*, HMSO, London.

Department of Health and Social Security (1990), *Children in Care of Local Authorities on March 31st 1989*, Department of Health and Social Security, London.

Giller H. and Rutter M. (1983), *Juvenile Delinquency : Trends and Perspectives*, Penguin, Harmondsworth.

Harragan, S. and Bullock, R. (1992), *Problem Adolescents : An International View*, Whiting and Birch, London.

Hazel N. (1988), 'Looking backwards, looking forwards', in J. Hudson and B. Galaway (Eds), *Special Foster Family Care*, Haworth, New York, 1989, pp. 17-22.

King R., Raynes N. and Tizard J. (1971), *Patterns of Residential Care*, Routledge and Kegan Paul, London.

Millham S., Bullock R. and Little M. (1984), 'Residential Education in Britain : Continuity and Conflict', in Y. Kashti and M. Arieli (Eds), *Residential Settings and the Community : Congruence and Conflict*, Freund, 1987, pp. 190-205.

Millham S., Bullock R., Hosie K. and Haak M. (1986), *Lost in Care*, Gower, Aldershot.

NISW (1988), *Residential Care : A Positive Choice*, HMSO/NISW, London.

Packman J. (1964), *Child Care - Needs and Numbers*, Allen and Unwin, London.

Packman J., Randall J. and Jacques, N. (1986), *Who Needs Care?* Blackwell, Oxford.

Parker R. (1966), *Decisions in Foster Care*, Allen and Unwin, London.

Parker R. and Dartington Social Research Unit (1988), 'Residential care for children', in NISW Op. Cit. pp. 59-124.

Rowe J., Cain M. and Hundleby M. (1988), *Child Care Now*, British Agencies for Adoption and Fostering, London.

Vernon J. and Fruin D. (1986), *In Care - A Study of Social Work Decision Making*, National Children's Bureau, London.

12 Residential and foster care in the EC

W. Hellinckx and M. Colton

Previous chapters have reviewed residential and foster care in each of the 12 countries which constitute the European Community. In closing, we want to highlight common developments among member states with regard to residential and foster care practice, emerging alternatives to residential and foster care, and developments in child care research.

These tasks are easier stated than accomplished, for in seeking to outline general tendencies, we were confronted with several difficulties. In addition to geographical and cultural variations, differences in political history and economic circumstances have to be taken into account. As a consequence, no comparisons can be made in relation to the proportion of public expenditure allocated to child care provision in member states, or about current spending on child care services. We are also unable to make comparisons between the legal and administrative frameworks of care in the different countries, because part of the requisite information is missing from foregoing chapters.

Merely indicating some striking common developments is a difficult enough task, owing to the differences that exist not only between the 12 member states but also between regions within certain countries. This is the case for both Italy and Spain. In Italy, for instance, it is clear that the quality of residential care practice in the South of the country lags behind that provided in other regions (Gugliemetti and Sapucci, 1991). In Spain, the geographical disparity of services is a consequence of the state's decentralisation into different autonomous communities (Casas, see chapter 10). This is also the case in Belgium, where the major two communities (the Flemish- and the French-speaking) have separate systems of youth care (Hellinckx, Van den Bruel and Vander Borght, see chapter 1). Moreover, the limited data available on Italy and Spain means that it is not possible to offer a detailed description of care in the whole of these countries (Casas, see chapter 10; Gugliemetti and Sapucci, 1991). The United Kingdom appears to represent a special case. Although the legal and administrative system in Britain is highly centralised, it is the local authorities that actually deliver most services and they have considerable freedom to define policy and fix budgets. In addition, different parts of the United Kingdom have their own history of welfare, and their own legislative and administrative systems. Hence, ... 'structures for decision making in England and Wales are not the same as in Scotland and Northern Ireland' ... (Bullock, see chapter 11).

The difficulties we encountered when undertaking this comparative study have inevitably led to shortcomings. Nevertheless, certain common trends can be distinguished among EC countries with regard to residential care, foster care and their alternatives for children and young people.

Common developments in the field of residential and foster care

Residential and foster care in the EC has recently been characterised by the following.

1. Decreasing numbers of residential provisions and children accommodated in residential care, along with an increasing number of children placed in foster care.
2. Changes in the population of separated children and adolescents.
3. A tendency towards small-scale provisions.
4. The development of an ecological perspective.
5. Greater differentiation of residential and foster care provision, and the development of alternative types of care.
6. Professionalisation.

1. In all countries of the EC *a decrease in the number of residential provisions, places and placed children can be observed along with an increasing number of children placed in foster care.* This shift away from residential care does not merely reflect the changing nature and needs of the client population - for example, the decline in the number of

orphans in most countries after the second world war; rather, it is indicative of much wider social processes. One obvious factor is the welter of criticism, dating back to the 1950's, that has created a negative image of residential care. Bowlby (1951), Pringle and Bossio (1960), and many others since, have stressed the adverse effects of residential care on children's psycho-social development.

However, according to Van der Ploeg (1984), three other factors have also contributed to the decline in residential care : (i) society seems to have become relatively more tolerant towards deviant behaviour; (ii) preventive care in the field work sector has been strengthened; and, (iii) in the past few years there has been a strong preference for keeping children in their home environments (see 5 below). It may also be noted that, partly as a consequence of increasing professionalism (see 6 below), the costs of residential care have risen considerably.

The decline of residential care has been accompanied by policies geared to stimulating the growth of foster care. In some countries, this trend is reflected in a change in the ratio of children accommodated in residential care to children placed in foster care. In the United Kingdom, for instance, the ratio of children in residential care to children in foster care is already 40:60. In other parts of the EC, the proportion of separated children placed in residential care is much higher. For example, in the Netherlands and Denmark, the ratio referred to is 50:50. In the Flemish-speaking region of Belgium, the ratio is 60:40. Whilst in Spain, a striking 88 per cent of separated children are accommodated in residential care, with the remaining 12 per cent placed in foster care. Traditionally, foster care has been the preferred form of care for younger children. Over recent years, however, increasing numbers of children in Denmark, Germany, Italy, the Netherlands, and the United Kingdom who were previously considered unsuitable for family placement, have been found foster homes (see 5 below). Indeed, one local authority in the United Kingdom, Warwickshire, has ceased to provide any residential services for child welfare cases (Bullock, see chapter 11).

To sum up, it can be said that the number of residential placements has decreased in all countries of the European Community. The case for placing children in residential care is no longer self-evident. Throughout the EC, residential institutions are fast becoming places of last resort. Before placing a child in residential care, other options are considered : foster care or alternative community based forms of care. In some countries - the Netherlands and the United Kingdom - many residential facilities have been closed. In others - Belgium, Germany, Ireland and Italy, traditional residential services have been transformed

234

into community care services, such as centres for day care, independent living under supervision, and family centres.

2. Changes in the population of separated children Both practitioners and researchers claim that recent years have witnessed changes in the population of children placed in residential care. Research findings by Van der Ploeg and Scholte (1988) have been compared with data from a study undertaken by Van der Ploeg in 1979. This comparison suggests that the family circumstances of children in residential care have become more problematic over the past 10 years. Relationship problems and divorce rates among the parents of such children seem to be increasing. At the same time, it appears that a rising proportion of separated children experience difficulties in their relationships with family members, peers, and teachers. Moreover, the two studies referred to indicate that children in residential care are not 'children without families', but rather, 'children from families with problems'. In the Netherlands and many other EC countries, an increasing number of children in residential care are drawn from one-parent families, from households effected by unemployment and poverty, and from families where the parents are addicted to illegal drugs. Further, children from ethnic minorities are disproportionately over-represented among the population of children in residential care, and this relative imbalance is increasing (Ligthart et al., 1991).

Thus, although the number of children placed in residential care is declining, it is believed that the needs of those currently accommodated are greater than was the case a decade or so previously.

That the problems presented by children in residential care are becoming more challenging, may also be related to the present trend towards strengthening foster care and various forms of community care with a view to preventing the placement of children in institutions. Young people are often admitted to residential care when foster care or some other alternative to residential care has failed to produce the desired effects. In the United Kingdom, for example, one of the main tasks of the residential sector involves helping to deal with the aftermath of fostering breakdowns (Colton, 1988). Further, young people with serious problems may be placed directly in residential care, because those responsible believe that foster care or alternative forms of help are unlikely to be successful (Van der Ploeg, see chapter 8).

Hence, it might be argued that residential care performs a valuable 'fail-safe' role in substitute child care (Berridge, 1985). Colton (1988) remarks that although the extent to which residential homes 'bail out' unsuccessful family placements is sometimes exaggerated, residential care is to community care what gold is to fiduciary or paper money.

Finally, it should be noted that the residential child care population in many countries, including Belgium, Denmark, Germany, the Netherlands, and the United Kingdom, contains far more adolescents than young children. In future, the proportion of young children accommodated in residential care is likely to decrease further.

3. The trend towards small-scale provision There is an increasing trend away from large-scale residential provision. The times are past when castles and other large structures were fitted out to accommodate separated children (Gottesman, 1991). However, the development of smaller living units has been very uneven in some countries. In certain regions of Spain - for example, the Basque Country, Catalonia, and Valencia - few large institutions remain. By contrast, in other parts of Spain, such as Extramadura and Galicia, the Canary Islands, and Castile and Leon the process of reform has only just begun (Casas, see chapter 10).

In most EC countries, the move towards small-scale provision has by no means resulted in the complete abolition of large institutions. Typically, the older, large-scale structures have been split up into a number of smaller units. Thus, several small units or group homes may be located on one site. In addition, a large institution may serve as the operational centre for a network of smaller units dispersed throughout the locality (Gilligan, see chapter 6).

Van der Ploeg argues that small-scale facilities can operate successfully as part of larger organisations, provided they conform to certain criteria. Among other things, this means that they must be located in residential areas, accommodate a limited number of residents and care workers, enjoy considerable autonomy from the larger organisation, and afford residents the opportunity to use social facilities (schools, clubs, libraries, etc.) that are available to other citizens (Van der Ploeg, see chapter 8).

However, research carried out in the Netherlands by Klüppel and Slijkerman (1983) shows that operating on a small-scale does not by itself ensure success. The study indicates that young people's satisfaction with living in a children's home is strongly shaped by the opinion they have of their group leaders. Moreover, it appears that the nature and seriousness of young people's problems influences how they evaluate their stay in a children's home.

That small children's homes do not automatically improve the performance of care workers can be seen in research by Van der Ploeg (1984b). It was found that child care workers employed in small-scale homes tend to display more symptoms of stress, as a result of receiving less support, than their counterparts in large facilities.

236

Nevertheless, such findings do not imply that small-scale provisions are undesirable. Rather, they only serve to indicate that small children's homes do not represent the most appropriate form of residential care as a matter of course. Factors other than size have to be considered in evaluating the relative merits of different kinds of residential provision - not least, for instance, the degree of support available to child care workers. However, even when such factors are taken into account, it remains the case that small-scale homes are more conducive to child-oriented care practice than large establishments (Zandberg, 1988). The same conclusion is reached in a study by Colton (1988), in which residential homes were compared with foster family homes. According to Colton (1992), reducing the number of youngsters in residential homes should diminish the need for bureaucratic management. This would allow caregivers to spend more time with the children.

4. The development of an ecological perspective In all countries of the European Community, there is increasing recognition that it is impossible to effectively help children without taking into account their origins, family networks and cultural environments. This notion was generated by systemic theory. From the systemic perspective, the child placed away from home is viewed as a product or 'symptom' of a dysfunctional family environment (Boszormenyi-Nagy and Spark, 1984; Boszormenyi-Nagy and Krasner, 1986). Therefore, in seeking to effectively help such a child, it is considered essential to involve the whole family in the care process. This idea has led to important changes in child care practice and the organisation of services in EC countries.

With regard to practice, more emphasis is placed on allowing the parents to exercise their rights and encouraging them to participate and share in decisions about their children. These principles are commonly expressed in laws concerning the care of separated children and young people in the different countries. However, less stress has been placed on involving parents in the care process by offering them very intense help and support in the form of family therapy focused on the parenting role, in order to prepare them for the child's return home.

Because the importance of children's family links are now widely recognised, the current tendency is to provide temporary, rather than long-term, care with the aim of returning the child home as soon as possible. However, research findings show that there are very considerable differences in children's length of stay. In the United Kingdom, for example, it is estimated that 10 out of every 100 children who enter care will have left it again within one week, half by three

237

months, three-fifths by two years, and five-sixths by five years (Millham et al., 1986). It should also be noted that runaways, whose stay varies from short to ultra-short, also contribute to the data on residential care (Van der Ploeg, see chapter 8).

It is generally acknowledged that length of stay is not only determined by prevailing views about care and treatment, but is also influenced by external factors (Van der Ploeg, see chapter 8). For example, the Dutch researcher, Vissers (1988), found that young people's length of stay in care is influenced by their family circumstances. Youngsters from particularly unfavourable family environments tend to remain longer in a children's home than those whose family circumstances are less adverse.

Other studies have shown that length of stay in residential care is not sufficiently conditioned by the progress made by residents (Edwards and Kelly, 1980). Research by Klüppel and Slijkerman (1983) revealed a curvilinear relationship between length of stay in residential care and the problems manifested by children. For a period after admission, a general reduction in the problems that led to the children being admitted was observed. Later on, however, the initial presenting problems tended to recur. Hence, it seems that treatment in a children's home ceases to be effective after a certain period. This suggests that many young people remain too long in children's homes.

Another idea that has gained international currency is the view that in order to be effective care services should be located near the child's family home. However, in many EC countries, this objective has not been fully realised, partly because of the legacy of institutional care provision that virtually all EC countries have to cope with. As already mentioned, large institutions have been transformed into small-scale facilities more in tune with contemporary ideas about care practice. In spite of this, the location remains the same. Many residential provisions are located in the countryside, far away from the residents' families. However, attempts are being made to solve this problem through the creation of small, autonomous, living units in children's communities of origin. Furthermore, these small units are part of local life. Children have access to services available to other youngsters in the locality.

The creation of this type of care illustrates a further trend, namely that of 'normalisation'. This principle holds that separated children must have access to the normal experiences of growing up. The price of being placed away from home should not involve missing out on opportunities that are taken for granted by the majority of children and young people. The child in care ... 'should receive the individual, personal care and attention which a child can be expected to receive in his own family, and ... should, as far as possible, share in the normal experiences of other children living at home. He ... (or she) ... should have a foot-hold in the ordinary community either through his ... (or her) ... own family or another family, he ... (or she) ... should attend an outside school with other children in the locality, take part in the ordinary activities of the community, and establish friendships with other children and adults there, unless there are clearly defined reasons relating to his ... (or her) ... own interests or the interests of others which require that he ... (or she) ... should not do so' (Task Force on Child Care Services, 1981 cited in Gilligan, see chapter 6).

There is also growing awareness that children's schools must be involved in intervention programmes. For example, although it can be observed that far fewer residential child care institutions now have a school on the premises, residential caregivers are beginning to place greater emphasis on the importance of maintaining links with children's schools.

Parker (1988) stresses that one of the reasons why children in care have such an insecure foothold in the labour market, is their generally poor level of educational achievement. This is not surprising given that children in care have often had a poor start and this effects their behaviour and progress at school. There is a strong association between low attainment and behaviour problems. The stress of separation and the adverse circumstances surrounding entry to care may also be contributory factors. Another possible cause is instability of placement, not only for the practical reasons that this often goes along with many changes of school, but because the effect of placement breakdown is to give children a sense of failure and to undermine their self-esteem. Lack of attention to children's educational needs and low expectations by caregivers, social workers and teachers also play a part, as does the poor quality of care experienced by some children (Colton et al., 1991; Colton and Jackson, 1993; Heath et al., 1989; Heath et al., 1993).

In view of this, the findings of a recent study on the educational attainment of foster children in the United Kingdom are especially disappointing. The children who took part were a particularly favoured group of children in care. The majority were in long-term, settled, foster family placements, with foster parents in comfortable circumstances who wanted them to do well at school. The children did make progress, but not nearly enough to catch up with other children of their age. The generally poor attainment of the children studied could not be explained by frequent placement breakdowns or the low expectations of teachers. Rather, it seems that damaging early experiences, especially abuse and neglect, continue to effect educational attainment many years later. Thus something more than 'normal' family life and 'normal' parental interest are required to overcome the effects of early deprivation : average inputs are not enough for children with above-average needs (Colton et al., 1991; Heath et al., 1989; Heath et al., 1993).

It is clear that much more attention must be given to the educational needs of separated children. Social workers and caregivers have an important role to play in helping separated children to overcome educational disadvantage.

5. Increasing differentiation of care provision   In all countries of the European Community, residential and foster care assume a variety of different forms. In general, care provisions can be classified in terms of the age of the youngsters accommodated or the particular type of service offered.

One form of residential care that is found across Europe is the 'children's home', accommodating children who do not have behavioural problems or whose difficulties in this respect are not severe. Children's homes vary from relatively large, multi-purpose, facilities to smaller hostel and family group provisions (Berridge, 1985; Colton, 1988). In Denmark, for example, some children's homes provide therapeutic help for troubled children. In these establishments, which may also be called 'treatment homes', the ratio of adults to children is generally higher than is ordinarily the case.

A number of countries - for instance, Belgium and Denmark - have 'assessment centres', which accommodate children of all ages for short periods, usually with the aim of observing the child's behaviour to ascertain what sort of help is required. Over the last decade or so, however, this form of residential care has been heavily criticised. Rather than being undertaken in 'artificial' residential environments, it is argued that assessment should take place in the family (Mesman Schultz, 1978; Bryce and Lloyd, 1981; Hellinckx and De Munter, 1990). Further, in practice it is very difficult to separate treatment from observation. In the Flemish-speaking part of Belgium, many children remain in assessment centres for long periods. As a consequence, the treatment process must be commenced in the assessment centre itself, which then makes it difficult to transfer the child to a long-term placement (Hellinckx and De Munter, 1990). Because of the disadvantages referred to, many residential assessment centres in countries such as the Netherlands and the United Kingdom have been closed (Harmonisatie, 1988). Interesting developments in the area of assessment have, however, occurred in Spain. Spanish child care law stipulates that assessment should be carried out by expert interdisciplinary teams. Thus, several Autonomous Communities in Spain have created special networks of such teams (Casas, see chapter 10).

Of late, new types of residential care have been introduced. As mentioned earlier, small-scale homes, many of which are linked to larger institutions, can be observed in most parts of the EC. A variation on this type of care is the 'Commune' which has been developed in Germany. Communes provide shelter for young people who volunteer to live together, and attend school for vocational training. In many countries - for example, Belgium, Germany, Ireland, and the Netherlands - houses located in residential communities provide accommodation for groups of older youngsters. Although adult care workers form part of some such groups, in other cases the group is exclusively comprised by young people who receive a minimum of adult supervision.

In Germany, small autonomous units have formed networks with one another in order to offer a wider range of programmes and activities which can be shared by youngsters from all the units within the network. This pooling of resources makes for economies of scale, and helps to overcome the high costs which discourage the development of small units.

Given the evidence suggesting that residential care is increasingly reserved for more challenging children and young people, there appears to be a need for small-scale facilities that are capable of offering effective help to such youngsters. In Germany and Ireland, small-scale, specialised facilities have been set up for children and adolescents with severe behavioural difficulties. A number of projects have also been developed in Germany for young drug addicts or runaways. Moreover, over the last few years, residential workers in Germany have given increasing emphasis to the problems experienced by girls in care, with particular attention devoted to helping sexually abused girls (Colla-Müller, see chapter 4). In the United Kingdom, attempts have been made to raise awareness of the special difficulties experienced by children and young people from different ethnic backgrounds (Ahmed et al., 1986).

Throughout the 1970's and 1980's, foster family care has also been in a state of transition, particularly in countries such as Germany, the Netherlands, and the United Kingdom. The traditional definition of fostering as 'bringing up someone else's child' is currently only appropriate for a proportion of foster placements. There is now a continuum of family placement running from short-term fostering - which can offer, for example, emergency care, assessment, placement prior to rehabilitation, respite care, and treatment - through to long-term foster care - either with or without contact between children and their birth families - and on to adoption (Colton, 1988).

Furthermore, in certain countries of the EC (Denmark, Germany, Italy, the Netherlands and the United Kingdom) a new type of foster family care has been developed, namely 'therapeutic' or 'specialist' foster care. This reflects attempts to provide children traditionally considered unsuitable for fostering - because, for example, they were deemed too difficult or too old - with family care.

6. Professionalisation   Special foster parents receive fees which are generous by comparison with the ordinary foster care allowances in recognition of the difficulties which their roles may entail; they are also given more intensive training and support than ordinary foster parents (Colton, 1988). In the United Kingdom, this type of fostering, which was pioneered in the 1970's by Nancy Hazel in Kent (Hazel, 1981), is now common practice (Bullock, see chapter 11). Rather than being asked to bring children up as their own, special foster parents are required to provide a professional caring service. A trend towards greater professionalism can also be observed in relation to residential care. Prior to the 1960's, residential care in many countries of the EC could be characterised as a response to the needs of orphans, abandoned and neglected children, and child poverty. Children in institutions were typically subject to a rigid daily regime of education, religion and work, and were kept under constant supervision. An identical approach was adopted for all children (Ligthart et al., 1991).

From the 1970's onwards, however, attempts have been made to meet children's needs on a more individual basis, and residential child care has become more professional. This has been attributed to two main factors, which were mentioned above. First, the population of children in residential care is said to have become more problematic; second, the quality of residential care practice has been heavily criticised from different points of view (see Spitz, 1945; Bowlby, 1951; King, Raynes and Tizard, 1971; Polsky, 1962).

Consequently, in most countries of the European Community, the number of care workers has been increased, along with their level of training. However, some countries have made less progress than others in this respect. For example, in Greece, Portugal and Spain, the proportion of qualified residential staff, and the standard of training provided for care workers, is lower than in the more industrialised countries. Insufficient numbers of staff have been recruited to the state child care centres in Greece due to economic constraints and the low political priority given to child care and protection (Agathonos, see chapter 5). In Spain, the process of professionalisation has been impeded by the lack of precise regulations concerning the educatie and training of care workers (Casas, see chapter 10).

However, problems have also been encountered in some of the northern countries. In the United Kingdom, for example, it has proved difficult to recruit appropriate staff for residential units, and turnover among care workers is very high. Young, inexperienced and untrained staff are often left to tend and work with the most problematic clients. Although attempts have been made to raise the status and skills of residential staff, through training courses, the adults looking after children are still more likely than not to be untrained and isolated from fellow professionals (Bullock, see chapter 11).

Some commentators consider that the rapid turnover of residential staff partly reflects the problematic nature of many youngsters now placed in residential care (Ligthart et al., 1991). In view of this, it is argued that care workers should receive higher salaries, and that the ratio of care workers to children should be increased.

There are also widespread calls for improved training and more intensive levels of support and supervision for care workers. As indicated above, the quality of training afforded care workers appears uneven across EC countries. In Greece, for example, the child welfare organisation 'Metera' provides in-service training programmes, but only 'as needs arise and conditions and time allow' (Agathonos, see chapter 5). A similar point can be made in relation to the supervision of care workers. For instance, although a good deal has been written about the need for effective supervision of group workers in the Flemish-speaking part of Belgium, such supervision is neither general, nor provided on a systematic basis.

Alternatives to residential and foster care

The idea that children in care represent a heterogeneous category with regard to the variety of their needs and possible ways of addressing such needs, together with the high costs of residential care and the criticism levelled against it, have led to the development of community-oriented alternatives. The main objectives of such provision are to prevent entry to care, and to keep the young person in his or her natural environment.

Before reviewing the different types of community alternatives to residential and foster care, it is important to note that in making comparisons between EC countries on the basis of the chapters comprising this book, it is sometimes difficult to establish whether a certain type of care does or does not exist in a given country. In the

not all authors have explicitly mentioned community based
s to care. Second, it is not always clear whether the authors
arious chapters mean the same thing when referring to
y alternatives. Consequently, reference cannot be made to all
rnatives that are found in the different countries of the EC.
the account which follows will be confined to the most
common alternatives to residential and foster care, namely : day
centres, centres for independent living under supervision, and home-
based treatment schemes.

1. Day centres are places where children and adolescents in need can go
after school. The child, the family, and school are all involved in the
intervention programme. Day centres focus help on youngsters who
are at risk of being placed away from home. Parents gain respite and
support, whilst maintaining responsibility for their children.

2. Centres for independent living under supervision typically involve young
people living in apartments, either by themselves or in small groups.
They are usually supervised by care workers based at larger residential
establishments, or by workers from services which specialise in this
form of care. The main objective is to offer young people the
opportunity to develop the skills essential for independent living. This
includes practical skills, such as household budgeting, cookery, etc.
However, youngsters also learn to make decisions about how to use
their time constructively, and how, more generally, to organise their
lives. This type of community care tends to focus exclusively on the
young people themselves. Parents and the wider family are often left
out entirely. However, recent research suggests that collaboration with
young people's families is vital in facilitating the transition to
independent living (Klomp, 1992).

3. Centres for home-based treatment are situated at the opposite end of
the care continuum from residential services, in that intensive help is
provided in the child's family home. A number of times each week,
family members receive training with regard to the material, practical,
and social aspects of family living. Intervention focuses on the
parenting process as a whole, rather than on specific, isolated,
problems; on family relationships, rather than on individual family
members (Philp, 1963). Home-based treatment is widespread in the
Netherlands, and it is currently being developed in Belgium and
Germany (Goldbrunner, 1989).

Research on residential and foster care

In many countries of the EC, research on residential care, foster care and their alternatives is very limited. This is particularly true of southern European countries such as Greece, Italy, Portugal, and Spain; and, somewhat surprisingly, also appears to be the case in France. Corbillon (see chapter 3) reports that although the 1989 yearbook on social research in France lists some 328 researchers and 97 research units, only 8 such researchers and 1 research unit are classified under residential or foster care.

In Belgium, Denmark, Germany, and Ireland the situation is somewhat more encouraging. Authors on the chapters concerning these countries all observe a growth in research over recent years (see chapters 1,2,4 and 6). Gilligan's (see chapter 6) comments on Ireland may also be applied to Belgium, Denmark and Germany. He notes : 'while the scale and scope of research has been limited by the availability of resources, much has been achieved within existing constraints'.

The Netherlands has a longer tradition of research on residential care and its alternatives than neighbouring Belgium, and the range of studies undertaken by Dutch researchers is quite impressive. Researchers in the Flemish-community of Belgium try to keep pace with their counterparts in the Netherlands, but are impeded by falling financial support from government and by the fact that university research units in Belgium are smaller than those found in the Netherlands.

It would appear from Bullock's contribution that child care research in the United Kingdom has established itself more firmly than in most other European countries. High quality information has been obtained about many aspects of the child welfare process, and a clear body of specialist knowledge has been built up. According to Bullock, this is the outcome of an enterprising approach towards research adopted by government (see chapter 11).

It is clear that lack of money has severely circumscribed research on separated children in a majority of EC countries. In turn, this can be explained, following Agathonos, by the low status generally accorded to social research (Agathonos, see chapter 5). Corbillon identifies two further reasons for the dearth of research on residential and foster care in France : firstly, because social workers are trained outside universities, research on child welfare is not routinely undertaken in university departments. In the second place, the strong doubts surrounding the efficacy of separating children from their home environments makes substitute child care an unattractive subject for research, both from the point of view of researchers and research funding agencies (Corbillon, see chapter 3).

A brief review of the current state of research on residential and foster care in EC countries will now be presented under the following five headings.

1. Major research funding agencies
2. Who carries out research?
3. Current trends in research
4. The relationship between research, policy and practice
5. Issues for future research

1. Major research funding agencies

In most European countries, research on residential and foster care is, to a greater or lesser extent, funded by central government and by the various forms of local government (eg. autonomous communities, counties, and municipalities). A range of administrative departments are involved in the different countries - for example, ministries of Health, of Social Affairs, of Welfare, of Education, of Cultural Affairs, of the Interior (Italy) and of Justice. Research is also sponsored by private agencies and charitable foundations (e.g. in Germany) or private foundations (e.g. banks, as is the case in Spain). However, such funding is the exception rather than the rule. In most EC countries, the private sector has so far shown little, if any, interest in promoting research.

Moreover, with the exception of the United Kingdom, research is funded by government on an entirely ad hoc basis. Many problems arise from this. Firstly, only proposals for projects that are directly relevant to the current policy concerns of the government in question stand any chance of being funded; secondly, it is impossible for research centres to plan research programmes on a long-term basis and, in some countries (e.g. Belgium), a change of government may mean that research programmes initiated by the previous administration may be terminated.

As we have seen, commentators in most countries complain about the lack of sufficient resources for research on child welfare. Agathonos (see chapter 5), for example, attributes the small sums that are allocated for research on child welfare in Greece to the economic problems and political turmoil which have characterised her country's recent history. By contrast, in Belgium and the Netherlands, the economic crisis of the 1970's appears to have stimulated research on child care. Van der Ploeg (1991), notes that although the connection

246

between economic decline and increased funding for child research seems somewhat paradoxical, in times of financial string governments raise questions about the role and functioning of c care provisions, their efficiency, and effects. Research is commissio to examine whether, and how, savings can be made.

However, Bullock reports that a sound research policy on child care has been conducted by successive governments in the United Kingdom since the 1970's, when child care matters became the responsibility of the Department of Health. The latter made an early decision that more research was needed, and that outside agencies should be contracted to undertake this. As a result, several external child care units were established to specialise in different areas of research. Each unit was funded on the basis of a full research programme, rather than on a single project. This offered greater job security to staff, and allowed them to develop a special area of expertise; it also facilitated cumulative knowledge founded on earlier work (Bullock, chapter 11). Current expenditure by the Department of Health on child care research totals over 3 million pounds.

Bullock observes that research arrangements in Britain may, at first sight, appear generous and satisfactory, because of the opportunities and freedom they afford to researchers. However, he highlights a number of important shortcomings in the British system. These include the fact that theoretical research rarely gets financial support, and empirical studies tend to reflect government policy priorities rather than academic relevance. Moreover, it is difficult for researchers in Britain to persuade government of the value of radical, as opposed to reformist, research. He further comments that investigators contracted to undertake applied studies, cannot afford to take too many risks in developing new methodologies or in pursuing interesting side issues.

Notwithstanding these points, the structure for child care research developed in the United Kingdom does appear to compare favourably with the approaches adopted by most other EC countries.

2. Who carries out research?

Governments in most member states do not have research agencies of their own. Research on child welfare is usually undertaken at universities or at research units affiliated to universities, as is the case in the United Kingdom. In France, there are national and regional research institutes. Research in Denmark and Greece is carried out at private research centres. In Portugal, the agencies responsible for providing child care services undertake research. University based research is done by members of faculties or departments of education,

247

criminology and law, psychology, social policy, social work and sociology.

It is important to note that in a good number of countries (e.g. Belgium, Germany, the Netherlands), much research is completed in pursuit of academic qualifications.

3. Current trends in research

Little reference is made in foregoing chapters to theoretical, historical or juridical research. Yet important theoretical research, developing concepts and typologies, has been carried out in the Netherlands and Germany. Despite the important historical dimension of child care research, many of the preceding authors (Calheiros from Portugal is an exception) have omitted to report historical studies in the field of residential and foster care. However, from our own knowledge, we are aware that important historical studies have been carried out in France, Germany, the Netherlands, and the United Kingdom.

Most research appears to be empirical and quantitative. In Germany, some attention has been paid to methodological innovation (Colla-Müller, see chapter 4) in the sense that more qualitative methods are employed, such as participant observation in the natural environment. A good deal of qualitative research has also been completed in the United Kingdom.

In the majority of countries, much more research has been carried out on residential care than on fostering. For example, in Greece no research seems to have been done on foster care. Research on foster care is also particularly scarce in Belgium, France, Germany and Portugal. Most research on residential care concerns the characteristics of children and their parents. Very often, however, this research involves small groups of children accommodated in one, or a small number of, facilities, who are studied at a fixed point (e.g. on admission, during their stay, or on discharge) on a limited number of variables. Another important type of research is process evaluation, which is used here in its broadest sense to denote a wide range of studies on care and treatment practice.

Judging from the research reported in previous chapters, it is difficult to escape the conclusion that more effect-evaluation or 'outcome' studies are required, as well as studies analysing the clients' perspective. In summarising the current state of research on residential care in EC countries, we may draw on Parker's (1988) critical remarks concerning British child care research, which seem to apply with even greater force to research on the European mainland :

1. There are virtually no large-scale and national studies (although to some extent they are to be found in the United Kingdom, the Netherlands and Flanders);
2. Few studies have surveyed the full range of residential care and important interconnections are liable to be overlooked;
3. Almost no comparative research can be found in which residential care is studied and assessed in conjunction with the major alternatives.

4. The relationship between research, policy and practice

Most of the contributors to this book do not expect research to have clear cut and positive effects on policy and practice. Nevertheless, as Gilligan notes, the influence of research remains significant (see chapter 6). Even in countries like Spain, where research is rather limited, measures taken to improve the quality of residential care and to restructure the community based framework of services for children have, according to Casas, often been based on fairly comprehensive research studies (see chapter 10).

In the United Kingdom, the impact of research on policy and practice is relatively impressive. Indeed, the Children Act 1989, which is widely seen as the most far reaching reform of child care law in England and Wales this century, was informed by a considerable body of research commissioned by government.

5. Issues for future research

Despite the marked differences between EC countries in the level and scope of research on residential, foster care and their alternatives, there is room in all member states for greater emphasis on evaluative studies of both the processes and outcomes of care. Longitudinal, rather than cross-sectional, studies of outcomes are required (see, for example, Heath et al., 1993), since the results obtained from well designed longitudinal research may be the exact reverse of those produced by cross-sectional studies (Banks and Jackson, 1992). Moreover, systematic comparative studies of different forms of provision are extremely useful. Studies should also be carried out on the views of children and their parents with regard to all aspects of the care experience. Further, Bullock (see chapter 11) rightly stresses the need for research that is broad in focus and which has an eye for the inter-relationships between different agencies concerned with children.

Finally, it is appropriate to end this book with a plea for research which adopts an international perspective. Regardless of the difficulties associated with making comparisons across national frontiers, it is our firm belief that much can be gained from studying child care policy and practice in different countries - both within and beyond the European Community. Researchers must join together with their counterparts in other countries in an effort to obtain knowledge that will ultimately result in better childhoods for vulnerable and troubled children everywhere. We hope that this book will serve as a contribution towards this goal.

References

Ahmed, S., Cheetham, J. and Small, J. (1986) (Eds), *Social Work with Black Children and their Families*, Batsford, London.

Banks, M. and Jackson, P. (1982), 'Unemployment and Risk of Minor Psychiatric Disorder in Young People, Cross-sectional and Longitudinal Evidence', *Psychological Medicine*, 12, pp. 789-96.

Berridge, D. (1985), *Children's Homes*, Blackwell, Oxford.

Boszormenyi-Nagy and Krasner, B.R. (1986), *Between Give and Take : A Clinical Guide to Contextual Therapy*, Brunner/Mazel, New York.

Boszormenyi-Nagy and Spark, G.M. (1984), *Invisible Loyalties : Reciprocity in Intergenerational Family Therapy*, Brunner/Mazel, New York.

Bowlby, J. (1951), *Maternal Care and Mental Health*, WHO, Geneva.

Bryce, M., and Lloyd, J.C. (Eds) (1981), *Treating Families in the Home : An Alternative to Placement*, Charles C. Thomas, Springfield (Illinois).

Colton, M. (1988), *Dimensions of Substitute Child Care : A Comparative Study of Foster and Residential Care Practice,*, Avebury, Aldershot.

Colton, M., Aldgate, J. and Heath, A. (1991), 'Behavioural Problems Among Children in and Out of Care', *Social Work and Social Sciences Review*, Vol. 2(3), 1991, pp. 177-191.

Colton, M. (1992). 'Social Climates and Social Support in Residential Homes and Foster Families : The Child's Voice', in J.D. van der Ploeg, P.M., van den Berg, M., Klomp, E.J., Knorth, and M. Smit, (Eds) (1992), *Vulnerable Youth in Residential Care, Part 1 : Social Competence, Social Support and Social Climate*, Garant, Leuven, pp. 261-272.

Colton, M. and Jackson, S. (1993), 'Failing Children', *Community Care*, (forthcoming).

Dinnage, R. and Pringle, M. (1967), *Residential Child Care : Facts and Fallacies*, Longman, London.

Dolan, P. (1991). Residential Care in Ireland, in M. Gottesman (1991) (Ed.), *Residential Care : An International Reader,* Fice International, London, pp. 171-178.

Edwards, D.W. and Kelly, J.G. (1980), 'Coping and Adaption : A Longitudinal Study', *American Journal of Community Psychology,* 2(6).

Goldbrunner, H. (1989), *Arbeit mit Problemfamilien : Systemische Perspektive für Familientherapie und Sozialarbeit, Edition Psychologie und Pädagogik,* Matthias Grünerwald Verlag, Mainz.

Gottesman, M. (Ed.) (1991), *Residential Care : An International Reader,* Fice International, London.

Gugliemetti, F. and Sapucci, G. (1991), 'Residential Education in Italy', in M. Gottesman, (1991) (Ed.), *Residential Care : An International Reader,* Fice International, London, pp. 194-198.

Harmonisatie (1992), dSO, 's Gravenhage.

Hazel, N. (1981), *A Bridge to Independence*, Blackwell, Oxford.

Heath, A., Colton, M. and Aldgate, J. (1989), 'The Educational Progress of Children in and Out of Care', *British Journal of Social Work,* 19 (6), pp. 447-460.

Heath, A.F., Colton, M.J. and Aldgate, J. (1993), 'Failure to Escape : A Longitudinal Study of Foster Children's Educational Attainment', *British Journal of Social Work* (forthcoming).

Hellinckx, W. et al., (1992), *Deelrapport : Consultatiegedrag en correlaten van gedrags- en emotionele problemen bij kinderen van 6 tot 12 jaar in Vlaanderen,* (unpublished).

Hellinckx, W. and De Munter, A. (1990), *Voorzieningen voor jongeren met psychosociale problemen, Onderzoek naar residentiële voorzieningen, diensten voor begeleid zelfstandig wonen en dagcentra,* Acco, Leuven/Amersfoort.

Kansen voor de jeugdhulpverlening? (1986-1990), WIJN, Utrecht.

King, R.D., Raynes, N.V., and Tizard, J. (1971), *Patterns of Residential Care : Sociological Studies in Institutions for Handicapped Children,* Routledge and Kegan Paul, London.

Klomp, M. (1992), *Hulpverlening aan adolescenten : Een bijdrage aan methodiekontwikkeling in Trainingscentra voor Kamerbewoning,* Rijksuniversiteit Groningen, Groningen (proefschrift).

Klüppel, J.E.J. and Slijkerman, A.J.M. (1983), *Gebruik en beleving van kindertehuizen door jeugdigen met psycho-sociale gedragsproblemen,* Instituut voor onderzoek naar psycho-sociale stress, Wageningen.

Ligthart, L.E.E., Van der Goes van Naters, J. and De Keyser, L.H. (1991), 'Residential youth care and protection : The Dutch situation', in M. Gottesman (Ed.), *Residential Care : An International Reader,* Fice International, London, pp. 222-238.

251

Mesman Schultz, K. (1978), *De COM-procedure, een methode om voor kinderbeschermingspupillen een advies te bepalen*, Coördinatie-commissie wetenschappelijk onderzoek, Rijswijk. kinderbescherming.

Millham, S., Bullock, R., Hosie, K. and Little, M. (1986), *Lost in Care*, Gower, Aldershot.

Nielsen, H. et al., (1986), *Sozialpädagogische Familienhilfe*, Juventa-Verlag, Weinheim.

Parker, R.A. (1988), 'Residential Care for Children', in I. Sinclair (1988) (Ed.), *Residential Care : The Research Reviewed*, Her Majesty's Stationery Office, London, pp. 57-124.

Philp (1963), *Family Failure : A Study of 129 Families with Multiple Problems*, Faber & Faber, London.

Polsky (1962), *Cottage Six : The Social System of Delinquent boys in Residential Treatment*, Russell Sage Foundation, New York.

Pringle, M.L. and Bossio, V. (1960), 'Early Prolonged Separations and Emotional Adjustment', *Child Psychology and Psychiatry*, 1, pp.37-48 .

Spitz, R.A. (1945), 'Hospitalism : An Inquiry into the Genesis of Psychiatric Conditions in Early Childhood', in A. Freud (1945) (Ed.), *Psychoanalytic Study of the Child*, New York.

Van der Ploeg, J. (1984a), Vormen van residentiële hulpverlening, in J. Van der Ploeg (Ed.), *Jeugd (z)onder dak : Theorieën, voorzieningen en jeugdigen in de residentiële hulpverlening*, Samson, Alphen a/d Rijn, pp. 91-116.

Van der Ploeg, J. (1984b), 'Het functioneren van de groepsleiding', in W. Hellinckx (Ed.) *Begeleiding van de groepsleiding in de residentiële orthopedagogische hulpverlening*, ACCO, Leuven, pp. 9-27.

Van der Ploeg (1991), 'Forces in innovation', in W. Hellinckx et al. (Eds), *Innovations in Residential Care*, Acco, Leuven/Amersfoort, pp. 1-8

Van der Ploeg, J. and Scholte E. (1988), *Tehuizen in beeld*, Vakgroep Orthopedagogiek, Centrum Onderzoek Jeugdhulpverlening, Leiden.

Vissers, J. (1988), *De residentiële carrière van jongeren in de kinderbescherming*, CWOK, Den Haag.

Zandberg, T.J. (1988), *Kleinschaligheid in de residentiële hulpverlening*, Stichting Kinderstudies, Groningen.

Biographical notes

Helen Agathonos-Georgopoulou is Director of the Department of Family Relations at the Institute of Child Health, Athens. She has published widely in Greece and abroad. Since 1982, Mrs Agathonos has been involved in international work on family and children's issues, primarily as a member of the Executive Council of the International Society for the Prevention of Child Abuse and Neglect (ISPCAN). She was President of ISPCAN between 1990 and 1992, and is now serving as Immediate Past President. Mrs Agathonos is also a member of the Executive Committee of the European Scientific Association on Residential and Foster Care for Children and Adolescents. She is President of the Hellenic Society for the Prevention of Child Abuse and Neglect, and is a member of the Executive Board of the Institute of Child Health, Athens.

Roger Bullock is Senior Research Fellow at Dartington Social Research Unit, University of Bristol, and was Open University Tutor from 1970 to 1984. His many publications (in conjunction with colleagues from the Dartington Social Research Unit) include *Chance of a Lifetime?* (Weidenfeld and Nicolson, 1975); *After Grace - Teeth* (Human Context Books, 1975); *Locking up Children* (Saxon House, 1978); *Learning to Care* (Gower, 1980); *Issues of Control in Residential Care* (HMSO, 1981); *Lost in Care* (Gower, 1986); *Access Disputes in Child Care* (Gower, 1989), and *Going Home* (Gower, 1992).

Maria Manuela de Amorim Calheiros studied psychology at the University of Lisbon, and psychotherapy at the Portuguese Association for Behavioural and Cognitive Therapy. Since 1990, she has worked at the Research and Planning Department of the Public School's Service in Lisbon, and is carrying out a research project on the socio-psychological factors associated with child abuse and neglect.

Ferran Casas is Professor of Applied Social Psychology and Social Welfare at Barcelona University. Since 1990, he has been Director of the Childhood Studies Centre (Centro de Estudios del Menor) at the Ministry of Social Affairs in Madrid. Dr. Casas is also an experienced and qualified social educator. Between 1985 and 1988, he was Director of the Programme for Children in Risk Situations administered by the Autonomous Government of Catalonia. He has published articles and books on children's problems, social services, quality of life and social and psycho-social indicators.

Herbert Colla-Müller is Professor at the University of Lüneburg; Institut für Sozialpädagogik, Germany. He has published several books and articles on residential and foster care, suicide, AIDS and other subjects. He is a member of the *Deutsche Gesellschaft für Erziehungswissenschaft* (DGFE), *Deutsche Gesellschaft für Selbstmordverhütung* (DGES), *Fédération Internationale des Communautés Educatives* (FICE) and member of the executive commitee of the European Scientific Association on Residential and Foster Care for Children and Adolescents (EUSARF).

Matthew Colton is Lecturer in Applied Social Studies, University of Wales, University College of Swansea. He is author of *Dimensions of Substitute Child Care: A Comparative Study of Foster and Residential Care Practice* (Avebury, 1989), is co-editor of *Innovations in Residential Care* (ACCO, 1991), (with W. Hellinckx, E. Broekaert and A. Vanden Berge) and has published many articles on children in public care. Dr. Colton is currently engaged in research on the education of separated children, and is undertaking a nationwide study of services for children in need in Wales. He is a member of the Executive Committee of the European Scientific Association on Residential and Foster Care for Children and Adolescents, and a member of the editorial board of *Community Alternatives: International Journal of Family Care*. He is a professionally qualified social worker, and has substantial practice experience with separated children.

Michel Corbillon began his career as a professional social worker, which included periods as a community worker and residential care worker. Dr. Corbillon then completed a sociological dissertation on intellectual deficiency. At present, he is responsible for the research group on social reproduction and innovation (GERIS, Groupe de recherche sur la reproduction et innovation sociales). In this capacity, he has participated in several research projects undertaken by the group, including a nationwide study of child welfare services in France. In 1989, he coordinated a UNESCO conference on French and international research on children placed away from home ('L'enfant placé, actualité de la recherche française et internationale'). In addition, he is responsible for the staff development and training unit at the school for care workers (L'Ecole d'éducateurs) d'Olivet, and is lecturer at the Universities of Orléans and Nanterre.

José João Seabra Dinis studied psychology in Italy, where he also began his studies in psychoanalysis. He completed his training in Lisbon, and has worked as a psychoanalyst with troubled children - including children in residential and foster care - for many years. He has a special interest in the problems associated with adoption.

Maria Margarida Peixoto da Eira Fornelos is a clinical psychologist at the Infancy Unit of the Department of Child and Adolescent Psychiatry, D. Estefânia Paediatric Hospital, Lisbon. She is former head of the DASE - the department responsible for the welfare of deprived infants and children in the Lisbon area.

Robbie Gilligan is Senior Lecturer in Social Work and Coordinator of the Advanced Diploma in Child Protection and Welfare in the Department of Social Studies, University of Dublin - Trinity College. He is the author of a range of publications on child welfare including *Irish Child Care Services* (Dublin, Institute of Public Administration, 1991). He was the Director of Studies for the Council of Europe Study Group which produced the report *Protection of Youth against Physical and Moral Danger* (Strasbourg, Council of Europe, 1990). He has a wide range of experience in child welfare services as social worker, foster parent, researcher, consultant and board member.

Walter Hellinckx is Professor at the Section of Orthopedagogics, Faculty of Psychology and Educational Sciences, University of Leuven, Belgium, where his teaching interests centre on work with troubled children. He is President of the European Scientific Association on Residential and Foster Care for Children and Adolescents, and a member of the editorial board of *Community Alternatives: International Journal of Family Care*. He has published widely on treatment for troubled children, and the different forms of care for such children - residential and foster care, and their alternatives - and on innovations in residential care. At present, he is co-ordinating a nationwide epidemiological research project on children with emotional and behavioural problems in Flanders.

Jill Melhbye was for eight years a clinical child psychologist and consultant to social workers involved with children at risk and their families. For the past nine years, however, she has undertaken research at the Danish Local Government Research Institute in Copenhagen, Denmark. She has specialised in empirical and theoretical studies on treatment for children and young people with serious problems, including those placed in residential and foster care. She has also completed evaluations of preventive strategies with regard to children and young people at risk. Currently, she is responsible for two major research projects: the first concerns help for children from divorced families; the second centres on integration strategies for children of migrant parents.

Benedikte van den Bruel is a researcher at the Section of Orthopedagogics, Faculty of Psychology and Educational Sciences, University of Leuven, Belgium. She has published many articles on care for troubled children.

Christine vander Borght is licentiate in Psychology of Université Catholique de Louvain and D.E.A. in Clinical Psychology of Nanterre University. She was formerly the Director of a residential home for children, and lecturer at the Université Paris VII. At present, she is responsible for a mental health agency in Brussels. She is co-author of *Placés, vous avez dit?*, Editions Matrice, 1987.

Jan van der Ploeg is Professor at the University of Leiden, the Netherlands. He is involved in empirical research and theory-development in relation to socially and emotionally disturbed adolescents. His published research includes studies on runaways, homeless young people, delinquent boys and girls and drop-outs in residential care. He has also written about theoretical concepts such as coping, social support, locus of control, stress scapegoating and self-image. He is President Elect of the European Scientific Association on Residential and Foster Care for Children and Adolescents.

Tiziano Vecchiato has been Scientific Director of the E. Zancan Foundation (Padova) since 1988. He was formerly Professor in Social Psychology at the School for Social Work, Trento (1982-1987) and Lecturer in Social Psychology at the University of Turin (1985-1989). He is the author of several publications on the development of children and adolescents, and has also written about social and health services for children and young people.